ARIZONA
Gardener's Guide

Mary Irish

COOL SPRINGS PRESS

Nashville, Tennessee
A Division of Thomas Nelson, Inc.
www.ThomasNelson.com

Published by Cool Springs Press, a Division of Thomas Nelson, Inc., P. O. Box 141000, Nashville, Tennessee, 37214.

Irish, Mary, 1949-
    Arizona gardener's guide / Mary Irish.
        p. cm.
    Includes bibliographical references (p.   ).
    ISBN: 1-888608-42-0 (pbk. : alk. paper)
    1. Landscape plants--Arizona. 2. Landscape gardening--Arizona.
    I. Title.
    SB407 .I75 2003

                                        2002011421

First printing 2003
Printed in the United States of America
10 9 8 7 6 5 4 3

Managing Editor: Billie Brownell
Designer: Sheri Ferguson
Horticulture Editor: Mike Wenzel
Production Artist: S.E. Anderson

On the cover: *Agave parryi*, photographed by Charles Mann.

Visit the Thomas Nelson website at www.ThomasNelson.com

Dedication

For all the Master Gardeners whose work and dedication give Arizona gardeners the know-how and inspiration to keep on creating their Southwestern gardens.

Acknowledgments

Gardens are generous places, full of the gifts both of nature and other gardeners. It is much the same with gardening books; they are full of the wisdom and experience of so many people it is nearly impossible to acknowledge them all. But the ones who helped most specifically with this book are: Marylou Coffmann, Donna DiFrancesco, Fern Elmore, Barry Golden, Mike Hills, Ardi Kary, Jeff Schalau, and the staff at Flagstaff Native Plant and Seed Nursery. Those gardeners whose information I received mainly through their writing are included in References, but conversations over the years with Matt Johnson and Warren Jones have added immeasurably to my understanding and joy in growing plants in the arid West. I thank you all.

But nothing good seems to come out of my garden, my life, or my writing without the devotion and care that my dear husband and gardening companion, Gary, offers. Thanks are rarely enough.

Featured Plants *for Arizona*

Table of Contents

Table of Contents

Welcome to
Gardening
in Arizona

I have designed gardens in a number of different places and, until I moved to Arizona, all were basically variations on the same theme. They consisted of large, spring-flowering shrubs set against the house in the typical American foundation planting, large, deciduous shade trees kept to a minimum to permit the most sunlight possible, and seasonally flowering perennials around the perimeter of the garden. These gardens were in Texas and Louisiana and therefore had a dash of both tropical and native plants, but still, each garden relied on a similar schedule for planting, pruning, and other general care. When I left the Gulf Coast and moved to Arizona, I imagined that I would have to begin entirely from scratch. I was certain that I would not recognize anything, and nothing I had grown would be part of my gardens in the West. While some of those imaginings were true, others were just myths, and I was delighted and surprised by how many outstanding new plants were added to my garden. However, I would never have predicted that the most interesting, exhilarating, and satisfying garden I had ever designed would be the one at my desert home.

Land of Challenges

Arizona presents many obvious challenges for gardeners, especially for recent arrivals. Soils do not appear as fertile as they were in a previous home, and rocks are a way of life, a fact that is daunting to some gardeners. The skies are clear and the abundant sunshine makes a welcome change, but rain is just a dream in some seasons and there never seems to be very much of it even in the best of times. What becomes clearer the longer you garden here is that the soils are absolutely fine for plants that are well-adapted to them, rocks are one of the treasures of a well-designed garden, shade is a great partner, especially in the lower zones to give your plants relief from that constant sunshine, and while you can't count on rain, you absolutely must be able to rely on your irrigation system.

While each zone in the state has its own distinct soils, it can be said that the soils in Arizona are alkaline, often thin with low humus content, and often just as rocky. It is time consuming and often impossible to correct the composition of any soil, especially its pH. On the other hand, it is impossible to correct the inherent physiology of plants, including their preference for or ability to survive in soils of varying composition and pH. Plants that love the acid soils of forests and bogs are not well suited to the basic soils of Arizona. They become chlorotic quickly, they often live much shorter lives, and in many

Desert Spoon

cases, they just refuse to flower and grow with the same vigor they would in a more congenial soil. It is much easier and less frustrating to look for and grow plants that are content with the soils that are found in your garden.

Much About Mulch

In the low zones, the great summer heat results in the rapid loss of soil moisture through evaporation. The easiest way to help plants cope with the heat is to provide mulch around the root zones to help slow down evaporation. There are two styles of mulch—organic and inorganic.

Organic mulch—leaves, pine needles, prunings—does two things for plants. Organic mulch cools the soil surface and thus slows down evaporation, thereby making more water available to the plants over a longer time. This can mean the difference between watering a plant every day or two and watering it every three or four days. As an added bonus, organic mulches provide tiny amounts of organic matter as they break down; they are essentially compost piles right next to a plant. Over the years, this action of decomposition enriches the bed, changes the texture of the soil, and makes it able to hold much more moisture.

It is popular to use inorganic mulch like crushed granite throughout the state, especially in the low zones. Rock mulch also cools the soil and slows down the rate of evaporation. Gravel mulch is hot on its surface and can create a lot of reflected heat if the rock covers more area than the plants. It is not always necessary to have a blanket of rocks to have useful rock mulch. Large rocks can be highly effective as an inorganic mulch. Succulents, in particular, which have shallow root systems, thrive in the shade of a nice rock. Under that rock mulch, the soil is just a bit cooler with just a bit more moisture, and that may be all that it takes to keep that plant fit through the long desert summer. Many of the desert species used in annual wildflower displays grow best with a rock mulch.

Rocks are also a treasured addition to a garden with their great presence and stunning regional appeal; rocks that come with the site always look better than the ones that are added to the garden. Rocks also are used in the garden to line a pathway, as walls, as well as accents. Use them for seating, to mark boundaries, or as a transition to tie together a highly cultivated area with a more natural area.

The Number One Issue

Water use is the overriding issue for gardening throughout Arizona. The entire state is arid, even in the mountainous areas where it is cool; water supplies that look abundant are really tenuous and ephemeral. Unless you garden exclusively with native plants and just let the entire garden rise and fall with the natural rainfall, you will have to provide some measure of supplemental irrigation to grow plants well. Managing how much and how often to water is the most challenging task that Arizona gardeners face.

It is a constant quest to find just the right schedule and just the right amount to water.

Drip irrigation is a popular style of irrigation in Arizona. Drip irrigation has the advantage of being relatively easy to install and maintain, delivers water exactly where a plant uses it—on the root zone, and can be modified and adapted to suit any kind of plant you have. Most people find that an irrigation system on a timer saves not only time and water but lots of plants.

Drip irrigation is an outstanding method for watering newly planted trees, shrubs, perennials, and vegetable gardens. It can be useful for succulents if the entire irrigation line is dedicated to succulents and the schedule is set specifically for them. Otherwise, it is better to water them by hand. Mature trees have root

Organ Pipe Cactus

systems that are so large and extensive that after a few years, a drip system doesn't do them much good. Watering with a slowly running hose over a long period of time works best. After a few more years, mature trees are mainly reliant on natural rainfall because they are just too large to water well without flooding the entire yard.

The greatest water users in a garden, other than pools, are lawns and trees. By planting well-adapted or native trees, you are able to free yourself from their continued watering as they mature. Eventually, well-adapted trees are sustained either on minimal, intermittent watering or natural rainfall. Lawns, of course, never survive without our intervention. You can keep their water use under control by planting only as much as is useful or by eliminating a lawn altogether wherever possible.

In Phoenix, it is estimated by the city water department that forty to sixty percent of a family's water use is outdoors. The number is not much different elsewhere in the state. It makes sense, therefore, that in this state where rain, and therefore water supplies, are severely limited, to look for plants that do not demand high levels of supplemental water to look their best. They are here in abundance. There are prolific numbers of low-water-use perennials, shrubs, and trees available in nurseries. More varieties are being introduced all the time that satisfy the need to be water-thrifty and still have a glorious, successful garden.

It's Not Boring

Using plants that demand little in the way of supplemental irrigation is not a sentence to boredom—far from it. The diversity of plants, whether native or from similar regions around the world, is astounding.

Toadflax

Whether you are gardening in the higher zones and have a short, but intensely colorful growing season, or in the low zones with their year-round growing season, the selection of well-adapted plants for Arizona gardens is large and diverse.

The low zones offer the most diversity in plant choices. In these zones, frost is only a brief consideration, and temperatures rarely plunge lower than the mid-twenties. Most of Zone 1, Yuma and the interior urban areas of Phoenix, are virtually frost-free. Here, a gardener can take advantage of the tropical and subtropical summer-flowering shrubs such as red bird of paradise, hibiscus, and yellowbells, as well as the vast numbers of flowering trees, shrubs, and perennials from the Sonoran and Chihuahuan deserts such as palo verde, cascalote, dalea, Texas sage, and chuparosa.

Prickly Pear

Although the range of choice in succulents is greatest in the warm, low zones, there is a group of succulents for gardens in every zone. The use of these plants is what sets many Arizona gardens apart from gardens elsewhere. In the higher zones, agaves, yuccas, and some species of cacti are easily mixed with evergreens and summer-flowering perennials. In the mid zones, adding the symmetry of desert spoon, the sculptural highlights of ocotillo and some of the hardier ice plants opens up the choices even more. In the low zones, in addition to all of these the mighty, treelike saguaro, countless prickly pears, cholla, hedgehog cactus, winter-flowering aloes, tiny dudleya, elegant sansevieras, and spectacular winter-flowering aloes are just a few of the succulents that offer tremendous interest and contrast to the garden.

These plants not only add texture, contrast, and striking form to the Arizona garden, they also give them a distinctive style. Liberal use of these plants not only helps the water bill, but gives a garden a gentle nudge toward the surrounding natural landscapes.

You Always Know Where You Are

Arizona is particularly fortunate to have an extremely well-developed network of growers and nurseries that offer native plants as well as well-adapted species from other parts of the world. All over the state, the

Douglas Fir

effect of having so many good native and well-adapted plants available is evident in the widespread use and acceptance of native trees, shrubs, and perennials that surround public plantings, and generously line freeways. Homeowners have responded in kind and have found that the durability and reliability of native and well-adapted plants are surpassed only by their great beauty.

Regional gardens are the absolute opposite of the uniform, one-size-fits-all approach to gardening that dictated two trees, foundation shrubs, and a lawn in front of every house in America. You never know where you are with those gardens. In Arizona, with the vast number of choices available and a liberal use of native and well-adapted plants, you always know where you are. Gardeners here are building some of the most exciting and varied gardens in the country, with a distinctive and unmistakable flair.

The West is once again the new land of the country. Most people in Arizona today have not lived here over ten years, and immense numbers of newcomers arrive every year. They come knowing a little something about the plants of their new home, bring more knowledge about how to garden in their old homes, and have a pretty good understanding of the seasons. Many things

Mixed Cacti

seem different and dauntingly new here for gardeners. But you will soon discover it is a marvelous place to build a garden once you have adjusted to the region and have acquired "desert eyes." Then you are looking at the new face of gardening—a place where "gardening where you live" becomes not just a catchy phrase but a watchword for the best that the area has to offer. Look for ideas and inspiration in the good examples that abound in the state—in public gardens, down the street in neighbors' yards, around city buildings, in community parks, and roadsides.

What Arizona does demand is that you lose a lot of the old ideas of what a garden "ought" to look like and what plants are "supposed" to be grown in gardens so that you can free yourself to look at all the enormous possibilities that this state offers. Do not be daunted, because you, too, are about to make a great Arizona garden.

Golden Barrel Cactus

How to Use This Book

Each entry in this guide provides you with information about a plant's particular characteristics, its habits, and its basic requirements for vigorous growth as well as my personal experience and knowledge of it. I have tried to include the information you need to help you realize each plant's potential. Only when a plant performs at its best can one appreciate it fully. You will find such pertinent information as mature height and spread, bloom period and seasonal colors (if any), sun and soil preferences, water requirements, fertilizing needs, pruning and care, and pest information. Each section is clearly marked for easy reference.

Sun Preferences

Symbols represent the range of sunlight suitable for each plant. "Full Sun" means to site the plant in a location receiving 6 to 10 hours of sun daily. "Part Sun/Part Shade" means dappled shade, or shade in the afternoon, or indirect light all day. "Full Shade" means a location protected from direct sunlight all day. Some plants grow successfully in more than one range of sun exposure, which is indicated by showing more than one sun symbol.

Full Sun

Part Sun/Part Shade

Full Shade

Additional Benefits

Many plants offer benefits that further enhance their appeal. The following symbols indicate some of the more notable additional benefits:

 Attracts Butterflies

 Attracts Hummingbirds

 Produces Edible Fruit

 Has Fragrance

 Produces Food for Birds and Wildlife

 Drought Resistant

 Suitable for Cut Flowers or Arrangements

 Long Bloom Period

 Native Plant

 Supports Bees

 Provides Shelter for Birds

 Good Fall Color

Companion Planting and Design

In this section, I provide suggestions for companion plants and different ways to showcase your plants.

Did You Know?

Some plants have interesting histories; others have important uses beyond the garden. Learn more about the life and lore of your plants in this section.

Cold Hardiness Zone Map

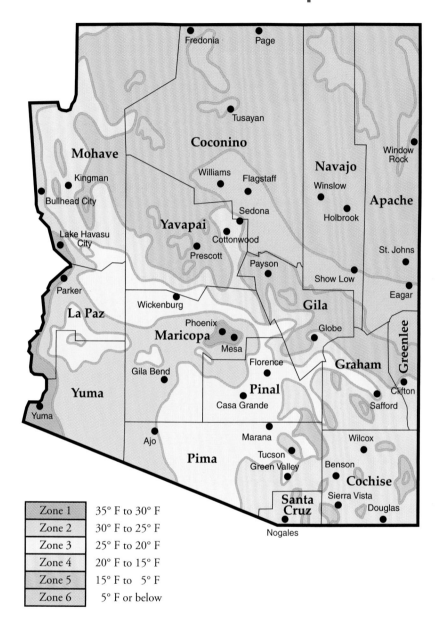

Zone 1	35° F to 30° F
Zone 2	30° F to 25° F
Zone 3	25° F to 20° F
Zone 4	20° F to 15° F
Zone 5	15° F to 5° F
Zone 6	5° F or below

Cold Hardiness Zones

Cold-hardiness zone designations were developed using minimum average temperatures and roughly follow elevation. With each zone, local changes in topography can create microclimates that may be one zone warmer or colder. Plants that are rated for one zone may well be grown in a colder zone if your site is warmer than the average for the zone, or if they are provided overhead protection, or if they are planted facing south. In addition, large urban areas are much warmer than other areas at their elevation or the surrounding areas; that is reflected on the map. All temperatures are Fahrenheit.

Annuals
for Arizona

Annuals are plants that live out their entire life cycle in one season. Whether this is a matter of months or weeks depends on the species and on the growing conditions. Annuals are nature's colonizers—these are the first plants to grow in an area that has been damaged by fire, flood, falling trees, road building, or housing developments. Many of the plants we call weeds are annuals. Some of the ones that we call wildflowers are annuals. The difference is only in our perception and our uses for these plants.

Cosmos

Garden Treasures

The combination of fast growth in disturbed areas and quick, reliable bloom is what makes annuals such treasures in the garden. In established gardens, annuals fill in small bare spots while providing brilliant seasonal color. Annuals are a terrific choice to plant in pots mixed with succulents, grasses, bulbs, or perennials to create a complete, but miniature, garden. I am especially fond of planting annual wildflowers—those colorful spring bloomers such as desert bluebell, farewell-to-spring, and tidy tips—in pots of agaves to offset the solid, hard-edged sturdiness of these plants with their riotous colors.

Annuals are irreplaceable to gardeners with brand new gardens. In the fast-growing cities of Arizona, many homeowners find themselves with a lovely new home sitting on a lot with a tree or two, a few shrubs, and little else. Annuals are a quick, inexpensive way to get a garden going and relieve some of the rawness of a new garden. The action of their roots and the litter of leaves and flowers they leave behind begin to enrich and enhance the soil.

The classic wildflower bed has great appeal and many gardeners want to recreate the sensational displays they see on the hillsides and plains of the state. This is generally more difficult to achieve than it looks. Plants tend to go naturally through up and down years, and weeds can become a tremendous problem in beds that are generously and continuously watered. For my money, annual wildflowers are much better when treated as a component of a bed, as colorful fillers in containers, or in small corners of the garden where they become an enhancement to the whole garden rather than the focus of a single bed.

Getting Off to a Good Start

Annuals such as corn poppy, bread poppy, and California poppy will grow in beds with a minimum of preparation. But most other annuals grow faster and bloom better if given a good start. To prepare the soil for annuals, rake the area once or twice to turn the soil while adding compost, mulch, and a light

dusting of fertilizer. Broadcast seed as evenly as possible. I sometimes mix seed with mulch or sand to insure an even planting because I am a hopelessly generous with seed and always end up spending too much time on my hands and knees thinning out the crowded seedlings. Be smarter, plant thinly. Finish by raking in the opposite direction to lightly cover the seed. Keep the bed well-watered until the seeds geminate, watering as often as daily depending on the weather. Water every day or two after germination until the plants have five true leaves, then water weekly.

Nasturtium

There are two ways to approach developing annual displays in a garden—use true annuals as described in this chapter or use perennial plants in a selected season as if they were annuals. This group of perennials often goes by the name "bedding plants" and includes old favorites such as pansy, petunia, stock, snapdragon, and geranium. In the low elevation zones, these bedding plants are planted through the fall for a quick, colorful spring show. In higher zones, they are planted in the spring and are the staple of summer gardens.

Annuals are so easy to grow and offer so many colors and styles that they can be used as a complement to any gardening style. Whether they are used as subtle additions to fill in odd spots or as reckless waves of seasonal color, we can all relish the diversity and appeal they bring to Arizona gardens.

Toadflax

African Daisy
Dimorphotheca sinuata

African daisy is an outstanding and reliable spring annual in low zones, coming back year after year. It is this very hardiness that makes it capable of growing in wild areas without a gardener's assistance. Be careful not to use it near parks, preserves, or other wild places. In high zones, plants are not so aggressive. The low, green leaves germinate early in fall, and by January, blooming begins. This is one of the first signals of spring, and many gardeners in the low zones use it to cover the entire front yard for an explosion of color. The daisylike flowers are usually in shades of yellow, gold orange with a pale disc. The closely related Dimorphotheca pluvialis has white rays with a violet disc, and hybrids are common between the two.

Bloom Period and Seasonal Color
Early winter and spring in low zones, spring and early summer in higher zones; yellow, orange, and white to mixes of all three.

Mature Height × Spread
4 to 12 inches × 4 to 8 inches

Zones
All

When, Where, and How to Plant
Sow seed in fall in low zones; as early as soil can be worked in high zones. Although African daisy will grow in almost any soil, including rocky, native soil, they grower larger and faster in well-drained, fertile soil. Prepare the bed by breaking the surface of the soil with a rake. Spread a light layer of slow-release or organic fertilizer and mulch on the surface and rake it in. Broadcast seed, mixing them with sand or mulch to help distribute them evenly. Cover lightly by raking the soil and press the soil gently to prevent seed from washing away. Water every two to three days until seed germinate, then water every five to seven days.

Growing Tips
African daisy does not need any supplemental fertilization. Once there are five leaves on the plant, reduce watering to once a week or less depending on temperatures. Plants are susceptible to collapse if overwatered. Water weekly when the plant is in bloom.

Care
To reduce aggressive reseeding, remove flowering heads as soon as they are finished blooming and begin to fade. African daisy is not susceptible to pests or disease.

Companion Planting and Design
Sow in mass plantings for spectacular effect around pools, walkways, or patios. Mix with other wildflowers such as tidy tips, desert bluebells, or Mexican poppies. African daisy is suitable for planters or large containers either individually or combined with other annuals for colorful displays. Their short blooming season allows them to be used in succession with other flowering annuals or perennials.

Did You Know?
Members of the sunflower family have unusual flowers. What we think is a single flower is actually a collection of dozens or even hundreds of tiny flowers in two distinct styles. One style has a single petal and is often a sterile or incomplete flower. It is known as a ray flower. The other type usually has no petals, produces seed and is called a disc flower.

Annual Chrysanthemum

Chrysanthemum paludosum

When, Where, and How to Plant

Sow seed or set out transplants in fall in low zones or as early as soil can be worked in high zones. Annual chrysanthemum grows best in well-drained, fertile soils. Prepare the bed by breaking the surface of the soil with a rake or turning lightly with a garden fork. Spread a thin layer of slow-release or organic fertilizer and mulch on the surface and rake it in. Broadcast seed, mixing the seed with sand or mulch to help distribute them evenly. Cover lightly by raking the soil and press the soil gently to prevent seed from washing away. Water every two to three days until seed germinate, then water every five to seven days. For transplants, prepare the bed in the same manner. Dig a hole that is just large enough to hold the roots. Space the plants 8 to 10 inches apart. Water transplants immediately, then every day until established.

Growing Tips

Water once a week while annual chrysanthemum is flowering. Water every two to three days when the weather is exceptionally hot or dry, or if temperatures remain over 90 degrees Fahrenheit. Mulch the roots to prevent soil from drying out too quickly.

Care

Remove spent flowers regularly—this will prolong the bloom. Not susceptible to pests or disease.

Companion Planting and Design

Use annual chrysanthemum to fill in barren spots in a newly planted garden. Annual chrysanthemum is excellent planted in mass groups and can be used in front of an annual or perennial bed for long seasonal color. Plant as an informal low border near walkways or in the front of beds. Mix with other annuals or perennials such as pansies, salvias, gaillardia, and coreopsis for colorful spring or summer displays. Use annual chrysanthemum in containers either in mass or as part of a mixed planting.

Did You Know?

Chrysanthemum comes from the Greek *chrysos* meaning "gold" and *anthemon* meaning "flower." *Paludosum* means "marsh-loving," referring to its natural habitat.

When we think of chrysanthemums, the huge corsages proudly worn to important school sports games or the florist's pot delivered at times of joy or grief come to mind. But there are numerous members of this widespread genus, from the fall-flowering garden perennials to the diminutive annual chrysanthemum. The 8-inch clumps look like tight, handheld bouquets with the pure white, ray flowers accented by yellow disc flowers completely covering the small, dark green leaves. In the low zones, annual chrysanthemum grows throughout the long, cool season, from early fall through winter and spring, but cannot survive summer. In higher zones, it blooms consistently through summer but cannot survive winter.

Other Common Name
Paludosum daisy

Bloom Period and Seasonal Color
Spring and early summer, occasionally surviving over two seasons; white ray flowers, yellow discs.

Mature Height × Spread
8 inches × 12 inches

Zones
All

Annual Coreopsis
Coreopsis tinctoria

Coreopsis is one of those flowers that just forces you to smile. The flat ray flowers are banded yellow and brown or maroon, held on whisper-thin stems above delicate, finely cut leaves. The slender appearance entirely belies how rugged this plant is for low zone gardens and how enduring it is for higher zone ones. Use it generously— coreopsis is better planted in mass groups—and give it some room for it can grow up to 3 feet tall. Best of all for low zones, it blooms late, beginning in May and lasting well into July. There are also dwarf and double forms. A perennial relative, Coreopsis lanceolata, has low tufts of hairy leaves with bright yellow flowers that bloom into summer even in low zones.

Bloom Period and Seasonal Color
Late spring to summer; yellow rays marked with brown or maroon, pure yellow, orange, bronze and reddish, discs are purple to brown.

Mature Height × Spread
2 to 3 feet × 1 to 2 feet

Zones
All

When, Where, and How to Plant
Sow seed in fall in low zones; as early as soil can be worked in high zones. Annual coreopsis grows both in well-drained, fertile soil or rocky, native soil; it does best if the soil is not too rich and is fairly dry. Prepare the bed by breaking the surface of the soil with a rake or turning it gently with a garden fork. Spread a thin layer of slow-release or organic fertilizer and mulch on the surface and rake it in. Broadcast the seed, mixing it with sand or mulch to help distribute it evenly. Cover lightly by raking the soil and press the soil gently to prevent seed from washing away. Water every two to three days until seed germinate, then water every five to seven days.

Growing Tips
Annual coreopsis needs no supplemental fertilization. Water once a week while the plants are growing and blooming. In areas with regular summer rainfall, take care that the soil is particularly well drained.

Care
Annual coreopsis is an effortless annual in Arizona gardens. Plants grow to 3 feet tall but may become floppy if grown in too much shade or if they have been crowded when young. Stake or support plants, but it is better to give them adequate light during their long growing phase to prevent the problem. Annual coreopsis is not susceptible to pests or disease.

Companion Planting and Design
Mix coreopsis with summer-flowering perennials such as salvia, gaillardia, or verbena. Coreopsis is particularly effective in the back of a bed where its height can be useful, and other plants will cover its sparse foliage. Because it appreciates dry soil, annual coreopsis may be mixed with agave, cactus, or other succulents to provide some late spring color. Sow generously for best effect; the wiry stems make it seem sparse when plants are isolated. Excellent when mixed with other annuals in large containers or planters or around pools, patios, or seating areas.

Did You Know?
Petals of this plant may be used to make a yellow or orange dye.

Canyon Lupine

Lupinus succulentus

When, Where, and How to Plant

Sow seed in fall. Many gardeners find that soaking seed in warm water overnight before sowing greatly improves germination. Although canyon lupine will grow in almost any soil, including rocky, native soil, plants are larger, more vigorous, and bloom best in well-drained, fertile soil. Prepare the bed by breaking the surface of the soil with a rake or gently turning with a garden fork. Spread a thin layer of slow-release or organic fertilizer and mulch on the surface and rake it in. Broadcast seed, mixing them with sand or mulch to help distribute them evenly. Cover lightly by raking the soil and press the soil gently to prevent seed from washing away. Water every two to three days until seed germinate, then water every five to seven days.

Growing Tips

Canyon lupine requires no supplemental fertilizer; in fact, fertilizer often encourages leaves at the expense of flowering. Water once or twice a week after plants are established and throughout the blooming season. Water more often if the weather is exceptionally hot or dry.

Care

Canyon lupine grows best with regular watering; do not allow plants to dry out. Canyon lupine is not susceptible to pests or disease.

Companion Planting and Design

This lupine is breathtaking when planted in mass plantings where the large leaves, and amazing, robust blooming stalks create a dramatic show. Use as a backdrop for smaller annuals such as tidy tips and poppies and with spring-flowering perennials such as pentagon and globemallow. Lupine is an excellent choice to fill in barren areas in the garden or close up gaps in newly planted beds. Like many lupines, this one does not reseed well, so save seed and replant each year.

Did You Know?

Like many legumes, lupines capture and hold free nitrogen from the air in their swollen roots. This gave rise to the old notion that such plants deplete the soil. In fact, it is just the opposite; turning under spent legumes such as lupine greatly enriches the soil.

For a dose of lupine magic in a desert garden, it is impossible to rival the spectacle of canyon lupine. In a garden setting, this California native grows numerous 3- to 4-foot tall stems with large, rounded leaves. Towering over the top are the 6- to 8-inch tall congested heads of indigo blue flowers. Bloom lasts over a month. The annual Lupinus sparsiflorus covers the roadsides of southern Arizona in spring with its deep blue, flowering heads and is a common component of native wildflower gardens. Another low zone native, Arizona lupine (L. arizonicus) is found in the desert flats around Phoenix and Tucson; it has light purple to rose flowers. Both of these species can be reluctant performers in a garden setting.

Bloom Period and Seasonal Color

February to April; deep indigo blue.

Mature Height × Spread

2 to 3 feet × 2 to 3 feet

Zones

1, 2, 3

Cosmos
Cosmos bipinnatus

It is hard to resist cosmos with its large, wide ray flowers in a range of bright, festive colors. I find it a cheerful plant—it lifts the spirits and places a bit of balm on a summer-weary garden. Plants can be tall, over 3 feet, but the tiny, pale green, threadlike leaves are so delicately lobed, they look like lace. Flowers emerge from the tips in a virtually endless array of white, pinks, and reds. Like sunflowers, they nod in the direction of the sun. Give your garden a generous dose of these summer-flowering plants; you will be rewarded for the entire summer. The closely related yellow cosmos (Cosmos sulphureus) has narrow lobed, hairy leaves and blooms in yellows, oranges, and reds.

Other Common Name
Mexican aster

Bloom Period and Seasonal Color
Spring and summer; shades of white, pink, rose, lavender, purple, crimson.

Mature Height × Spread
1 to 6 feet × 1 to 2 feet

Zones
All

When, Where, and How to Plant
Sow seed in fall in low zones; as early as soil can be worked in intermediate and high zones. Although cosmos will grow in almost any soil, including rocky, native soil, plants are larger, more vigorous, and bloom best in well-drained, fertile soil. Prepare the bed by breaking the surface of the soil with a rake or gently turning with a garden fork. Spread a thin layer of slow-release or organic fertilizer and mulch on the surface and rake it in. Broadcast seed, mixing them with sand or mulch to help distribute them evenly. Cover lightly by raking the soil and press the soil gently to prevent seed from washing away. Water every two to three days until seed germinate, then water every five to seven days.

Growing Tips
Cosmos need no supplemental fertilizer during the growing and blooming season. Water once or twice a week during the blooming season in low zones. Water once a week or less during the blooming season in high zones. Cosmos thrives on a regimen of benign neglect and overwatering or overly rich soils will cause plants to become floppy, unkempt, and reduce bloom.

Care
Deadhead spent flowers throughout the season to prolong bloom. Cosmos make excellent cut flowers. Plants that have become overly large, or begin to flop can be staked or propped to keep them upright. Cosmos is not susceptible to pests or disease.

Companion Planting and Design
Mix generously with other summer-flowering annuals such as sunflowers, zinnias, or coreopsis. Mix with flowering perennials such as Mexican oregano, gaillardia, or salvias for long-standing color. Smaller or dwarf varieties make good container plants, either singly or in mixed plantings. Plant generously near walkways or patios. Butterflies are strongly attracted to cosmos; place where you can enjoy these visitors.

Did You Know?
The name *cosmos* derives from a Greek word for harmony in recognition of the orderly arrangement of the petals.

Desert Bluebell
Phacelia campanularia

When, Where, and How to Plant
Sow seed in fall in low zones; as early as soil can be worked in high zones. Desert bluebells will grow in any soil, including rocky, native soil, or well-drained fertile soil. Prepare the bed by breaking the surface of the soil with a rake or gently turning with a garden fork. Spread a thin layer of slow-release or organic fertilizer and mulch on the surface and rake it in. Broadcast seed, mixing them with sand or mulch to help distribute them evenly. Cover lightly by raking the soil and press the soil gently to prevent seed from washing away. In rocky areas, broadcast seed over the surface and water the area immediately. Water every two to three days until seed germinate, then water every five to seven days.

Growing Tips
Desert bluebells do not need supplemental fertilizer and will grow excessive leaves at the expense of flowers if grown under conditions that are too rich. Water once a week through the blooming season, although those planted in rocky locations or in partial shade will require less frequent watering.

Care
This is one of the easiest of all wildflowers to grow and enjoy and requires no special care. Desert bluebell is not susceptible to pests or disease.

Companion Planting and Design
The classic wildflower combination in low zones is to mix desert bluebells with Mexican gold poppies or California poppies in large wildflower beds, small corners, or in containers. The color contrasts are stunning. This species reseeds freely, especially in rocky soils, and plants tend to find their way to charming locations at the base of rocks, near doorways, or in nooks of a patio. Use as a filler in containers with succulents for extra spring color or plant generously so that the rich blue flowers cover barren spots.

Did You Know?
The genus name comes from the Greek, *phakelos*, meaning "a bundle," which refers to the bunched flowers. The epithet is from the Latin *campana* meaning "bell," referring to the shape of the flowers.

Desert bluebells are lush, thick plants with dark, gray-green, heart-shaped leaves that are dimpled along the surface and crimped along the edge. Plants are tidy, looking like a bouquet in the garden. These charming leaves are the backdrop for the brilliant deep purple to indigo blue flowers that are held in loose heads above the foliage. This is one of the easiest of all wildflowers to grow. There are other annual phacelias which do well in low zone annual gardens. Look for lacy phacelia (Phacelia tanacetifolia) that, as the name suggests, has finely cut foliage, grows to 3 or more feet tall, and has long clusters of lavender to purple flowers. The native scorpion weed (P. crenulata) has fingers of purple flowers that curl much like a scorpion's tail.

Bloom Period and Seasonal Color
Spring; indigo-blue flowers.

Mature Height × Spread
6 to 12 inches × 6 to 15 inches

Zones
1, 2, 3

Farewell-to-Spring
Clarkia amoena

After the big splash of spring-blooming desert wildflowers begins to fade, it is encouraging to find that farewell-to-spring has just begun to bloom. There are two basic types of this plant—a small, thin-stemmed, low, trailing plant, and the taller, more upright form. Most of the plants sold from seed are the shorter version. Both have large flowers held on short stalks with wide open, flared petals. Farewell-to-spring has a great color range in reds, pinks, and sometimes white, but almost all flowers have a darker throat to contrast with the petals. Numerous selections of this species include 'Dwarf Gem' that grows to only 10 inches tall, and 'Tall Upright' that grows, as the name suggests, up to 3 feet tall.

Other Common Name
Godetia

Bloom Period and Seasonal Color
Late spring through summer; pink, lavender, mauve, and white.

Mature Height × Spread
4 to 5 inches (some to 3 feet) × 12 to15 inches

Zones
1, 2, 3, 4

When, Where, and How to Plant
Sow seed in fall in low zones; as early as soil can be worked in high zones. Farewell-to-spring grows well both in well-drained, fertile soil or rocky, native soil. Prepare the bed by breaking the surface of the soil with a rake or gently turning with a garden fork. Spread a thin layer of slow-release or organic fertilizer and mulch on the surface and rake it in. Broadcast seed, mixing them with sand or mulch to help distribute them evenly. Cover lightly by raking the soil and press the soil gently to prevent seed from washing away. Water every two to three days until seed germinate, then water every five to seven days.

Growing Tips
Farewell-to-spring needs no supplemental fertilizer; in fact, too rich a soil will cause the plants to become floppy and unkempt. Water once or twice a week during spring and while the plants are blooming. Increase watering if the weather becomes exceptionally hot or dry.

Care
Farewell-to-spring makes a good cut flower. Remove spent flowers to encourage continued bloom. Farewell-to-spring is not susceptible to pests or disease.

Companion Planting and Design
When used in a mixed planting with early season and spring-flowering annuals, farewell-to-spring helps extend the season. Low-growing forms are effective as a mixed border in front of larger annual or perennial plantings. Use farewell-to-spring in pots of succulents or agaves to give some spring color to the container. Useful in large containers as part of a mixed planting. Whether in the ground or in a container, plant generously when used alone; the plants look wispy and spare by themselves.

Did You Know?
Like many plants, farewell-to-spring has undergone name changes. The original genus was *Godetia*, but when it was changed to *Clarkia* in honor of the explorer Captain William Clark, the name godetia hung on as a common name. Selections of this species used extensively in the florist trade are still known as godetia.

Mexican Gold Poppy

Eschscholzia mexicana

When, Where, and How to Plant

Sow seed in fall in low zones; as early as soil can be worked in high zones. Mexican gold poppy grows best in native, rocky soil while California poppy grows best in well-drained, fertile soil, but survives in rocky, native soil. Prepare the bed by breaking the surface of the soil with a rake or gently turning with a garden fork. Spread a thin layer of slow-release or organic fertilizer and mulch on the surface and rake it in. Broadcast seed, mixing them with sand or mulch to help distribute them evenly. Cover lightly by raking the soil and press the soil gently to prevent seed from washing away. Water every two to three days until seed germinate, then water every five to seven days until there are five leaves.

Growing Tips

Neither of these species needs supplemental fertilizer. Water once a week through the growing and blooming season. Water more frequently to extend bloom if the weather becomes exceptionally hot or dry.

Care

Apply a thin layer of gravel or other inorganic mulch to keep soil moist and reduce watering. Neither of these poppies reseeds abundantly and should be over-seeded each year. The color selections in California poppy do not come true from seed. Neither of these poppies is susceptible to pests or disease.

Companion Planting and Design

Mix Mexican gold poppy with desert bluebells for a classic Sonoran wildflower look. Use either species abundantly; poppies are most dramatic and effective planted in mass groups. California poppy mixes well with other spring-flowering perennials such as penstemons, salvia, or spring-flowering bulbs, or in the high zones with other summer-flowering perennials and annuals. Both are excellent in large containers or planters placed near a patio or walkway for abundant spring or summer color.

Did You Know?

It is said that the hills of present day Pasadena, California were so thick with blooming poppies in spring that Spanish sailors came to call the coast the "Land of Fire."

Drive anywhere in southern Arizona in spring and you will see roadsides and hills painted in the golden hues of the diminutive Mexican gold poppy. In good years, the one-inch yellow flowers are so prolific that hillsides glow yellow and gold for miles in the distance. These charming natives have been brought into the garden to form the basis of many wildflower gardens. The dusky gray-green leaves are arranged in a rosette growing low to the ground. The bright golden flowers are held on thin stalks above the foliage. California poppy (Eschscholzia californica) is a taller plant with numerous finely-cut leaves and deep gold-orange colored flowers. This species has been extensively planted along highway rights-of-way. California poppy has many color forms with the pure white 'Milky White' and deep red 'Red Chief' among the best.

Bloom Period and Seasonal Color
February to April; gold, yellow, occasionally white.

Mature Height × Spread
4 to 8 inches × 2 to 6 inches

Zones
All

Nasturtium

Tropaeolum majus

Nasturtiums are an old-fashioned plant full of nostalgia and pleasant memories carried from generations of gardeners before us. Older forms are loose rambling vines that crawl away from their trellis. Flowers are prolific on the plant and open for a long season in a stunning range of colors from red to maroon, to butter yellow to orange. 'Empress of India' is a striking bushy plant with dark, dusky green leaves and vivid scarlet flowers. Nasturtium blooms in winter and spring in the low zones and through summer in intermediate and high zones. A delightful vining relative—canary creeper (Tropaeolum peregrinum)—has bright yellow flowers with frilly-edged petals that look ready to fly. Like nasturtium, it is a spring-flowering plant in low zones and summer-flowering in high zones.

Bloom Period and Seasonal Color
Spring to summer; yellow, gold, red-orange, orange, reddish, white, cream, and red, including combinations and bicolored forms.

Mature Height × Spread
2 to 10 feet × 2 to 10 feet

Zones
All

When, Where, and How to Plant
Sow seed in fall in low zones; as early as soil can be worked in high zones. Nasturtium grows in either full sun or partial shade. Nasturtium will grow in almost any soil, including rocky, native soil, but plants are larger, more vigorous, and bloom best in well-drained, fertile soil. Prepare the bed by breaking the surface of the soil with a rake or gently turning it with a garden fork. Spread a thin layer of slow-release or organic fertilizer and mulch on the surface and rake it in. Broadcast seed, mixing them with sand or mulch to help distribute them evenly. Cover lightly by raking the soil and press the soil gently to prevent seed from washing away. Water every two to three days until seed germinate, then water every five to seven days.

Growing Tips
Nasturtium needs no supplemental fertilizer; in fact, too much fertilizer results in excessive vegetative growth and poor flower production. Water established plants every week while they are blooming, more often if the weather turns hot.

Care
Vining varieties need a trellis or arbor for support (check the seed packet). Nasturtium reseeds vigorously and most varieties come true from seed. Not susceptible to pests or disease.

Companion Planting and Design
Use vining forms on arbors or trellises to provide extra spring color. These forms can also be allowed to run along the ground or spill over a raised planter creating a carpet of spring flowers. Nasturtium mixes well with vegetables adding interest and color to vegetable gardens. This is an excellent annual to provide quick cover for bare areas in a new garden. Mix with bulbs or spring-flowering annuals or use it to mask winter dormant perennials. All forms grow well in containers or hanging baskets.

Did You Know?
The leaves and flowers are edible and have a spicy, peppery flavor. Use them to add zest to a salad of spring greens or mix them into butter as a tasty spread.

Scarlet Flax
Linum grandiflorum 'Rubrum'

When, Where, and How to Plant
Sow seed in fall in low zones; as early as soil can be worked in high zones. Scarlet flax grows in full sun or partial shade. Although scarlet flax will grow in almost any soil, including rocky, native soil, plants are larger, more vigorous, and bloom best in well-drained, fertile soil. Prepare the bed by breaking the surface of the soil with a rake or gently turning it with a garden fork. Spread a thin layer of slow-release or organic fertilizer and mulch on the surface and rake it in. Broadcast seed, mixing them with sand or mulch to help distribute them evenly. Cover lightly by raking the soil and press the soil gently to prevent seed from washing away. Water every two to three days until seed germinate, then water every five to seven days.

Growing Tips
Scarlet flax does not need supplemental fertilizer. Water established plants every week through the growing and blooming season. Sow seed at two-week intervals to extend the blooming period.

Care
Scarlet flax is effortless in most gardens and requires no special care or attention. It is not susceptible to pests or disease.

Companion Planting and Design
Mix with other spring-flowering annuals such as Shirley poppy, nasturtium, or coneflower. Because of its height, plant flax as a background for flowering perennials such as salvia and penstemon. Plant generously; the spare stems make an individual plant seem sparse, while they are glorious in groupings. Scarlet flax is an excellent choice to use in mass plantings around patios, seating areas, and pools or to fill in barren spots in a newly planted garden.

Did You Know?
There are numerous species of flax both annual and perennial. All types of flax can produce linen of varying quality and many species have been grown since at least 3000 B.C. for this purpose. Today, the annual flax, *Linum usitatissimum*, which has extremely fine fibers, is the flax of commerce.

Many annuals promise long-lasting blooms, brilliant color displays, spontaneous reseeding—all with little or no effort on our part. Few live up to this pledge, but gardeners throughout Arizona can count on scarlet flax. I could never be without these plants again in my garden, and they seem to agree. Plants are tall, with erect stems that branch toward the ends. Among the earliest annuals to germinate, plants emerge in early fall and may begin blooming as early as January in Zone 1. The true species has rosy pink flowers, but this selection presents one-inch wide, scarlet red blooms and has now become the most common form. The variety 'Bright Eyes' has white flowers with a dark, red-brown eye.

Bloom Period and Seasonal Color
Spring through summer; pure red.

Mature Height × Spread
18 to 24 inches × 6 to 12 inches

Zones
All

Shirley Poppy

Papaver rhoeas

Shirley poppy is perfectly at home in gardens in all zones of the state. The dark green dissected leaves grow as a low basal plant through fall and winter until suddenly in late spring, the plant stretches out and the nodding flower buds form on thin stalks. Flowers are large, with paper-thin petals lasting only one day. There are countless forms in a host of colors, but it is the pure, deep red with the black cross at the petal's base that has won my devotion. Bread poppy (Papaver somniferum) is a heftier plant with large, powdery gray-green, cabbagelike leaves and 4-inch flowers in a vast array of colors. Iceland poppy (P. nudicaule) has low, light green basal leaves and bright, multihued flowers on tall, thin stalks.

Other Common Names
Flanders field poppy, corn poppy

Bloom Period and Seasonal Color
Spring to summer; red, pink, white, salmon, blue, and purple.

Mature Height × Spread
2 to 3 feet × 1 to 2 feet

Zones
All

When, Where, and How to Plant
Sow seed in fall in low zones; as early as soil can be worked in high zones. Shirley poppy will grow in any kind of soil including hot, rocky, native soil in the low zones or well-drained, fertile soil in all zones. Prepare the bed by breaking the surface of the soil with a rake or gently turning it with a garden fork. Spread a thin layer of slow-release or organic fertilizer and mulch on the surface and rake it in. Broadcast seed, mixing them with sand or mulch to help distribute them evenly. Cover lightly by raking the soil and press the soil gently to prevent seed from washing away. Water every two to three days until seed germinate, then water every five to seven days.

Growing Tips
Shirley poppy requires no supplemental fertilization. Plants become floppy and bloom poorly if grown with too much fertilizer or too much water. Water established plants sparingly through winter or spring as they are growing. Water once a week or less when the plants are blooming, depending on the temperatures.

Care
Shirley poppy grows with minimal care and little attention. It is not susceptible to pests or disease.

Companion Planting and Design
Plant generously—Shirley poppies are spectacular in mass plantings. Unlike other poppies, there are multiple flowers on each stalk that open in succession through the season. Because of its height, use as a background plant for smaller spring-flowering bulbs, penstemons, or salvias or to cover over winter weary summer-flowering perennials such as red bird-of-paradise or lantana. This is an excellent plant to hide barren spots or empty corners in a newly planted garden.

Did You Know?
My father's family is Czech and his aunts always had bread poppy planted in the front yards of their farmhouses. They grew them for the seeds that were used as a filling for their delicious poppy seed cakes and buns, a treat that we all adored.

Sunflower
Helianthus annuus

When, Where, and How to Plant

Sow seed in fall in low zones; as early as soil can be worked in high zones. Sunflowers grow best in well-drained, fertile soil in full sun. Prepare the bed by breaking the surface of the soil with a rake or gently turning it with a garden fork. Spread a thin layer of slow-release or organic fertilizer and mulch on the surface and rake it in. Broadcast seed, mixing them with sand or mulch to help distribute them evenly. Cover lightly by raking the soil and press the soil gently to prevent seed from washing away. Water every two to three days until seed germinate, then water every five to seven days.

Growing Tips

Sunflowers do not require supplemental fertilizer. Apply mulch to the ground around the stems but do not let it touch the stems. Water regularly, two or three times a week in low zones and do not allow the soil to dry out while plants are blooming.

Care

Flowers may be cut anytime and regular removal of flower heads promotes continued blooming. Plants are susceptible to mildew on the lower leaves—a condition that is exacerbated by overhead watering. Prevention is the best remedy.

Companion Planting and Design

Mix with other summer-flowering annuals such as zinnias, coreopsis, and nasturtium. Sunflowers liven up vegetable or herb gardens and mix well with these plants. Plant among gaillardias, coneflowers, and salvias to add height and bright color. Use compact varieties planted generously as an informal border or edging. Small varieties work well in containers or planters either planted solely or in mixed groups. Birds are drawn to the seeds and will help spread seed around the garden.

Did You Know?

To save seed, cut off the sunflower head when the disc is dark brown and the rays begin to fade and put it in a paper bag. Keep the bag dry and out of the sun until the seeds mature. Seeds are dry and ready to store in about three weeks.

Known all over the country for their large, yellow-rayed flowers, sunflowers are an icon of summer. In the low zones, most varieties begin to bloom in late spring and continue until mid-summer. In high zones, plants bloom throughout summer. Native from the central United States south into South America, there are endless forms and cultivars. Many of the large varieties are grown commercially for their edible seed. Native American farmers in the Southwest selected many varieties for their oily seeds as well. Colors range from the traditional yellow with brown disc to white, gold, orange, brownish red, and maroon. These flowers make wonderful cut flowers and the delicious seeds are ravaged by birds as soon as they are ripe.

Bloom Period and Seasonal Color
Late spring through summer; yellow, reddish, brown, or orange rays, and dark brown discs.

Mature Height × Spread
2 to 10 feet × 2 to 4 feet

Zones
All

Tidy Tips

Layia platyglossa

Tidy tips is a low-growing, spring-flowering annual that perfectly lives up to its name. The light green lance-shaped leaves are entirely covered by the prolific bloom. One of the first wildflowers to begin blooming, tidy tips continues to bloom until the weather becomes very warm. In high zone gardens, it blooms through summer. The flowers have yellow ray flowers that are rimmed in white. The disc flowers are light yellow. The flower is so symmetrical and the colors so regular it looks crisp and cool, like a snappy linen suit. Although very small, these plants are prolific both in nature and in the garden. The related *Layia glandulosa* is native to Arizona. This species has pure white flowers that also bloom prolifically in early spring.

Bloom Period and Seasonal Color
Spring; yellow rays with white edges and yellow discs.

Mature Height × Spread
4 to 10 inches × 5 to 10 inches

Zones
All

When, Where, and How to Plant
Sow seed in fall in low zones; as early as soil can be worked in high zones. Tidy tips will grow in any soil from well-drained, fertile soil, to heavy clay, and rocky, native soil. Prepare the bed by breaking the surface of the soil with a rake or gently turning it with a garden fork. Spread a thin layer of slow-release or organic fertilizer and mulch on the surface and rake it in. Broadcast seed, mixing them with sand or mulch to help distribute them evenly. Cover lightly by raking the soil and press the soil gently to prevent seed from washing away. Water every two to three days until seed germinate, then water every five to seven days.

Growing Tips
Tidy tips need no supplemental fertilizer. Water every week during the blooming season.

Care
Tidy tips is an easy and effortless species to use for vivid spring color and requires no special care or attention. It is not susceptible to pests or disease.

Companion Planting and Design
Mix tidy tips with other annuals such as desert bluebells or poppies to provide interest and contrast in a spring wildflower bed. Plant generously to use it as a low border in front of taller perennials or annuals. This species is particularly effective used in mass plantings along a walkway or around a seating area, courtyard, or pool. Look for a place to plant tidy tips where the stunning regularity of the flowers and their bright colors can be viewed from above. Tidy tips mixes well with succulents and adds a splash of color to potted succulents, cactus, or agaves. Tidy tips can be used in containers or planters either alone or mixed with other annuals or perennials.

Did You Know?
The sunflower family is among the largest in the plant kingdom with 1,300 genera and over 21,000 species. There are sunflower species found on every continent, including Australia.

When, Where, and How to Plant

Sow seed in fall or early winter in full sun or partial shade. Toadflax is not particular about soil and will grow in well-drained, fertile soil, heavy clay, or rocky, native soil. It grows larger and blooms more prolifically in fertile soil. Prepare the bed by breaking the surface of the soil with a rake or gently turning it with a garden fork. Spread a thin layer of slow-release or organic fertilizer and mulch on the surface and rake it in. Broadcast seed, mixing them with sand or mulch to help distribute them evenly. Cover lightly by raking the soil and press the soil gently to prevent seed from washing away. Water every two to three days until seed germinate, then water every five to seven days.

Growing Tips

Toadflax does not need supplemental fertilizer. Once plants are established, water weekly through the blooming season. Water more frequently if the weather is exceptionally hot or dry.

Care

Some strains continue to grow and bloom through summer if they are grown in partial shade. Toadflax requires no special care or attention to continue to grow and bloom successfully. It is not susceptible to pests or disease.

Companion Planting and Design

Mix toadflax with other spring-flowering annuals such as tidy tips, bluebells, or poppies. Toadflax, with its huge array of colors, is outstanding in mass plantings to fill in a barren spot in a newly planted garden or to line a drive or walkway. Toadflax mixes well with succulents such as cactus, aloes, or agaves, and brings a dash of color to odd corners or small beds near seating areas and pools. Toadflax is excellent in containers or planters either alone or mixed with perennials or annuals.

Did You Know?

There is a variety of toadflax that has brilliant purple and orange flowers and is locally grown in Phoenix. A close friend proudly growing them pointed out to me that they bloom in the colors of the local basketball team—the Phoenix Suns.

den in arden, ierous inning t does nge is s, and ts are t look quet' astel les of

C
Ba.

Bloo.
Spring and summer in red, gold, rose, pink, blue, and purple.

Mature Height × Spread
6 to 24 inches × 6 inches

Zones
All

Bulbs, Corms, and Rhizomes *for Arizona*

Bulbs are a natural for Arizona gardens because many bulbs are from semiarid to desert regions, often with strongly seasonal rainfall patterns. The term "bulb" is a catchall word for a large and variable group of plants that may or may not actually grow true bulbs. Plants such as tulips, daffodils, and amaryllis grow from true bulbs, which are congested leaves wrapped around a short stem or basal plate. Moraea and freesia, also called bulbs, grow from corms, which are odd flattened stems often with scaly sheaths. Iris grow from rhizomes, which are swollen underground stems with nodes that produce new plants along the stem, although there are iris that grow true bulbs as well. Each of these organs serves as a storage unit for the plant enabling it to endure long periods of dormancy with little or no water.

Let Sleeping Bulbs Lie

Because most bulbs are dormant during at least part of the year, it is important not to interrupt their growth cycle by removing leaves prematurely. The energy to grow and flower is established in most bulbs during the previous year. Therefore, it is also important to provide ample water and a little fertilizer while the leaves are actively growing. The growing season for a bulb is variable by species. Some, such as freesia, send up the leaves first and grow them awhile before the flowers emerge. Then the whole plant dies quickly after flowering. Others, such as rain lilies, shoot up the flowers first, followed by the leaves, which last for a few weeks or months until the plant becomes dormant. And still others, such as spider lilies, are ever green, and while they may rest and grow less during certain times of the year, they never completely die away. Except for evergreen bulbs, relocate bulbs only when they are dormant.

Fringed Tulip

Rain Lily

While we tend to think of bulbs as needing chill, that is not necessarily the case for most bulbs. Low zone gardeners find that bulbs requiring a chill, such as hybrid tulips or hyacinths, are often difficult plants to grow with tedious requirements of artificial chill needed to induce bloom. High zone gardeners, on the other hand, find that these bulbs are some of the easiest and most consistent bloomers for their gardens. But there are numerous winter-growing, summer-dormant bulbs such as sparaxis, moraeas, and freesia, chiefly from South Africa, which are perfectly suited to low zone gardens. In addition, the long, warm summer of the low zone makes it an ideal area for Mexican summer flowering species such as rain lilies and some of the tropical species of *Crinum* and *Hymenocallis*.

The Versatility of Bulbs

Bulbs blend beautifully into perennial beds by providing vivid, spectacular flowering in season, then obligingly fading away to make way for other flowering plants. The summer-growing, largely tropical species of crinums and spider lilies have large, strappy leaves that are usually a vivid green. These large, fountain-shaped plants make an excellent background or filler plant even when they are out of bloom.

Small species add extra drama to the garden as a low border to a perennial bed or when planted in mass. In every area of the state, there are some species that naturalize and spread freely with minimal effort creating splendid color displays in their season. Bulbs can also be tucked into very tiny spots or fill in small, barren areas of the garden. Many of the South African species grow extremely well in the rough, rocky, native soils of the low zones and can be used in newly planted beds or hot, dry corners of the garden. Some species, especially spider lilies, are excellent in the shade, even the dry shade of the desert regions.

Bulbs also make outstanding container plants. They can be planted closely together to create an intense display during their blooming period. They also mix well with other bulbs, annuals, or perennials to create miniature gardens in a pot. It is easier to control the conditions for plants grown in containers which provides the opportunity for growing a wider variety of bulbs than may be possible in the ground.

There is such a vast range of choices in bulbs that it is possible to find the perfect fit for your garden's conditions and style. Make a garden resolution to use bulbs generously as the seasoning for a perennial bed, to lighten up a succulent bed, or as a dash of seasonal color.

Amaryllis
Hippeastrum species and hybrids

These beloved garden ornamentals come to American gardens from South America. Although there are about eighty species, most of the garden forms are hybrids and their resulting cultivars and forms. Flowers arise on tall, sturdy stalks in spring and produce a wheel of large trumpet-shaped flowers in reds, pinks, and whites. Flowers may be as few as three or as numerous as eight and are either single or double. Cultivars grown for the floral trade produce immense flowers on hefty stalks, but these can also be reluctant rebloomers. Good garden forms are just as striking and rebloom better in the ground. Amaryllis are effortless repeat bloomers in the ground in the low and intermediate zones but are not reliably hardy in Zones 3 and 4. In those areas, pot culture, lifting the plants before winter, or mulching the bulb heavily is advised.

Bloom Period and Seasonal Color
April to June; hues of red, pink, and white, often with bicolors and combinations of these colors.

Mature Height × Spread
2 to 3 feet × 1 to 2 feet

Zones
1, 2, 3, 4
Hardy to 20 degrees Fahrenheit with some protection.

When, Where, and How to Plant
Plant bulbs in early spring. Amaryllis grow in full morning sun or partial shade. Dig a hole in well-drained, fertile soil that is as large as the bulb and add bonemeal or organic fertilizer to the hole before planting. Place the bulb so that the neck is well above the surface of the soil. Some gardeners recommend that the bulb be halfway above the soil line. Water every two to three weeks until leaves emerge, then water weekly.

Growing Tips
Apply bonemeal, balanced or organic fertilizer annually after bloom is finished and again in summer. Container-grown plants need regular applications of soluble fertilizer while they are growing. Amaryllis bulbs may be left in the ground year-round in the low elevation zones and will tolerate regular watering during dormancy.

Care
Amaryllis leaves and bulbs continue to grow long after blooming. Maintain regular watering and fertilization during that time. In mid to late summer, when leaves begin to yellow, it is best to quit fertilizing plants, reduce watering, and let them die down naturally. Remove leaves that come away easily in your hand. Reduce watering and stop fertilizing plants grown in containers in late summer to bring on dormancy. Amaryllis are susceptible to slugs and snails, particularly in poorly drained soils.

Companion Planting and Design
Plant generously for a spectacular show during the short, blooming season. Use amaryllis as part of an informal border or mixed perennial planting. Amaryllis bloom at roughly the same time as roses and iris and look splendid when interplanted among these two perennials. Amaryllis are excellent in containers. This is the most reliable way to ensure reblooming in cold areas.

Did You Know?
Plant names are rife with confusion. The genus *Amaryllis* has only one species and it is from South Africa. But the common name "amaryllis" applies to the over eighty species and hundreds of hybrids in the South American genus, *Hippeastrum*.

When, Where, and How to Plant

Plant bulbs in spring or early summer in any sun exposure, but shade is best in the hottest zones. Bulbs grow well in rocky, native soil, or well-drained, fertile soil. Dig a hole as large as the bulb and add bonemeal or organic fertilizer to the hole before planting. Plant the bulb so that the entire neck is above the surface of the soil. Water every week for the first month; every week or two through the first summer.

Growing Tips

Apply slow-release or organic fertilizer annually in spring. Keep plants well mulched, even when they are in the shade, to prevent the soil from drying out completely. Water established plants every week in summer, much less in winter.

Care

Evergreen crinums grow vigorously for months after their summer bloom. In early summer, plants often lose some of their leaves and appear to decline. Do not remove the leaves unless they come away easily in your hand. Continue watering as before. Remove spent flowering stalks anytime after blooming. Crinums resent disturbance and should not be lifted or moved unless necessary. Crinums are not susceptible to pests or disease when grown in very well-drained soil.

Companion Planting and Design

Crinums are excellent specimen or accent plants. The large, deep green, strap-shaped leaves give a lush appearance to a shady bed, perennial planting, or patio garden. Use white flowering forms to brighten dark, shady places or offer a spot of bright color in the hottest part of the summer. Many varieties are sweetly fragrant and should be used near seating areas, entryways, or other gathering areas to fully enjoy the scent. Crinums grow well in large containers or planters.

Did You Know?

A bulb is an underground storage organ that is made up of a basal plate from which the roots grow and a compressed stem that looks like a bud. That stem is then enclosed by leaf bases and by fleshy, modified leaves called scales.

If you are familiar with crinums in the southeastern United States where they grow in ditches, ponds, and waterways, it is hard to imagine that they would be successful in southern Arizona. But Crinum is a large genus, and many of these subtropical bulbs, especially the evergreen varieties, do well in the low zones. Most of the plants sold are hybrids of Crinum bulbispermum, a South African species, or are part of the hybrid complex Crinum × powellii. One or more tall, sturdy, flowering stalks arise in summer, topped with the large, colorful, trumpet-shaped flowers. There can be up to six flowers on each stalk. These are extremely long-lived bulbs that gain girth every year. Old bulbs may become the size of a football.

Bloom Period and Seasonal Color
Summer; white, pink, mauve, and reddish.

Mature Height × Spread
3 to 4 feet × 3 to 5 feet

Zones
1, 2, 3, 4
Hardy to 23 degrees Fahrenheit when well protected.

Daffodil
Narcissus species

Prized for their early and prolific bloom, daffodils do remarkably well in all zones of the state. The tubular petals open like wide-mouthed trumpets and are surrounded at the base by a ruffled collar of sepals. In good, garden soil, these are long-lived bulbs; they multiply generously, but are rarely invasive. For low and intermediate zones choose between the Cyclamineus types, with their swept back petals and one bloom per stalk, or Jonquilla with narrow leaves and one to five blooms per stem. The Tazetta types are the best for the hot desert regions—they require no winter chill and have up to twenty flowers per stem. There are hundreds of varieties but most are colored in whites and yellows with smooth, ruffled, or double-flowered forms.

Other Common Names
Narcissus, Jonquil

Bloom Period and Seasonal Color
Early spring; yellow or white.

Mature Height × Spread
6 to 8 inches × 4 to 8 inches

Zones
All
Hardiness depends on the variety but most are hardy to at least 20 degrees Fahrenheit, many much lower.

When, Where, and How to Plant
Plant in fall in all but the coldest zones. Plant varieties that need a cold chill in high zone gardens. Although some low-zone gardeners prechill bulbs in the refrigerator for six weeks before planting, it is better to use varieties that do not need prechilling. Plant in full sun or partial shade in well-drained, fertile soil. Dig a hole the size of the bulb. Apply bonemeal or organic fertilizer to the hole before planting. Set bulbs deeply in the ground, about twice their height and cover well. Water thoroughly. Water weekly until leaves or flowers emerge.

Growing Tips
Apply slow-release or organic fertilizer annually in fall in low zones; early spring in high zones. Water daffodils that are growing and blooming every week or two depending on the temperatures. Bulbs do not have to remain entirely dry when they are dormant but they should not be kept continuously wet either.

Care
Allow leaves to yellow and dry out naturally. Remove them when they can be pulled away easily by hand. Cut flowering stalks anytime. Daffodils are not susceptible to most disease, although gophers find the bulbs irresistible. Most varieties multiply readily and can be divided every four or five years.

Companion Planting and Design
Daffodils, especially the multiflowered Tazetta types, mix well with spring-blooming penstemon, red justicia, and other bulbs such as alliums and freesia. Use daffodils to create an informal border or edge for a larger bed, along a drive, or walkway. Daffodils make excellent plants for containers. The ones known as paperwhites require no chilling period to grow and are extremely easy to force into late winter bloom for indoor or holiday use.

Did You Know?
The roots of bulbs are generally annual. They die when the plant goes dormant and regenerate completely when the plant begins to grow again.

Flowering Onion
Allium neapolitanum

When, Where, and How to Plant

Plant dormant bulbs in fall or container-grown plants in spring. Flowering onions will grow in full sun or partial shade and need a well-drained, fertile soil. Dig the hole the size of the bulb or container and add bonemeal or organic fertilizer. Set bulbs in holes leaving the top of the bulb an inch below the surface. Cover and water thoroughly. Water every week or two until leaves emerge, then water weekly through flowering.

Growing Tips

Apply slow-release or organic fertilizer to the bed annually in fall. While the flowering onion is actively growing and blooming, water every seven to ten days. This bulb will tolerate some water when dormant and can be left in the bed through summer even in low zones.

Care

Alliums lose their leaves quickly after flowering. Allow the leaves to dry naturally on the plant and remove them when they can be pulled away easily in your hand. Spent flower stalks may be removed anytime. Divide bulbs in fall every five or six years. The flowering onion is not susceptible to pests or disease.

Companion Planting and Design

The pure white flowers make the flowering onion an excellent contrast when planted among colorful spring-flowering annuals such as desert bluebells and godetia or perennials such as salvia, penstemon, and desert marigold. Place bulbs where the plant can multiply without crowding or use in mass along the edges of large beds, drives, or walkways. The flowering onion grows well in a large container or planter, a method which is particularly useful in areas where the plant may become invasive.

Did You Know?

Common kitchen onions (*Allium cepa*) have been cultivated for over 5,000 years. They were considered the food of the poor in Medieval Europe but were a sacred vegetable suitable for offerings to the gods in ancient Egypt.

Flowering onions are an effortless garden plant in the low and intermediate zones of Arizona. A highly reliable spring-flowering bulb, it is closely related to the onion of the dinner table. Native to southern Europe, the long, strap-shaped leaves of the flowering onion begin appearing in early spring. Soon after emerging, they are topped by open heads of small, pure white flowers. Considered an aggressive garden pest in cool summer climates, in the hot low zones of the state, it is well behaved, multiplying gently in the garden. For low zone gardeners it is more reliable and easier to grow than most other ornamental onions. The variety 'Grandiflorum' has white flowers with a dark eye and is often mistakenly sold as Allium cowanii.

Other Common Names
Daffodil garlic, Naples garlic

Bloom Period and Seasonal Color
February and March; pure white loose heads.

Mature Height × Spread
8 to 10 inches × 10 to 24 inches

Zones
1, 2, 3, 4
Hardy to 20 degrees Fahrenheit.

Freesia

Freesia species

Many low zone Arizona gardeners are surprised to learn how easily this lovely bulb can be grown in the garden. Hybridized for a long time and well known in the floral trade, this South African species can be found in a wide range of colors and forms, including double flower forms. All are fragrant, some extravagantly so. In early spring, a fan of flat leaves emerges first, followed quickly by a nodding head of wide, tubular flowers. Individual flowers remain open for a week or more and the entire blooming sequence lasts about six weeks. The diminutive species, Freesia alba, fills the spring garden with its sweet, spicy aroma. The flowers are white with a bright yellow throat and it, too, blooms well over a month.

Bloom Period and Seasonal Color
Spring; reds, blue, lavender, purple, white, and yellow.

Mature Height × Spread.
3 to 6 inches × 3 to 6 inches

Zones
1, 2, 3
Hardy to 20 degrees Fahrenheit.

When, Where, and How to Plant
Plant corms in fall. Freesia tolerates any kind of soil from well-drained, fertile soil to heavy clay but grows particularly well in rocky, native soil. Plant in full sun or filtered shade. Dig the hole about 2 inches deep, setting the corms in with the root bud in the bottom of the hole. Cover completely and water thoroughly. Water every two to three weeks until the leaves emerge and then increase watering to once every seven to ten days.

Growing Tips
Apply slow-release or organic fertilizer annually in fall. Water weekly when the plant is flowering and continue to water every seven to ten days while the leaves remain on the plant. Freesia can be kept entirely dry when it is dormant. In areas that have regular summer rain or where summers are cool, it is best to lift the corms and replant them in fall.

Care
Leaves continue to grow for a month or more after blooming. Allow them to dry naturally and remove them when they can be pulled away easily by hand. Cut flowering stalks anytime. Corms multiply quickly and may be divided every three or four years. Freesia is not susceptible to pests or disease.

Companion Planting and Design
This colorful species is an outstanding addition to any spring plantings. Because freesia grows well in dry conditions, it is a good choice to mix with succulents such as aloes and agaves. Use freesia to fill barren spots in a newly planted garden. Freesia grows well in containers or planters either individually or mixed with other bulbs, annuals, or perennials. This reliable rebloomer, with its dry summer dormancy, is a perfect choice for a garden that is left on its own for the summer.

Did You Know?
Freesia grows from a corm, which is a thickened underground stem that serves as a food storage organ for the plant. Most corms are annual; numerous new corms form around the base every year.

When, Where, and How to Plant

Set out rhizomes in fall in low zones; in spring in higher zones. Plant in full sun, although partial shade is fine in the low zones. Dig a hole or trench in well-drained, fertile soil. Apply bonemeal or organic fertilizer to the bed before planting. Place the rhizome just at the surface of the soil and cover lightly. Water thoroughly. Water weekly until leaves begin to emerge.

Growing Tips

Apply slow-release or organic fertilizer in fall and again in spring a month before bloom. Fertilize monthly from September to April. Water established plants weekly while they are growing and flowering. Water carefully in summer to keep plants on the dry side; in low zones water weekly, in higher zones, water less often.

Care

Iris grow leaves through fall and winter and continue to grow them for a couple of months after bloom. Allow leaves to age and die in late summer and remove them when they can be pulled away easily in your hand. Remove blooms anytime. Cut back all remaining leaves to within 6 inches of the soil in early fall in low zones and early spring in higher zones. Divide clumps every three to four years, replanting newer rhizomes to maintain vigorous plants. Iris are susceptible to snails, slugs, and borers particularly in areas that have wet, warm summers.

Companion Planting and Design

Mix iris with spring-flowering perennials such as salvia, globemallow, and spring-flowering bulbs such as amaryllis for a grand spring show. Iris and roses are a classic combination because their blooming periods often coincide. Arilbreds need a very dry summer dormancy. This makes them a good choice to mix with Mediterranean perennials such as lavender and rosemary.

Did You Know?

There are over 250 species of iris and untold thousands of hybrids. Iris shows are held around the year, and iris societies are a great source of interesting and unusual varieties.

Iris have seduced gardeners all over the world with their rare and exotic beauty, and they grow well in Arizona in all but the coldest parts of Zones 4 and 5. Iris flowers have three large petals that fall away toward the stem and three that stand upright. In the class of bearded iris, each petal carries the characteristic caterpillar-like "beard." Aril iris have slender flowers and bizarre color schemes, and hybrids form the group called arilbred. They are particularly well suited to the hot, dry summers of the low zones. For low zones, the arilbred 'Heart Stealer', 'Dawn Caress', and the bearded 'Larry Gaulter', 'Mesmerizer', and 'Superstition' are among the best. For intermediate and high zones try 'Orange Slices', 'Old Black Magic', and 'Raspberry Splendor'.

Bloom Period and Seasonal Color
February to May; blue, purple, pink, white, yellow, and reddish tones including bicolors.

Mature Height × Spread
2 to 4 feet × 2 to 4 feet

Zones
1, 2, 3, 4, 5
Most hardy to at least 25 degrees Fahrenheit.

Rain Lily
Zephyranthes species

In the summer, shortly after a good drenching rain, rain lilies pop up out of the ground, burst into bloom, then quickly fade leaving only their leaves as a reminder that they will return if the rain returns. The large pink rain lily common in low and intermediate zone lawns and older gardens is Zephyranthes grandiflora. The tall, thin white flowers of Z. drummondii (formerly known as Cooperia drummondii and still sold under that name) reach up to 12 inches in height and like most rain lilies, spread prolifically over time. The clear yellow flowers of Z. citrina bloom later in summer as does the white flowered evergreen species, Z. candida. There are many hybrid forms, of which 'Ajax' is the most common.

Bloom Period and Seasonal Color
Summer; pink, white, yellow, and light orange.

Mature Height × Spread
4 to 6 inches × 4 to 6 inches

Zones
1, 2, 3, 4
Hardy to 23 degrees Fahrenheit.

When, Where, and How to Plant
Plant dormant bulbs in fall and container-grown plants either in fall or spring. Rain lilies grow well in either full sun or partial shade. Dig a hole or trench that is up to two inches deep in well-drained, fertile soil. Apply a thin layer of bonemeal or organic fertilizer to the hole. Set bulbs in the hole or trench to about twice their height and cover completely. Set container-grown plants in a hole that is the same size as the root zone. Cover the bulbs and roots, pressing the soil gently to remove air pockets. Water thoroughly after planting.

Growing Tips
Apply slow-release or organic fertilizer in fall and spring. Water established plants weekly in summer; rely on natural rainfall during winter. Plants will survive winter dormancy in beds that are regularly watered as long as there is good drainage. *Z. candida* should be watered every two to three weeks in winter.

Care
Leaves of rain lilies grow for only a short time after the blooming period and will dry and wither quickly. Remove when they can be pulled away easily in your hand. Evergreen species lose some leaves in summer and these, too, can be removed by hand. Remove spent flowers anytime. Divide crowded clumps every four or five years in fall. Rain lilies are very sturdy and are not susceptible to pests or disease.

Companion Planting and Design
Mix rain lilies with summer-flowering perennials such as salvia, gaillardia, lantana, or vinca. Rain lilies grow well in large containers or planters alone or in mixed plantings. Use evergreen species generously to form a loose, informal border or provide the edge for a large perennial bed. Most species of rain lily, and *Z. grandiflora* in particular, tolerate growing in a lawn.

Did You Know?
Arizona is home to one native member of this genus, *Z. longifolia*, which has thin, blue-green leaves and gold flowers.

Spider Lily
Hymenocallis species

When, Where, and How to Plant
Plant bulbs in spring or summer in any well-drained soil, even rocky, unamended, native soil. There are species that grow naturally in swamps and these require moist, fertile soil. Place spider lilies in partial to deep shade or full morning sun. Dig a hole that is slightly larger than the bulb, adding bonemeal or organic fertilizer to the hole before planting. Place the bulbs so that two thirds of the bulb and all of the neck are above the soil surface. Cover and water thoroughly. Water weekly until leaves emerge.

Growing Tips
Spider lilies grow with or without additional fertilizer but mulching the base of the plants helps keep them from drying out. Apply slow-release or organic fertilizer around the base annually in spring. Water established bulbs every seven to ten days in summer. Reduce watering to every other week in winter.

Care
Remove spent flower stalks anytime. Spider lily leaves grow for a long time after flowering—many are nearly evergreen. As leaves yellow and dry they may be removed when they can be pulled away easily by hand. Spider lily bulbs multiply slowly and resent being disturbed. Spider lilies are not susceptible to pests or disease.

Companion Planting and Design
The bulbs of the large, hybrid varieties grow in size over the years and produce many blooming stalks, making them especially dramatic as a specimen or focal plant. Mix with summer-flowering plants such as four o'clocks, California fuschia, and salvia. Smaller varieties do well in containers or planters particularly in areas where it is too cold to leave them in the ground year-round.

Did You Know?
Like most night-flowering plants, spider lilies are white—making them easier to see in low light, fragrant—making them noticeable with little light, and pollinated by night-flying moths, including the spectacular hawk moth.

The first spider lily that I planted in Arizona was given to me by a friend who was moving. I casually parked the large bulb in a shady spot out of the way, thinking I would move it later. Despite the rocky soil and neglect, it has thrived and blooms every summer, lighting up that dreary corner with its elegant, dangling white flowers. It is the common hybrid form of the large semievergreen plant with deep green strappy leaves. The flowers are extraordinary, with a thin, saucer uniting the thin, draping petals on tall, sturdy stalks high above the foliage. Some of the smaller species Hymenocallis maximillianii or H. littoralis are deciduous in the winter, growing and blooming only in the hottest part of summer.

Bloom Period and Seasonal Color
July to September; white or yellow.

Mature Height × Spread
1 to 4 feet × 1 to 3 feet

Zones
1, 2, 3
Hardy to 25 degrees Fahrenheit, but some species are tropical and need to be grown only in frost-free areas.

Tulip (Lady)
Tulipa clusiana

I have always thought tulips were way too much trouble—a big burst of overdone flowers for a terribly short time. I changed my mind when I started growing lady tulip (Tulipa clusiana), candia tulip (T. saxatilis), and T. sylvestris. The vast numbers of hybrid tulips require a long chill period and exacting cultivation, but these are real garden plants requiring only ordinary garden soil and minimal care, for which they reward you by multiplying rapidly and reblooming faithfully every year. Lady tulip has petals that are cream to yellow inside but red or coral outside. Candia tulip flowers are large and open in shades of pink, mauve, and lavender, often with bright yellow centers. T. sylvestris flowers range from lemon yellow to gold and are sweetly scented.

Bloom Period and Seasonal Color
March to May; yellow, white, pink.

Mature Height × Spread
6 to 36 inches × 3 to 6 inches

Zones
1, 2, 3, 4
Hardy to about 20 degrees Fahrenheit, perhaps more.

When, Where, and How to Plant
Plant bulbs in fall in full sun or partial shade. All three types described in the introduction grow larger and bloom more reliably in well-drained, fertile alkaline soil. Candia tulips grow and bloom in rocky, native soil as well. Dig a hole that is slightly larger than the bulb and apply bonemeal or organic fertilizer to the hole before planting. Place bulbs so that the tip of the bulb is 2 inches below the surface, cover completely and water thoroughly. Water every week or two until the leaves emerge.

Growing Tips
Apply slow-release or organic fertilizer in fall and early spring. Water growing and blooming plants weekly, more often if the weather is exceptionally hot or dry. These tulips need a long, dry summer dormancy and can be left in the ground or lifted and replanted.

Care
Leaves continue to grow for about a month after flowering and should be left to die off naturally. They may be removed when they can be pulled away easily by hand. Flowers may be cut anytime, and if picked early in the bloom cycle, make good cut flowers. Unlike hybrid forms, these species are not susceptible to pests or disease.

Companion Planting and Design
Mix tulips with other spring-flowering perennials, bulbs, or annuals. These species are shorter than the hybrids and should be used in the front of a border or in groups. All grow extremely well in containers or planters either in mass or mixed with other bulbs or perennials. They spread by stolons (underground stems) and fill in small, barren corners or odd ends of beds.

Did You Know?
The history of tulips is long and fascinating. They came to Europe in the 16th century from Turkey where they had already been cultivated for a long time. The lady tulip was recorded as growing in an Italian garden in 1606 and has been in continuous cultivation since that time.

Cacti, Succulents, and Desert Perennials *for Arizona*

It is easy to take succulents for granted in Arizona, especially in the low zones. Throughout the southern section of the state, saguaros, the giant succulent trees of the desert, rise up along rocky hillsides. Ocotillos, with their flashy, red sparklers of bloom, ignite rocky slopes, and blue-gray globes of desert spoon dot the canyon walls. Spring makes it clear how abundant cacti are in the desert when thousands of hedgehog, prickly pear, and cholla cacti crown the desert with their gaudy flowers.

Desert Specialists

Succulents are specialists, designed with a number of unique adaptations to living in hot, arid places where rainfall is low and infrequent. The most important feature is specialized water storing tissue in their leaves, stems, or roots. Leaf succulents such as agaves and aloes are arranged in rosettes to direct water to their wide, spreading, fibrous root systems. The leaves are thick, hard, and coated with a waxy cuticle to hold in as much water as possible. Cacti have succulent stems and their leaves are reduced to the spines that daunt us all. They, too, cover their skin in a waxy cuticle and like many succulents lose most of their root system during drought, growing it back in a matter of days when rain returns.

Mixed Cacti

47

Aloe

All these adaptations give succulents a huge advantage in their desert homes where rain is scarce and unreliable, but it also means that these remarkable plants are some of the most dramatic and unusual elements of Arizona gardens. While in most parts of the country gardeners constantly seek plants to provide a hard, sharp texture to contrast with all the billowy perennials, Arizona gardeners can find succulents of almost any size or style to add a bit of zing in the garden and give our gardens a recognizable and unique style.

Great Choices

Of all the succulent plants available for gardens, it is the cactus that comes first to mind when using succulents. Cacti may be tall, with single or multiple stems, giving height and weight to a garden. Some, like prickly pears and chollas, are virtually shrubs with their numerous stems, stacked and clustered and twisted into a shrublike shape. Smaller cacti like hedgehogs or pincushions fill in small spaces in the garden and are particularly attractive around rocks, as accent to larger succulents, or along slopes. Choose cacti for the garden carefully, not only for their scale and colors, but for their pungent spines. While they aren't the best choice around a play area or a pool, they are spectacular at the edge of the garden or mixed into large desert perennial or annual plantings.

Arizona is home to about fourteen species of agaves. The tight symmetry of most agaves gives them elegance and grace and makes them one of the most useful plants in a garden. Coupled with their

Hedgehog Cactus

hard-edged leaves, agaves provide outstanding textural contrast for perennial beds, bring drama to annual plantings, and their colorful skin, teeth, and spines can light up a dull corner of the yard. There are sizes and colors for almost any garden, and many are remarkably cold-hardy, making them useful for high zone gardens as well.

Yuccas are closely related to agaves but offer a completely different look. They, too, have large heads of leaves that can be stiff or relaxed and are often held high on tall trunks that are actually fibrous stems. Yuccas are stately plants and unlike agaves that die when they bloom, yuccas show up every spring with their large, crowded heads of creamy white flowers.

Africa is home to more succulent plants than any other continent and many of them have found their way into Arizona gardens. Aloes, with their vivid winter blooms in corals, pinks, yellows, and reds, are abundantly used in southern Arizona. Along with the well-known sansevieria, aloes are some of the best choices for that implacable problem area, dry shade.

Bear Grass

Although most succulents are too sensitive to cold temperatures to be used in higher zone gardens, they are easily grown in containers. The shallow, spreading roots systems and tolerance of dry, hot soils allow these plants to thrive in pots in any climate. Most succulents require plenty of light (although they do best in the light shade in the deserts) and fast draining soils.

Agave
Agave species

Agaves have stiff, well-armed leaves arranged with tight regularity into a rosette. The yellow to gold flowers occur on huge stalks and the plant generally dies after flowering. Many species produce rhizomatous offsets (pups) and a few produce plantlets on the flowering stalk (bulbils). There are agaves for all zones of Arizona from the native Parry's agave (Agave parryi) with gray leaves rimmed in maroon that grows in all zones of the state to the soft, unarmed, celadon green leaves of foxtail agave (A. attenuata) that grows only in the low zones. Other choices include the large blue-gray A. americana, the solitary A. victoriae-reginae with rigid, dark green leaves marked with white, or the rapidly spreading A. lophantha with flat, deep green leaves rimmed with white.

Other Common Name
Maguey

Bloom Period and Seasonal Color
Summer, occasionally in winter; flowers in yellow, gold, wine-red, white.

Mature Height × Spread
6 inches to 5 feet × 6 inches to 7 feet

Zones
All
Hardiness varies by species.

When, Where, and How to Plant
Plant in low zones in fall or very early winter; in higher zones, plant in spring or summer. In low zones, plant most species in light shade; in higher zones, full sun is best. Agaves are tolerant of a wide range of soils from well-drained, fertile soil to rocky, native soil. They do not tolerate heavy or poorly drained soil. Dig a hole that is two to three times wider than the container and as deep. Soil amendments are not necessary. Fan out the roots and set the plant in the hole slightly above the soil line. Fill the hole and press the soil gently to remove air pockets. Water immediately following planting. Water every four days for the first month.

Growing Tips
Most agaves do not need supplemental fertilization although the tropical species benefit from an annual application of slow-release or organic fertilizer. Water established plants every two weeks in summer in low zones; every month in higher zones. Water sparingly over winter in all zones.

Care
Remove dead leaves or spent, flowering stalks anytime. Resist pruning living leaves—it invites infection. If plants crowd a path or walkway, prune just the terminal spine for greater safety. Pups may be removed anytime. Many species are susceptible to infestation of the agave snout weevil; preventive measures are few. Weevils lay eggs inside the bud, and once the telltale wilting and death of the leaves appear, leaving only the folded bud, it is too late to save the plant.

Companion Planting and Design
Agaves provide interest and contrast to succulent plants. Many species tolerate supplemental summer watering enough to be mixed with perennials. Their shallow root system and dramatic forms make agaves an excellent choice to grow in containers. Native species are useful in areas of the garden that receive minimal care.

Did You Know?
Fiber from agave leaves has been used for centuries for mats, baskets, rope, and clothing. The liquor, tequila, is a distilled version of the ancient fermented beverage known as pulque made from agave sap.

When, Where, and How to Plant

Plant aloes in late fall or early winter in low zones; early spring in intermediate zones. Aloes grow best in full morning sun or partial shade, especially in Zones 1 and 2. Aloes grow in a wide range of soil from well-drained, fertile soil to rocky, native soil. They do not grow well in heavy or poorly drained soil. Dig a hole two to three times wider than the container and as deep. Soil amendments are not necessary. Set the plant in the hole slightly above the soil line. Fill the hole and press the soil gently to remove air pockets. Water immediately following planting. Water every five to seven days for the first month.

Growing Tips

Aloes need no supplemental fertilizer. Water established plants carefully and be sure the soil is dry between waterings. Water every one to two weeks in summer, once every two to three weeks in winter.

Care

Remove spent, flowering stalks or dead leaves anytime. Do not prune living leaves of aloes; it invites infection. Aloes are not susceptible to pests or disease but can develop black, oozing rot on the stem that is indicative of a root rot when they are overwatered or grown in poorly drained soils. Prevention is the only remedy.

Companion Planting and Design

Mix aloes with other succulents to provide winter color. Many aloes are tolerant of supplemental watering and can be mixed with perennial or annual beds. Plant them generously near seating areas, patios, or pools both for their long, cool season blooms and for the hummingbirds they attract. Aloes are excellent plants in containers and the flowering stalks make good cut flowers. Aloes are particularly useful in areas of dry shade.

Did You Know?

Aloes are from Africa and the Middle East where the people enjoy countless uses and tales about them. However, only three or four species have the remarkable healing properties of aloe vera, whose sap has been used medicinally since ancient times.

Aloes are one of the most beautiful succulents for low zone gardens. The thick, glossy leaves may be dark green, pale blue-gray or nearly white. The winter-blooming flowers occur on long stalks in soft shades of coral, pink, and red. Hummingbirds are strongly attracted to the flowers making them a welcome winter food source. Coral aloe (Aloe striata) has wide, light green leaves bordered in pink and dark, coral flowers. A. ferox is a heavy-leaved aloe with spikes of brilliant red flowers. A. saponaria is a small, clumping aloe with yellow to orange flowers arranged in loose heads. This aloe is quite cold hardy. The mainstay of medicinal gardens, A. vera, with its spikes of yellow or orange flowers, grows prolifically in the low zones.

Bloom Period and Seasonal Color

From November to April, a few flowers through summer; red, orange, yellow, and pink; some species have bicolored flowers.

Mature Height × Spread

1 to 5 feet × 1 to 5 feet

Zones

1, 2, 3, 4
Hardiness varies by species but most are hardy to 25 degrees Fahrenheit.

Bear Grass
Nolina species

The Arizona native bear grass (Nolina microcarpa) has coarse, grasslike leaves and is distributed throughout the central and southern portions of the state. It strongly resembles a large bunch grass but bear grass is not only very heat- and drought-tolerant but is evergreen as well. The more refined looking sacahuista (N. texana) has thin, light green leaves, rarely grows over 3 feet tall and is cold hardy enough for the high zones. Desert nolina (N. bigelovii), also an Arizona native, has broader leaves, a short trunk, and a towering blooming stalk and is the most drought hardy of all nolinas. Sonoran tree bear grass (N. matapensis) with broad, dark green leaves and blue nolina (N. nelsoni) with stiff, blue-gray leaves both have trunks up to 4 feet tall and are showy specimens in low zone gardens.

Bloom Period and Seasonal Color
Summer; cream to yellow.

Mature Height × Spread
3 to 6 feet × 3 to 5 feet

Zones
All
Hardy to 10 degrees Fahrenheit, some species to 15 degrees Fahrenheit.

When, Where, and How to Plant
Plant native species in fall or spring in full sun. All other species are planted in fall or spring in full morning sun or partial shade in the low desert. All species in the intermediate and high zones grow best in full sun. Plant nolinas in well-drained, fertile soil or rocky, native soil. Nolinas do not tolerate heavy or poorly drained soil. Dig a hole that is two to three times wider than the container and as deep. Soil amendments are not necessary. Set plants in the hole slightly higher than the soil line. Fill the hole and press the soil gently to remove air pockets. Water immediately following planting. Water every four days for the first month.

Growing Tips
Nolinas do not need supplemental fertilizer. Water established plants every two to three weeks in summer in low zones, monthly in other zones. In winter, water monthly in low zones; in other zones, rely on natural rainfall.

Care
Remove spent, flowering stalks anytime. If dead leaves become prominent, remove by cutting back to the base but do not shear them as you would a grass. Nolinas are not susceptible to pests or disease although blackened leaves and loss of the crown indicate root and crown rots that may occur in heavy or poorly drained soil. Prevention is the best remedy.

Companion Planting and Design
Mix the shorter, grasslike species with other desert perennials such as globemallow and fairyduster or shrubs such as black dalea or Texas sage. Nolinas add a soft form to plantings of agaves, cacti, or other succulents. Plant in mass groups to create an informal border or site them in areas of the garden that receive minimal care. The trunked forms make excellent specimen plants. Nolinas grow well in large planters and their soft leaves make them useful along walkways or around pools.

Did You Know?
Although often called bear grass, nolinas are not grasses but are in the same family as desert spoon (*Dasylirion*) and ponytail palm (*Beaucarnea*). The family is called Nolinaceae.

Cholla

Cylindropuntia species

When, Where, and How to Plant

Plant chollas in spring or summer in any well-drained soil, including rocky, native soil. All chollas grow best in full sun. Dig a hole two to three times wider than the container and as deep. Soil amendments are not necessary. Position the plant in the hole until it is level with the original soil line. To handle chollas, use scraps of carpet, plastic bread wrappers, strips of cloth, or used garden hoses. Fill the hole and press the soil gently to remove air pockets. Water immediately following planting. Water every five to seven days for the first month. Then water every one to two weeks during the first summer.

Growing Tips

Chollas need no supplemental fertilizer. Water every three to four weeks in summer in low zones; rely on natural rainfall in other zones. Rely on natural rainfall in all zones in winter.

Care

Prune dead or damaged stems in warm weather by cutting away at a joint. The greatest risk to chollas is when the root rots from too much water or poorly drained soils. Symptoms include black or oozing areas on the stem and loss of all or part of a stem. Chollas are also susceptible to infestations of cochineal scale. Remove the white, cottony masses by spraying the plants regularly with strong jets of water.

Companion Planting and Design

Mix chollas with other succulents in a native garden or areas that receive minimal care. Plant generously to create a barrier where trespassing is a problem. Many chollas are striking when used as specimen or accent plants.

Did You Know?

The flower buds of cholla were roasted and eaten by native peoples in the Southwest. They taste like artichokes and when picked very young do not have the dangerous spines and fine bristles (glochids) they acquire as they mature. Jumping cholla does not really jump; the brittle joints and barbed spines loosen easily and attach to fur or clothing with the merest breeze or touch.

Like their near relatives—prickly pear cactus—chollas are cacti with short, rounded stems that are linked together by brittle joints. Each stem segment is coated with sharp, barbed spines that are covered with a paper-like sheath. Sheath color varies by species and may be tan, silver, gold, or white. These sheaths reflect light and make chollas stunning when backlit. In the garden, chollas are long-lived, extremely drought tolerant shrubby succulents. Jumping cholla (Cylindropuntia fulgida) has light purple flowers and cascades of fruit that continue to accumulate from year to year. Staghorn cholla (C. versicolor) has thin, intricately branched stems and blooms in colors of purple, pink, yellow, or bronze. Cane cholla (C. spinosior) has deep purple flowers followed by bright yellow, persistent fruit; it is very cold hardy.

Bloom Period and Seasonal Color
Late spring through summer; yellow, greenish, red, pink, purple, or white depending on the species.

Mature Height × Spread
3 to 10 feet × 3 to 15 feet

Zones
All
Hardiness varies by species, but most are hardy to the low 20s, some to 0 degrees Fahrenheit.

Desert Spoon
Dasylirion wheeleri

Desert spoon occurs in vast numbers through the central sections of the state. It has also become a prominent ornamental species in the low and intermediate zones of Arizona. Hundreds of leaves crowd onto a virtually invisible short stem and overflow to form the characteristic globe shape. The blue-gray caste of the leaves and the extremely regular form result in an elegant, refined plant that is both drought and heat resistant. The leaves are well-armed with hooked, yellowish teeth and are generally frayed at the tips. Dasylirion acrotriche has thin, bright green leaves and the frayed tips are so regular they look like a swirled maze from above. Mexican grass tree (D. quadrangulatum) has a 6-foot stem and wide, green leaves that fall gracefully, almost touching the ground.

Other Common Name
Sotol

Bloom Period and Seasonal Color
Summer; inconspicuous creamy white in a showy plume.

Mature Height × Spread
3 to 4 feet × 4 to 5 feet

Zones
1, 2, 3, 4, 5

When, Where, and How to Plant
Plant in fall or early spring in full sun or partial shade in low zones; full sun in other zones. Plant desert spoon in any fast draining soil from well-drained, fertile soil to rocky, native soil. Dig a hole that is two to three times wider than the container and as deep. Soil amendments are not necessary. Set the plant in the hole slightly higher than the soil line. Fill the hole and press the soil gently to remove air pockets. Water immediately following planting. Water every four days for the first month.

Growing Tips
Desert spoon does not need supplemental fertilizer. Water established plants every two weeks in summer in low zones, every three to four weeks in higher zones. Water plants monthly in winter in low zones; rely on natural rainfall in other zones.

Care
Desert spoon has excellent natural form and never needs pruning to shape. Remove dead leaves by pulling out those that will come off in your hand, otherwise leave them to protect the trunk. Remove spent blooming stalks anytime. The oldest leaves will eventually die off at the base. Desert spoon is not susceptible to pests or disease but will die out quickly in heavy or poorly drained soils.

Companion Planting and Design
Mix desert spoon with other desert shrubs or perennials to provide contrast to a mixed planting. Plant generously to create borders or for areas where care is minimal. Desert spoon makes a striking specimen or focal plant, particularly in a small garden. It grows well in large containers.

Did You Know?
The base of the leaf widens at the stem and if it is removed, it looks just like a spoon. Although accounts vary, it may have been used as a spoon or vessel in historic times. Leaves of desert spoon are still used to make a wide range of woven ornaments in Mexico known as *flor de sotol*.

Golden Barrel Cactus

Echinocactus grusonii

When, Where, and How to Plant

Plant in fall or early spring in partial shade or full morning sun, although plants can be acclimated slowly to full sun. Golden barrel cacti need very sharp drainage and grow best in rocky, gravel soil. Remove from the container, place the plant in a dry, shady location, and let the roots dry out before planting. Dig a hole two to three times wider than the container and as deep. Soil amendments are not necessary. Position the plant until it is level with the original soil line. To handle the plant, use scraps of carpet, plastic bread wrappers, strips of cloth, or used garden hoses. Fill the hole and press the soil gently to remove air pockets. Water immediately following planting. Water every five to seven days for the first month. Then water every seven to ten days for the first summer.

Growing Tips

Golden barrel cactus does not need supplemental fertilizer. Water established plants every two weeks in summer. Water every month or two in winter.

Care

Golden barrel cactus is not susceptible to pests or disease. Like all cacti, its worst enemy is too much water collected around the roots, making the plant susceptible to root rot. Good drainage and minimal watering when the weather is cool are the best ways to prevent root rot.

Companion Planting and Design

Plant golden barrel cactus singly or in groups mixed with prickly pear cactus, agaves, and desert spoon. Interplant with very drought-tolerant shrubs such as creosote bush, black dalea, and Texas sage. This is a spectacular species to use as a specimen plant, particularly in a small garden. Golden barrel cactus grows well in containers but avoid using the plant near areas where the sharp spines might present a danger.

Did You Know?

Golden barrel cactus is known to exist in nature in only a few locales in southern Mexico. Because of habitat destruction and the building of a dam in the region, it is thought to be virtually extinct in the wild. For many years, all plants sold have been grown from seed of cultivated plants.

Cacti come in three general shapes; columnar ones are much taller than they are wide such as saguaro or organ pipe, jointed stemmed ones have round or flat stems that are stacked together such as prickly pear or cholla, and round or globular plants. Of the globular cacti, one of the most beautiful and widely grown in low zone gardens is the golden barrel cactus. The plant is almost round and the ribs are thickly lined with stiff, bright yellow spines. The spines overlap enough to form a light web over the dark, green skin. Most plants are solitary and grow to about 3 feet tall. But occasionally golden barrel cacti form large clumps of plants of varying sizes. The flowers that occur in the top of the plant are bright yellow with strawlike petals.

Bloom Period and Seasonal Color
Early summer; yellow.

Mature Height × Spread
1 to 4 feet × 2 to 3 feet

Zones
1, 2, 3
Hardy to about 25 degrees Fahrenheit.

Hedgehog Cactus
Echinocereus engelmannii

Hedgehog cactus blooms are always a surprise; one day there are small, spiny knobs on the stems, then overnight they erupt into glorious riots of color. Hedgehogs are short, multistemmed cacti that cover the hills and mountain slopes of the state. Plants may have a few or dozens of stems. Their hardiness, colorful spines, and gorgeous flowers have made hedgehogs a favorite for low and intermediate zones. Flowers are prolific and bloom in vivid shades of purple and magenta. The variety bonkerae has exceptionally short spines and deep purple flowers; the variety nicholii has long, golden spines and bright lavender flowers. Claret cup (Echinocereus triglochidiatus) is a compact species that grows on high mountain slopes and has hundreds of cup-shaped, scarlet flowers in spring.

Bloom Period and Seasonal Color
March and April; purple and magenta.

Mature Height × Spread
1 to 2 feet × 2 to 4 feet

Zones
1, 2, 3
Hardy to 15 degrees Fahrenheit.

When, Where, and How to Plant
Plant in spring or fall in full sun. Hedgehog cacti are sensitive to compacted or poorly draining soil or soil that is too fertile. Hedgehog cacti grow best on rocky or gravel soil. Remove from the container, place the plant in a dry, shady location, and let the roots dry out for at least a week before planting. This allows tiny tears in the roots to heal and prevents the introduction of bacteria and fungus. Dig a hole two to three times wider than the container and as deep. Soil amendments are not necessary. Position the plant until it is level with the original soil line. To handle hedgehog cactus, use scraps of carpet, plastic bread wrappers, strips of cloth, or used garden hoses. Fill the hole and press the soil gently to remove air pockets. Water immediately following planting. Water weekly for the first month.

Growing Tips
Hedgehog cacti do not require supplemental fertilizer. Water established plants carefully; they are subject to rot with too much water in late summer. Water every three to four weeks in summer; rely on natural rainfall in winter.

Care
Prune diseased or damaged stems in late spring or summer by removing the stem as close to the base as possible. Hedgehog cacti may develop bacterial infections or be preyed upon by borers in summer. In both cases, the interior of the stem is hollowed out. Prevention is difficult and unreliable, but both conditions are most common in plants that are old or overwatered.

Companion Planting and Design
Mix with other succulents such as saguaro, prickly pears, ocotillos, desert spoon, and agaves. Hedgehog cacti make an attractive specimen plant for small succulent gardens or in areas of the garden that receive minimal care. Hedgehog is an excellent choice for containers either alone or as part of a mixed succulent planting.

Did You Know?
The genus comes from the Greek *echinos* meaning "a hedgehog" and the Latin *cereus* which means "a wax taper, or candle," and refers to the shape of the stems. Engelmann was an imminent botanist working in America in the 19th century.

When, Where, and How to Plant

Plant evergreen species in fall or early spring; plant deciduous species in spring. Plant in full morning sun or partial shade. In low zones, manfredas grow well even in deep shade. Manfredas are tolerant of a wide range of soil from well-drained, fertile soil, moderately moist soil, as well as rocky, native soil. Dig a hole the size of the root system and as deep as the container. Apply a thin layer of compost or mulch to the backfill. Set the plant in the hole well above the soil line. Fill and gently press to remove air pockets. Water thoroughly. Water weekly through the first summer.

Growing Tips

Manfredas require no supplemental fertilizer. Water established plants weekly in summer, more often if the weather is exceptionally hot or dry. Water evergreen species twice a month or less in winter; rely on natural rainfall for deciduous species. In well-drained soils, manfredas are tolerant of more water, especially in summer.

Care

Remove spent, flowering stalks as soon as they dry out. Lift and divide clumping species in early summer. Manfredas are not susceptible to pests or disease.

Companion Planting and Design

Mix manfredas with small shade-loving succulents such as aloes, gasterias, dudleyas, or sansevieras. Plant manfredas generously to form a low, succulent border for a shady garden or along a dry walkway. In beds with very well-drained soil, manfredas can be mixed with perennials such as salvia, penstemon, red justicias, and plumbago. The striking foliage and small size make manfredas especially useful in large containers or planters.

Did You Know?

The name, "Rattlesnake Master," comes from the practice by many native peoples to use the plants to treat snakebite. The name, "Amole," is widely applied in Mexico to any plant that can be used as a cleanser. The roots of many manfredas can be pounded, mixed with water, and used as soap.

I am fond of manfredas with their spotted, soft but brittle leaves and almost clownish blooms. Their low-growing rosettes thrive in dry, shady locations. All manfredas grow well in low and intermediate zone gardens, but only the deciduous Manfreda virginica is cold tolerant enough for the high zones. Related to agaves, manfredas send up tall flowering stalks in spring, but plants do not die after blooming. The flowers are unusual with stiff, open blooms in chartreuse, maroon, red-brown, or creamy pink. The diminutive M. maculosa has evergreen, thin, green leaves marked in purple with fragrant, white flowers that fade to dusky pink. A vigorous form with long, folded, light green, evergreen leaves variously marked with purple and chartreuse flowers is a garden hybrid but is commonly sold as M. variegata.

Other Common Names

Rattlesnake master, Amole

Bloom Period and Seasonal Color

May and June; chartreuse, maroon, red-brown, cream to pink.

Mature Height × Spread

4 to 6 inches × 6 to 18 inches

Zones

1, 2, 3, 4, 5
Hardiness varies by species.

Ocotillo
Fouquieria splendens

Ocotillos are tall, multistemmed plants with a number of long stems, called canes, emerging from the base of the plant. In late winter and spring, the hillsides of southern and central Arizona come alive with the showy, red, tubular flowers that hang like tassels from the tips of the stems. The dark green leaves are held on long, thin petioles that stiffen as they age into dark, gray spines. Ocotillos shed their leaves at the first sign of drought, but when it rains, they can regrow them within days. This cycle can be repeated five or six times a year. The related palo adan (Fouquieria macdougalii) is an intricately branched shrub with bright, red flowers like sparklers at the ends of the stems in spring.

Bloom Period and Seasonal Color
April to July; red, red-orange, and rarely in yellow or white.

Mature Height × Spread
8 to 25 × 5 to 12 feet

Zones
1, 2, 3, 4
Hardy to 5 degrees Fahrenheit.

When, Where, and How to Plant
Plant ocotillo in fall or early spring in full sun. While ocotillo will tolerate a wide range of well-drained soil, they grow best in rocky, fast draining native soil. Dig a hole as wide and deep as the root system. No soil amendments are necessary. Set the plant in the hole slightly higher than the soil line. Fill the hole and press the soil gently to remove air pockets. Water weekly for the first summer, every two to three weeks through the first fall.

Growing Tips
Ocotillo need no supplemental fertilization. Large, bare-root plants are slow to establish a new root system and it may take up to two years before they leaf out regularly. Continue watering as described until the plant leafs out regularly. Water established plants monthly in summer in the low zones, every other month in winter. In Zones 2 and 3, established plants grow on natural rainfall alone.

Care
The natural form of ocotillo is graceful with the upright stems cascading gently at the tips. Prune only dead or damaged stems and remove them back to the base. Cuts made high on living stems produce irregular, thin branches rather than the sturdy, single canes characteristic of this species. Ocotillo is not susceptible to pests or disease, although borers may invade unhealthy or deeply stressed plants, killing the stem. Prevention is the best remedy.

Companion Planting and Design
Ocotillo is unrivaled for its graceful form and makes a wonderful specimen plant. Ocotillo is particularly effective when planted against a wall or building that will reflect its dramatic shadows. Mix ocotillo with desert shrubs such as creosote bush, black dalea, and ruellia or with large succulents such as saguaro, organ pipe cactus, and agaves. Hummingbirds feast on the nectar of the flowers and use the stems as perches.

Did You Know?
The canes are very long-lived, and even dead wood will stand for many years before it begins to rot. This makes the canes—living and dead—useful for fences, corrals, and ramadas.

Organ Pipe Cactus

Stenocereus thurberi

When, Where, and How to Plant

Plant in spring or summer in any well-drained soil, including rocky, native soil. Organ pipe cactus grows best in full sun. Remove small plants from their container, place in a dry, shady location to let the roots dry out before planting. Dig a hole two to three times wider than the container and as deep. Soil amendments are not necessary. Position the plant in the hole until it is level with the original soil line. To handle the plant, use scraps of carpet, plastic bread wrappers, strips of cloth, or used garden hoses. Fill the hole and press the soil gently to remove air pockets. Water immediately following planting. Water every five to seven days for the first month. Then water every one to two weeks during the first summer.

Growing Tips

Organ pipe cacti need no supplemental fertilizer. Water established plants every two weeks in summer; every month or two in winter.

Care

Organ pipe cactus can be damaged in a hard freeze. Protect the tips of the stems with Styrofoam™ cups or frost cloth. Water carefully in the winter; organ pipe cactus is susceptible to the black oozing wounds indicative of root rot when they are grown in cool, wet soils that do not drain well. Organ pipe cactus is not susceptible to pests or disease.

Companion Planting and Design

Use organ pipe cactus in naturalistic plantings or areas of the garden that receive minimal care. This cactus blends well with other desert shrubs and succulents such as creosote bush, ruellia, prickly pear cactus, ocotillo, and agaves. Organ pipe cactus grows well in large containers and is also a striking specimen or accent plant.

Did You Know?

The Seri Indians of northern Sonora found numerous uses for organ pipe cactus. The thin ribs were used as construction materials. Soft tissue from the plants was applied as boat caulking. And the delicious fruit was part of their diet.

Found naturally only in the Sonoran Desert, organ pipe cactus stands in striking contrast to the single columns of saguaro and the short, shrubby forms of prickly pears and chollas. Mature plants are 9 to 25 feet tall and have 20 or more deep green stems that are lined along the ribs with short, deep brown spines. The plant is trim, neat, and elegant and even small plants have great presence in the garden. This handsome cactus is slow-growing and although frost tender, is resistant to great heat and drought. The small, white flowers are found at the ends of the stems and open at night providing food for night-flying insects and bats and birds. The sweet, red fruit is edible and prized by both men and animals.

Bloom Period and Seasonal Color
April to June; white.

Mature Height × Spread
4 to 26 feet × 5 to 10 feet

Zones
1, 2, 3
Hardy to 25 degrees Fahrenheit.

Prickly Pear Cactus
Opuntia species

Prickly pear cacti are such unlikely plants with their flattened pads (actually stems), united to each other by brittle joints, and protected by both long, sharp spines (modified leaves), and minuscule bristles called glochids. Dangerous and delightful, these shrubby cacti are excellent garden plants if given the space and respect they deserve. There are hundreds of types but in Arizona the purple prickly pear (Opuntia santa-rita) with its deep gray-green skin tinged with purple is a particular favorite. The purple color is intensified in cold weather. Other attractive species include beavertail prickly pear (O. basilaris) with dimpled, gray-green skin and brilliant magenta flowers, and desert prickly pear (both O. engelmannii and O. phaeacantha) with deep green skin, fewer spines, and clear yellow flowers.

Bloom Period and Seasonal Color
Late spring to summer in yellow, orange, pink, reddish, or deep magenta, depending on species.

Mature Height × Spread
2 to 5 feet × 2 to 8 feet

Zones
1, 2, 3, 4
Hardiness varies by species; most native species are hardy to at least 20 degrees Fahrenheit; many species are hardy to much lower.

When, Where, and How to Plant
Plant in spring or fall in any well-drained soil. Some, like the huge Indian fig (*Opuntia ficus-indica*), will grow in garden soil with regular irrigation, but most prefer well-drained, rocky soil. Dig a hole two to three times wider than the container and as deep. Soil amendments are not necessary. Position the plant in the hole until it is level with the original soil line. Fill the hole and press the soil gently to remove air pockets. Water immediately following planting. Water every five to seven days for the first month. Then water every one to two weeks during the first summer.

Growing Tips
Prickly pear needs no supplemental fertilization. To prevent shriveling and deep stress, water established plants (those that have been in the ground at least two years) twice a month in summer, monthly or less during winter.

Care
Prune diseased, damaged, or unneeded pads anytime in the summer but always cut them off at the joint. Cochineal scale, identified by the white, cottony mass that covers a pad, can infest plants, particularly in the summer. Control by regularly spraying plants with strong jets of water; pesticides are rarely effective.

Companion Planting and Design
Mix with desert perennials or other succulents for a contrast and exquisite late season color. Excellent when used as a specimen or accent plant, particularly species that have colorful skin or spines. Many of the smaller species are excellent in containers or planters. Take care not to place them near play areas, walkways, or pools; the spines and glochids are unpleasant.

Did You Know?
Although spines are long and can usually be avoided when handling a prickly pear, glochids are nearly invisible. To minimize problems when handling pads, never use gloves but rely on tools like tongs, or lengths of hose, or other cloth. Wrapping your hands in discarded plastic bread wrappers is also effective in handling these plants.

Red Hesperaloe

Hesperaloe parviflora

When, Where, and How to Plant

Plant in fall or spring in the low zones; in spring or summer in the higher zones. Plant in full sun or partial shade. Red hesperaloe tolerates almost any type of soil from well-drained, fertile soil, to rocky, native soil as long as it is alkaline and sharply drained. Dig a hole that is two to three times wider than the container and as deep. Soil amendments are not necessary. Set the plant in the hole slightly higher than the soil line. Fill the hole and press the soil gently to remove air pockets. Water immediately following planting. Water every four days for the first month.

Growing Tips

Red hesperaloe does not need supplemental fertilizer. Water established plants every two to three weeks in summer in the low zones, every three to four weeks in higher zones. In all zones, rely on natural rainfall in winter unless the weather is exceptionally warm or dry.

Care

Remove spent, blooming stalks anytime. Remove dead leaves only if they can be pulled away in your hand. Divide crowded clumps in early spring. Red hesperaloe is not susceptible to pests or disease.

Companion Planting and Design

Red hesperaloe mixes well with perennials such as globemallow, ruellia, black dalea and desert milkweed. Mix with succulents such as agaves, yuccas, and prickly pears for contrast and their long colorful bloom. Plant red hesperaloe generously to form an informal border, fill in barren spots in a newly planted garden, or to line drives, walkways, or large beds. Red hesperaloe is excellent around pools, against hot walls or other areas where reflected heat is intense. It also grows well in a large container or planter.

Did You Know?

The coral to pink flowers of this plant reminded early botanists of aloes. That is why it was named western (*hesper*) aloe (*aloe*) despite the fact that this genus is in the agave family, not the aloe family.

Red hesperaloe is one of the most reliable desert plants for either low or high zone gardens. The short, thin leaves turn inward to look almost round and crowd together in a tight rosette. Plants spread quickly to form large, dense clumps. Tall, straight, or arching blooming stalks emerge in spring, and the coral and cream flowers open intermittently through summer, staggering their opening up and down the stalk for months. Birds and insects are strongly attracted to the bloom. The closely related Hesperaloe funifera has large, stiff leaves and a massive, branched flowering stalk with night opening, white flowers. Hybrids between the two abound but are unnamed. The newly introduced H. tenuifolia has deep, pink flowers, and leaves so fine they resemble grass.

Bloom Period and Seasonal Color

April to September; the outer petals are pink, coral, or red; inner petals are cream or white, occasionally salmon and yellow.

Mature Height × Spread

3 to 4 feet × 3 to 6 feet

Zones

All
Hardy to 0 degrees Fahrenheit.

Saguaro

Carnegiea gigantea

This gigantic cactus is native to the Sonoran Desert of Arizona and Mexico. Notable for the numerous and variously arranged stems (arms), this Arizona icon needs some room and good care in the garden. Readily grown from seed, it is now easy to find artificially propagated plants in almost any size. Because of their mature size, saguaros are home to a grand parade of desert birds, especially the Gila woodpeckers that drill holes to create nests for their young. The crown of large, night opening, white flowers in spring is quickly followed by large, juicy, red fruit. It is some of the tastiest fruit produced by any cactus, and its arrival marked the new year to the native peoples of southern Arizona.

Bloom Period and Seasonal Color
May and June; white.

Mature Height × Spread
30 to 60 feet × 10 to 20 feet

Zones
1, 2
Hardy to 25 degrees Fahrenheit.

When, Where, and How to Plant
Plant in early spring or fall in full sun. It's fine to plant in partial shade if the plant is small; a saguaro will outgrow and outlive anything it is planted beneath. Saguaros grow best in rocky, dry, or gravel soil. Remove it from the container and place in a dry, shady spot for a week to dry the roots. This allows the roots to heal tiny tears resulting from handling and prevents the introduction of bacteria and fungus. Dig a hole two to three times wider than the container and as deep. Soil amendments are unnecessary. Set the plant slightly higher than the soil line. Handle cacti carefully. Fill the hole and press the soil to remove air pockets. Water at once. Water every five days for the first month. Then water every seven to ten days the first summer.

Growing Tips
Saguaro does not require supplemental fertilizer. Although established plants tolerate extreme drought, water deeply once a month in summer to maintain vigorous plant growth. Rely on natural rainfall in winter unless the weather is exceptionally warm or dry.

Care
Saguaros may be damaged in a hard freeze. Protect the tips of the stems with frost cloth or other covering. Root rot develops in plants with too much water or grown in poorly drained soils. Damage to the skin may result in a lethal bacterial infection known as bacterial necrosis. Symptoms of either are a black liquid oozing from a hole in the plant with a strong, rotten smell. Often plants begin to lean as a result of the death of part of the root system. There is no cure; prevention is the only remedy. Gila woodpeckers drill holes for nests but only cause cosmetic damage.

Companion Planting and Design
Place saguaros among other desert plants such as creosote bush, ocotillo, globemallow, and penstemons. Use in succulents beds with prickly pear, hedgehogs, agaves, and yuccas. Saguaros do not live long in areas that are regularly watered.

Did You Know?
The saguaro flower is the Arizona state flower. The fruit is sweet and when it's dried, it can be chewed like candy or cooked down into syrup. The seeds may be dried and used in cooking like poppy seeds.

When, Where, and How to Plant

Plant in fall or spring in low zones; in spring or summer in high zones. Yuccas have a high tolerance for soils from moist, heavy soil to well-drained, fertile soil and rocky, native soil. Plant in full sun, although species native to eastern areas prefer partial shade in low zones. Dig a hole that is two to three times wider than the container and the same depth. No soil amendments are necessary. Set the plant in the hole slightly higher than the soil line. Fill the hole and press the soil gently to remove air pockets. Water immediately following planting. Water every four days for the first month.

Growing Tips

Apply slow-release or organic fertilizer annually in spring to the eastern species. Western species do not require supplemental fertilizer. Water established plants every week for eastern species in low zones, less often in higher zones. In summer water established plants of western species every two to three weeks in low zones, relying on natural rainfall in higher zones unless the weather is exceptionally warm or dry. Western species need minimal water in winter.

Care

Remove dead leaves when they pull away in your hand or cut them off, leaving them attached to the stem. Be careful not to puncture or damage the stems. Remove spent flowering stalks anytime. Yuccas are occasionally infested with borers, which kill all or part of a stem, but otherwise are not susceptible to pests or disease.

Companion Planting and Design

Blend smaller yuccas with perennials or plantings to provide good texture and color contrast. Taller species are outstanding specimen or accent plants. Use native or drought-tolerant yuccas in areas of the garden that receive minimal care, or mix them with succulents such as saguaro, prickly pear, and agaves. Many yuccas grow well in containers.

Did You Know?

Fibers from many species of yucca are revered by basket makers for their color, durability, and silky texture.

Although yuccas are strongly associated with the West, there are yuccas native to the eastern coast of the United States, the forests and plains of northern and central Mexico, as well as the western deserts. Generally, the eastern species are very cold hardy, rarely over 10 feet tall, and include familiar species such as Yucca filamentosa, Y. recurvifolia, *and* Y. aloifolia. *Western species are taller, generally have stiffer leaves, and include the Arizona native banana yucca (*Y. baccata*), soaptree yucca (*Y. elata*), and beaked yucca (*Y. rostrata*). These species are extremely heat- and drought-tolerant. One of the loveliest yuccas for Arizona gardens is the Mexican blue yucca (*Y. rigida*) with its large head of powdery blue-green leaves and plumes of bright white flowers.*

Bloom Period and Seasonal Color
Summer; white.

Mature Height × Spread
3 to 25 feet × 4 to 10 feet

Zones
All
Hardiness varies by locale; most common ones are hardy to 10 degrees Fahrenheit.

Grasses *for Arizona*

Grasses are an astounding family of plants and one that has been tied closely to human needs and endeavors since the very dawn of agriculture. The grains that dominate agriculture—rice, corn, wheat, and barley—are grasses. Cattle, sheep, and to a great extent goats, graze extensively on any available grass so that they in turn may provide food and other goods to men. Horses and other useful animals—not to mention wild game—are dependent, to a greater and lesser extent, on grass as food. It makes you wonder what kind of world it would be if there were no grasses.

When You're Hot, You're Hot

From a gardener's perspective, however, grasses break into two distinct categories—those that are low-growing, usually spreading from underground stems (stolons) to cover wide areas, and those that are taller, growing in a congested bunch with hundreds of individual upright stems. We call the former style, "turf grass," and it is used chiefly for lawns while the latter goes by the catchall phrase, "ornamental grasses," serving a role in the garden similar to perennials and other showy plants.

Ornamental grasses are one of the hot trends in gardening right now and while the craze has not overwhelmed most of Arizona yet, it probably will get here sooner or later. Grasses grown for their

Deer Grass

form, size, and color, rather than as a lawn, can be a beautiful addition to a garden. They add softness to a garden scene, a feature that helps when dealing with our abundance of sharp, hard textured plants.

Although any grass could be considered ornamental in the right circumstances, what is generally meant by the term, "ornamental grass," is a perennial bunch grass that has an attractive, even showy, flowering style as well as attractive foliage. In the low elevation zones, the best ornamental grasses on the market right now are in the genus *Muhlenbergia,* a large, wide-ranging group of plants that are native to the southwestern United States. In the higher elevation zones, there are many more choices than could be described here.

The Role of Grasses

Ornamental grasses act like an anchor in a garden. Like shrubs and trees, they hold their shape and maintain a strong presence, even if they change appearance through the year. In cold winter areas, where many perennials go dormant, or die out over the winter, the late season bloom of grasses extends the gardening season to provide color and interest long after the riot of summer bloom has quieted. The graceful blooming heads of grasses are often loveliest when backlit by autumnal light shifting from the bright greens of summer to the subdued gold, dusty pink, and silver shades of autumn.

Tall ornamental grasses make a good background for perennial plants by providing a solid wall to frame the colorful show of summer-flowering perennials and annuals. Many gardeners interplant ornamental grasses of varying size and color throughout a large perennial bed to carry the whole bed through the fall.

Ornamental grasses are often used to best effect in great numbers as mass plantings. Planted generously, ornamental grasses can soften and add drama and excitement to a difficult spot at the edge of the garden or a small bed along a driveway or road. Grasses, particularly bunch grasses, hold soil tenaciously in their fine, wide network of roots. Planted along a steep slope where soil erosion has been especially dire, these grasses will stabilize the slope and begin the long process of building and restoring the soil.

A Note of Caution

When choosing an ornamental grass, well-adapted or locally native grasses make the most sense. Not only are they happy to live with the soil, temperatures, and rainfall of the area, but also like all well-suited plants, they resist disease and pests better and provide their vigor and beauty to the garden with minimal effort on the part of the gardener. Even more endearing, local creatures do not tend to run amok and become hated regional pests.

There is a note of caution regarding the use of ornamental grasses, particularly those from analogous, but distant locales. Many of them are fierce competitors, sending out oceans of seed to set up home in the new land without any of the controls that would have been at work in their native land. Too many lovely and attractive garden plants have been introduced into Arizona and elsewhere that have overtaken their hosts. Fountain grass (*Pennisetum setaceum*) in the low elevation zones is now wild, growing at will among the rocky desert hills of low elevation zone parks and natural areas, cramming its way into all the available space leaving little room for new seedlings of native species. It is much harder to remove aggressive invaders than it is to be careful about planting them in the first place. Look for grasses that are sterile hybrids, female plants, or those that have a demonstrated history of remaining where they are planted before you consider adding them to your garden.

The Demands of Lawns

I should say it right now—I do not care for lawns. First of all, they are very thirsty. Over the entire life of the lawn, it will use more water than anything you could plant. Not only do they demand enormous amounts of care—feeding and mowing are just the beginning—a lawn never achieves the independence that well-adapted trees and shrubs gain over time. You must water and care for a lawn always; it never grows up and leaves home. In the low elevation zones, a bermuda grass lawn requires the equivalent of 40 to 42 inches of rain a year to stay green, and that is for a winter-dormant grass. Low elevation zones are areas that receive between 3 to 12 inches of rainfall annually; the remaining water that bermuda requires has to be supplied by irrigation.

But their tremendous need for water isn't my main objection to lawns, formidable though it is. My objection is how they look—blank, boring, and so irrevocably green. The longer I garden, the more I find that the old maxim, "Garden where you live," resonates in my gardening mind. Swards of green do not blend well in my eye with the rich textures of desert shrubs or the blue-gray tones so common in the perennials of the entire region. A backdrop of deep, evenly colored green does not enhance succulents. Ribbons of mowed lawn clash with the rocks, hills, and stunning backdrops found throughout the state, as well as with the shrubs and trees that form the native vegetation.

However, lawns are popular with many people in Arizona and some gardeners feel they cannot do without a lawn. I know many ardent fans of native and drought-adapted plants that still believe there must be at least a little touch of lawn to set off the perennials, or run as a balance to the pond, or provide a haven for children's feet and pets' paws.

Lawns came to Arizona gardens early and form part of the historic garden landscapes of all cities in the state. In the older parts of Phoenix and adjacent cities, abundant sources of cheap water during the

Lawn Grass (magnified)

initial settlements made lawns easy and affordable. This water was delivered in canals and lots were formed to hold a flood of water at prescribed intervals. The geographic limits of this water delivery system are fixed, and many of these lawns are well established and continue to be maintained with this flood irrigation.

The best news in lawns is that there is a lot of research and development going on to develop lawns from grasses that are well adapted to the areas where they are used, and therefore, are considerably more water conservative than older varieties. Buffalo grass leads the way and has already become a favored grass in the higher elevation zones of Arizona. In the two highest zones, established buffalo grass lawns need only intermittent irrigation—in fact, they are killed by overwatering—and grow slowly enough to require minimal mowing.

In the desert zones, bermuda is still king of the lawn grasses. It is hard to beat its heat tolerance, but it is hardly a water conserving choice. To add to the problem, most lawns are vastly overwatered. Most grasses are healthier and thrive better if they are given long, deep soaks at weekly or biweekly intervals to water the root zone. The light, daily sprinklings so commonly applied are often an invitation to shallow rooting, fungal disease, and other lawn problems.

There are strategies to maintaining a lawn without breaking the bank on the water bill. Choose a grass that works well in your area and is as water conservative as you can find. Plant only what you will use, forgoing that huge, front lawn for a smaller but more active area around a playground or patio in the backyard, then be sure to water correctly. In addition to providing only what the lawn actually needs, watch the time of day you water. Water in the early morning in the summer when evaporation is less. Set sprinklers low to the ground or let them bubble out to reduce evaporation; fine mists running in the middle of the day are sending more water out into the air than onto your lawn.

Choose grasses carefully and never be afraid to consider how lovely your garden can be without a wide, expansive lawn. If you are not mowing and constantly caring for your lawn, just think how much time you will have to sit back and enjoy your Arizona garden!

Bermuda Grass
Cynodon dactylon

Bermuda grass is ubiquitous in the low zones of Arizona; it is one of the few turf grasses that can take the heat of the desert summer. Common bermuda is a coarse plant with widely spaced blades and tall, blooming stalks. Bermuda not only reseeds easily but spreads from trailing stems called stolons. Bermuda grows only in warm weather; it goes dormant when temperatures are routinely 60 degrees Fahrenheit or lower. Both common and so-called improved bermuda grows from seed, plugs, or sod. The hybrid varieties are sterile and must be planted from plugs or sod. 'Tifgreen 328' is a very fine-textured grass that holds up well to traffic. 'Tifway 419' and 'Santa Ana' are medium- to fine-textured cultivars that form very dense lawns.

Mature Height × Spread
4 to 18 inches × 2 to 4 feet

Zones
1, 2, 3, 4
Hardy to 20 degrees Fahrenheit.

When, Where, and How to Plant
Plant in late spring or summer in full sun. To prepare an area that has never had lawn before, level, clean, and thoroughly water the area then let it dry for two days. Apply a generous layer of compost, mulch, and/or gypsum, soil sulphur, and lawn fertilizer. Turn the soil, working in the amendments to a depth of 6 inches, but 10 or 12 inches is better. Water the soil to a depth of 2 inches and let it dry for three days. Water lightly just before broadcasting seed (1 to 2 pounds per 1,000 square feet), setting out plugs, or laying sod. When laying sod, be sure the mats touch or are close enough to knit together quickly. Water two to four times a day for the first two weeks, then once a day for the next two weeks or until established.

Growing Tips
Apply lawn or organic fertilizer two weeks after seedlings emerge or plugs or sod were installed. Fertilize weekly until the lawn is entirely filled in. Fertilize established lawns once a month while the grass is actively growing. Water established lawns one inch of water per week. When temperatures are below 90 degrees Fahrenheit, water one inch of water every other week, and water one inch of water once a month in winter.

Care
Mow regularly to about 1 inch tall but mow often enough so that no more than one-third of the blade is removed each time you mow. Bermuda lawns can be susceptible to the intermittent dead spots (indicative of pearl scale or fungal disease) when the soil is compact, when there is too much shade, or when the drainage is poor. Treatments are not reliable, so prevention is the best remedy.

Companion Planting and Design
Lawns form a frame or background for colorful perennials and annual beds. Lawns are often planted for play areas and to cool reflected heat.

Did You Know?
The Spanish brought bermuda grass to the Caribbean. It is thought that it first reached the United States as early as the 17th century in crates of goods from Bermuda where it was used as packing material.

Blue Grama

Bouteloua gracilis

When, Where, and How to Plant

Plant in late spring or summer in full sun. Remove all rocks, old turf, and weeds from a new planting area, then level the area and water it to a depth of at least 6 inches and up to 12 inches. Let it dry for two days. Apply a generous layer of compost, mulch, or lawn fertilizer, turn the soil to a depth of 4 to 6 inches, and then work in the amendments. Water again but to about half the original depth and let the soil dry for up to three days. When ready to plant, water lightly or use a lawn roller half filled with water, sowing seed evenly at the rate of 1 to 4 pounds per 1,000 square feet. Water every day or two, keeping the bed evenly moist until the seeds begin to germinate. Once grass is up, water two to three times a week until your lawn is well established.

Growing Tips

Apply lawn or organic fertilizer in April. An iron/sulphur fertilizer may be applied in late summer to help green up the lawn but do not use nitrogen-based fertilizer then. Water established lawns weekly when temperatures are above 85 degrees Fahrenheit, every two weeks when they are between 70 and 85 degrees Fahrenheit, and monthly thereafter.

Care

Mow regularly to about 2 inches tall but mow often enough that no more than 1 inch is removed each time. Blue grama is resistant to most turf grass pests and diseases.

Companion Planting and Design

The soft color and gentle texture of blue grama blend well with low-growing native perennials and evergreen shrubs. The fine texture makes it useful for play areas. Like all lawns, it provides relief from reflected heat.

Did You Know?

Grasses have two types of growing points. The *meristem*, located at the base of each leaf, can grow one-sided and allows stems to right themselves after being trampled. The *culm* is just above the leaf base on the stem and allows the stem to continue to grow even if it's cut, grazed, burned, or destroyed.

Blue grama is native to the Southwest and the Great Plains. Its pale green color and soft texture mesh beautifully with the sturdy perennials and shrubs of the high desert. However, this bunch grass also serves as an excellent and more water conservative lawn for high zone gardens. Blue grama is a cool-season grass that grows naturally into flat topped clumps. Because it does not spread by underground stems, it must be densely seeded and given supplemental summer watering to crowd the clumps together into a fine sod. 'Lovington' and 'Alma' are selections developed from populations of blue grama growing in New Mexico. 'Hachita', also selected from New Mexico, is considered particularly well suited to be used as a lawn grass because of its fine texture and dense growth.

Mature Height × Spread
18 to 24 inches × 12 to 18 inches

Zones
3, 4, 5, 6
Hardy to 0 degrees Fahrenheit, perhaps lower.

Buffalo Grass
Buchloe dactyloides

Buffalo grass is native to the short grass prairies of the Great Plains as far south as New Mexico. Blades of buffalo grass are blue-green to pale green during summer but fade to a warm, golden-brown through winter when it is dormant. Buffalo grass is a short bunch grass that spreads slowly from stolons and is often mixed with blue grama to fill a lawn area more completely. It is becoming widely used as a turf grass in intermediate and high zones in Arizona for its durability and low water use. 'Prairie' and '609' are female selections that grow to 8 inches tall, while 'Cody' and 'Tatanka' are shorter. 'Topgun' and 'Plains' are planted from seed and are dense, short-leaved grasses with darker blades.

Mature Height × Spread
4 to 8 inches × 2 to 4 feet

Zones
3, 4, 5, 6
Hardy to 0 degrees Fahrenheit or lower.

When, Where, and How to Plant
Plant in late spring or summer. Buffalo grass grows best in heavy or well-amended soils in full sun. Remove all rocks, old turf, and weeds from the planting area. Level the area and water up to 12 inches deep, then let it dry for two days. Apply a generous layer of compost, mulch, or lawn fertilizer. Turn the soil and work in the amendments to a depth of 4 to 6 inches (10 to 12 is even better). Water and then let the soil dry for up to three days. When ready to plant, water lightly or use a lawn roller half filled with water. Broadcast seed (2 to 4 pounds per 1,000 square feet) or set in plugs. Water every day or two to keep the bed evenly moist until seeds begin to germinate, then water weekly until the lawn is well established.

Growing Tips
Apply lawn or organic fertilizer in April. An iron and sulphur fertilizer may be applied in late summer to help green up the lawn but do not use nitrogen-based fertilizer then. Water established lawns weekly when temperatures are above 85 degrees Fahrenheit, every two weeks when they are between 70 and 85 degrees Fahrenheit, and monthly thereafter.

Care
Mow regularly to about 2 to 4 inches tall but mow often enough that no more than 1 inch is removed each time. Buffalo grass grows much shorter than most bunch grasses and it can be left unmowed in many situations. Buffalo grass is resistant to most turf grass pests and diseases.

Companion Planting and Design
Mix with faster-growing blue grama to establish a lawn quickly. Use a buffalo grass lawn as a frame for colorful perennials and annual beds. The fine texture makes it useful for play areas for children and pets. Like all lawns, it provides a relief from reflected heat.

Did You Know?
"Dioecious" means that plants have flowers of only one sex on a plant. Buffalo grass is dioecious; therefore, clones of female plants do not produce pollen—a definite plus for those who suffer from grass pollen allergies.

Common Blue Fescue

Festuca glauca

When, Where, and How to Plant

Plant in early spring as soon as the soil can be worked. Common blue fescue is very shade tolerant but also does well in full sun. Grow in well-drained, fertile soil. Dig a hole that is two or more times the width of the container and as deep. Mix in a generous amount of compost or mulch with the backfill. Fill the hole, gently pressing the soil to remove air pockets. Water thoroughly. Water every three to four days for a month; then every seven to ten days through the first summer.

Growing Tips

Apply slow-release or organic fertilizer annually in spring. Use a thin layer of mulch to keep the soil evenly moist. Established plants are very drought tolerant and, in cool summer climates, grow well on natural rainfall. If the weather is exceptionally hot or dry water twice a month in summer.

Care

Plants often die out in the center after a few years and need to be divided and replanted. Cut established plants back to within a few inches of the ground in early spring to remove spent, blooming stalks, decrepit leaves, and reinvigorate the plant. Divide overgrown clumps in fall. Common blue fescue is not susceptible to pests and disease.

Companion Planting and Design

The stunning blue or silvery leaves make this an excellent choice to mix with smaller perennials for color contrast. Blend common blue fescue with other colorful ornamental grasses or small native or alpine perennials to create a dry garden. With its small size, common blue fescue makes a tidy edge to a large bed or border along a drive or walkway. This species is very dramatic in containers, particularly the silver-leaved forms.

Did You Know?

Grasses are flowering plants although their flowers are unlike those of most plants. All floral parts are greatly reduced or missing, with the stigma, anthers, and ovary barely visible to our eyes and enclosed within scalelike sheaths.

Sometimes I wonder how any plant ever makes it into horticulture, but in the case of common blue fescue, there is no mystery why gardeners in the high zones treasure this perennial bunch grass. Formerly known as Festuca cinerea *and often erroneously sold as* F. ovina, *the numerous and remarkable powder blue, thin leaves are so brilliant they look painted. Plants are generally small and take up only a square foot of space in the garden. Many color forms have been selected over the years. 'Elijah Blue' has silver blue foliage, 'Blue Silver' is one of the best of the silver-leaved forms, and 'Siskiyou Blue' has bright, shimmering blue foliage. This European species spreads nicely but is rarely invasive. The lacy flowering stalk is held above the foliage through summer.*

Bloom Period and Seasonal Color
Summer; tan spikes.

Mature Height × Spread
4 to 12 inches × 6 to 10 inches

Zones
3, 4, 5, 6
Hardy to 0 degrees Fahrenheit and perhaps more.

Deer Grass

Muhlenbergia rigens

Deer grass is a large, narrow-leaved bunch grass that is one of most dependable ornamental grasses for Arizona gardens. Deer grass is extremely drought tolerant, immune to heat and aridity, and rarely invasive. The countless, light green leaves form a fountain of a plant that, when mature, is nearly round. Tan, flowering spikes shoot up in late summer, arch over, and fade to a reddish hue as they age. Pink muhly (Muhlenbergia capillaris) is a shorter, more graceful plant with striking, airy rosy red plumes in fall. M. lindheimeri has wider leaves with a bluish caste that turns delicate silver after the first frost. M. emersleyi has deep green leaves topped with purple to red flowering stalks in late summer and fall.

Bloom Period and Seasonal Color
August to December; tall spikes well above the foliage ranging from tan to pink and reddish.

Mature Height × Spread
4 feet × 4 feet

Zones
1, 2, 3, 4, 5
Hardy to 10 degrees Fahrenheit but root hardy to 0 degrees Fahrenheit.

When, Where, and How to Plant
Plant in fall or early spring in low zones; in spring as soon as soil can be worked in the high zones. In low zones grow in full or partial sun, elsewhere in full sun. Deer grass grows in well-drained, fertile soil, heavy clay, or rocky, native soil. Dig a hole that is two or more times the width of the container and as deep. Mix in generous amounts of compost or mulch with the backfill. Fill the hole, gently pressing the soil to remove air pockets. Water thoroughly. Water every two to three days for a month, then weekly through the first summer.

Growing Tips
Apply slow-release or organic fertilizer annually in spring. Water established plants every two to three weeks in summer in low zones. In high zones, water monthly in summer although well-established plants thrive on natural rainfall. In all zones, rely on natural rainfall in winter.

Care
Deer grass is evergreen in low zones, but is semi-dormant in winter in high zones. Prune severely, to within a few inches of the ground, in early spring to remove spent, flowering stalks, dead leaves, and reinvigorate the plant. Deer grass is not susceptible to pests or disease.

Companion Planting and Design
Deer grass is striking when planted in mass groups, almost as a ground cover for large areas. Plant generously to use as an informal border, to create a low screen, or line walkways and drives. The tremendous drought and heat tolerance of deer grass make it a good choice for succulent beds or in other areas that receive minimal care. The soft form and striking autumn color make it particularly effective near seating areas, patios, or around pools. In smaller gardens, use as a specimen or focal plant or place in large containers.

Did You Know?
The genus *Muhlenbergia* is the largest genus of grasses in Arizona, numbering about fifty species.

Fescue

Festuca arundinacea

When, Where, and How to Plant

Plant in fall in mild winter areas and spring in all other zones in full sun. Prepare the planting area by tilling or scratching the soil, and removing rocks, old turf, and weeds. Level the area and water at least 6 inches or up to 12 inches deep, then let it dry for two days. Apply a generous layer of compost, mulch, or lawn fertilizer. Turn the soil, working in the amendments, to a depth of 4 to 6 inches. Water and then let the soil dry for up to three days. Spread to smooth, water well, and then sow the seed evenly at the rate of 7 to 10 pounds per 1,000 square feet. Keep evenly moist until the seed begin to germinate, then water two to three times a week until the lawn is well established.

Growing Tips

Apply lawn or organic fertilizer once in fall and once in spring. An iron and sulphur rich fertilizer may be applied in late summer to help green up the lawn but do not use nitrogen based fertilizer that late in the season. Water established lawns twice a week when temperatures are above 85 degrees Fahrenheit, once a week when they are between 65 and 85 degrees Fahrenheit, twice a month when they are between 50 and 65 degrees Fahrenheit, and monthly in winter when the grass is dormant.

Care

Mow regularly to about 4 inches tall but mow often enough that no more than 1 inch is removed each time. New varieties are quite resistant to most grass pests and diseases although beetle grubs can cause dead spots in summer. Control is difficult and unreliable, but damage is usually short-lived and rarely extensive.

Companion Planting and Design

Soft color and gentle texture make it a soothing lawn near a house or around a play area or pool. Fescue mixes well with bluegrass or perennial rye. When left unmowed, it offers excellent erosion control.

Did You Know?

The genus comes from the Latin meaning "a grass stalk." The epithet means it looks like another type of grass in the genus *Arundo* which are tall, stalked, and look somewhat like bamboo.

Fescue is a European and Asian grass that naturalized in the United States many decades ago. Long known as a pasture grass that could grow to 4 feet tall, with breeding and selection it has taken its place among the cool-season lawn grasses for Arizona. Fescue is evergreen and does best in the intermediate and high zones, but it can be planted as a cool-season grass or in the shade in the low zones. Fescue is a bunch grass and does not spread from underground stems so it is necessary to plant it densely to create a full lawn effect. Blades of modern varieties are fine textured and deep green and include 'Rebel', 'Shenandoah', 'Masterpiece', 'Silverado', and 'Dynasty', among many others.

Mature Height × Spread

18 inches × 1 to 2 feet

Zones

2, 3, 4, 5, 6
Hardy to 0 degrees Fahrenheit.

Tufted Hair Grass
Deschampsia caespitosa

This is one of those plants that are in desperate need of a new common name. Nothing about the name suggests the delicacy and gentle form of this charming ornamental grass. Delicate, wide blades form the base of the small plants and look like green sea urchins early in the season. But the evergreen leaves are just a platform for the clouds of airy, arching flowering heads of summer, which completely transform the plant. As the season turns to fall, the leaves turn bright orange to gold and the flowering heads fade to tan. All this color is seen to best advantage when backlit by the setting autumnal sun. The variety 'Bronze Veil' has bronzy-yellow flowering heads.

Bloom Period and Seasonal Color
Late spring to early summer; light green to green-gold, fading to tan.

Mature Height × Spread
1 to 2 feet × 1 to 4 feet

Zones
4, 5, 6
Hardy to 0 degrees Fahrenheit.

When, Where, and How to Plant
Plant in early spring as soon as the soil can be worked. Grow tufted hair grass in well-drained, fertile soil in full sun. Dig a hole that is two or more times the width of the container and as deep. Mix generous amounts of compost or mulch into the backfill. Fill the hole, gently pressing the soil to remove air pockets. Mulch lightly to keep the soil from drying out. Water thoroughly. Water every two to three days for a month, then weekly through the first summer.

Growing Tips
Apply slow-release or organic fertilizer annually in spring. Water weekly in summer, more often if the weather is exceptionally hot or dry. This charming grass does poorly where summers are long and hot.

Care
Prune severely to within a few inches of the ground in late winter to remove spent flowering stalks, dead leaves, and to reinvigorate the plant. Tufted hair grass is not susceptible to pests or disease.

Companion Planting and Design
Plant tufted hair grass closely to create a ground cover in large areas. Use generously at the edge of lawns where the dramatic and colorful foliage and lovely, flowering heads are highlighted. Plant generously to create a low border for large beds, or to line a drive or walkway. Mix with other small ornamental grasses or low-growing alpine perennials to create a striking dry garden. Tufted hair grass is useful around patios, seating areas, or pools to soften the hard edges of pavement and provide autumn color.

Did You Know?
Grasses are one of the plant families most widely used by mankind both historically and in the present day. All-important grain crops such as corn, rice, barley, wheat, and oats are grasses that have been domesticated, grown, and cultivated for thousands of years. Rice is the major food source for nearly half the world's population.

Ground Covers *for Arizona*

The term "ground cover" actually describes a function in the garden more than a specific type of plant. There are many occasions when it is useful or desirable to cover bare dirt not just by an umbrella of perennials, shrubs, or trees, but right down on the surface of the soil. And that is what ground covers do for us; they lay directly on the soil well beneath the larger plants of the bed providing a visual unity to an area. While ground covers may be sturdy perennials, tender annuals, trailing succulents, or even vines running on the ground, all ground covers share a few traits in common.

Many Sources

The best ones are perennials that have long, loose stems or have stems that root at intervals along the ground. Perennial ground covers provide permanence to the planting. Once in place you can design around the color of their bloom or the texture of their foliage so it becomes part of the ensemble of plants in the bed. Using perennial ground covers to stabilize slopes or other erosion-prone areas assures that over the years their increasing size and wider root system will continue to hold the slope.

Ground covers that have exceptionally long, trailing stems instead of sturdy, branching, or upright stems are preferred. The advantage of this type of growth is obvious — it allows one plant to spread over more ground that just the location where the roots are growing. From a gardening perspective this is a useful trait, especially in water-restricted locations. Plants can be watered only at their root zone, but they grow to cover a much larger area that does not need to be watered.

Plants whose stems are quick to root anywhere they touch the soil are also useful.

Ice Plant

Prairie Zinnia

Ground covers like these are especially good for protecting against soil erosion. In addition, this trait means that your plant will multiply readily to cover even more ground than the original plantings.

Special Uses for Ground Covers

Ground covers are useful in difficult spots such as sites in full sun or deep shade, in dry spots, or along rocky slopes. Plants such as Mexican evening primrose and trailing smokebush are especially adept at combining stems that root quickly along the ground and abundant reseeding to take firm hold of a steep slope or other area that is subject to erosion.

Sometimes ground covers come from unexpected sources. Almost any vine can be a good ground cover if it's grown in the right conditions or if it gives the garden the right look. There is nothing that mandates that all vines must grow up, many are just as happy to be left running along the ground.

Jamming plants very close together can form a ground cover. This is particularly effective with small plants such as desert marigold or Angelita daisy. In this case, small, dense plants form a continuous covering to the soil by their proximity to each other rather than the mass of one or a few plants. This is actually the principle by which bunch grasses create lawns, which, when you think of it, are the ultimate ground cover.

Although ground covers are extremely useful in most gardens, they take on special significance in hot, dry areas such as the low zones of Arizona. There, the sun's heat plays havoc with barren soils. Not only do the soils simply heat up to astonishing temperatures, but moisture held within the soil evaporates rapidly when the soils remain uncovered. All of this can dramatically affect the performance of your plants, causing them to dry out too quickly. Ground covers provide a living protection that cools the surface of the soil and help retain every ounce of soil moisture possible.

Ground covers also help to protect buildings from absorbing too much heat. When the sun bears down on the ground, especially bare ground, much of its heat is reflected upward at an angle. What is often in the path of that angle is the wall or window of a building. Plants absorb a tremendous amount of that heat, significantly reducing the amount of heat reflected onto the building wall. The plants do not have to be against the wall for this to work. Working like a staircase, low ground covers first absorb heat

and reflect it onto taller perennials or shrubs, which then collect more of the heat, until finally only a tiny amount of heat is reflected onto the building.

Ground covers can also keep the soil where it belongs. Loose, barren soil blows around easily in the wind, creating volcanic amounts of dust. Rain falling on barren soils gathers up soil and washes it away. Ground covers, especially those that root along the ground as they grow, stabilize soil whether the surface is flat or on a slope and help prevent such losses.

Finally, if we needed another good reason to grow ground covers, they gently enrich the soil under them over the years. All plants continually lose leaves and flowers and collect those of other plants as they blow around. Steadily, over the years, this acts like a miniature compost pile making the soil a bit richer with a finer texture. It gives the plants growing among and around ground covers a little leg up on those growing in barren soil.

Ground covers are such useful plants, especially in dry or hot areas, that it is easy to have an abundance of them in various parts of the garden. When chosen carefully so they suit the size and style of the bed where they grow, these tenacious, low-growing plants will delight you for years to come.

Moss Verbena

Copper Ice Plant
Malephora crocea

For many years the only ice plants sold in the low zones of Arizona were short-lived species that were excellent as winter annuals but unable to survive the desert summers. Gradually species with a greater tolerance for the rigors of the desert summer began to be grown by local growers, and the star performer of this group is copper ice plant. Dusky gray-green fingerlike leaves thickly cover the woody, wandering stems. The 2-inch, daisylike flowers in shades of burnished copper red or dark orange bloom longer than all other ice plants, and this species easily withstands the intense heat of the low zone summer. Another long-lived, winter-blooming succulent ground cover for the low zone is the Rocky Point ice plant (Drosanthemum sp.) with large, bright yellow flowers throughout winter.

Bloom Period and Seasonal Color
November to March; copper red, orange, or yellow.

Mature Height × Spread
1 to 4 feet × 3 to 6 feet

Zones
1, 2, 3
Hardy to about 25 degrees Fahrenheit.

When, Where, and How to Plant
Plant in fall or winter in full sun or partial shade. Copper ice plant grows in almost any soil, including salty and very alkaline ones, but demands excellent drainage. Dig a hole that is just large enough to hold the root system. Soil amendments are not necessary. Copper ice plant is not a heavy feeder and grows best in soils that are low in organic matter. Rock mulches help maintain soil moisture, but organic mulch will encourage rot around the roots of the plants. Water every two or three days for two weeks, then every week through the first winter.

Growing Tips
Apply balanced, but low nitrogen, slow-release or organic fertilizer to container grown plants in fall. Plants in the ground need no supplemental fertilizer. Water established plants weekly during the winter growing and blooming season. Reduce watering to every two to three weeks in summer or just often enough to keep plants from shriveling. Plants are semidormant in very hot weather and will rot quickly if watered regularly in summer.

Care
Prune in late fall or early winter to remove damaged stems, or to cut back the size of the plant. Ice plants are not susceptible to disease, but rabbits and other rodents will eat the succulent foliage.

Companion Planting and Design
Copper ice plant mixes well with other succulents, particularly the winter-growing aloes. Use as a succulent filler among winter-flowering, summer dormant bulbs such as homeria, freesia, and chasmanthe. This species makes an excellent, colorful ground cover in succulent gardens where its need for a fairly dry summer can be accommodated. Ice plants are an excellent choice for containers or planters by providing a brilliant splash of winter color.

Did You Know?
Malephora is part of an immense family of succulents from South Africa that is collectively known as mesembs. "Mesemb" is short for their old family name, *Mesembryanthemaceae*. Go ahead, try to say it.

Ice Plant
Drosanthemum species

When, Where, and How to Plant

Plant in fall or spring in intermediate zones, or set plants out in spring in high zones after all danger of frost is past. Plant in full sun, although ice plant does well in partial shade. Dig a hole that is just large enough for the root system. Soil amendments are not necessary because ice plants grow best in soils low in organic matter. Use rock mulches to keep the soil evenly moist; avoid organic mulch as it can encourage rot around the roots of the plants. Water every two or three days for two weeks, then every week or two through the first winter.

Growing Tips

Apply balanced, but low nitrogen, slow-release or organic fertilizer to container grown plants once in spring. Plants in the ground need no supplemental fertilizer. Water established plants every week or two while they are growing and blooming if rainfall is scarce; most survive well on natural rainfall once established. Reduce watering to every three weeks in the hottest part of the summer. Plants are semidormant in hot weather and will rot quickly if overwatered at that time.

Care

Prune in early spring to remove damaged stems or to cut back the size of the plant. Ice plants are not susceptible to disease, but rabbits and other rodents will eat the succulent foliage.

Companion Planting and Design

Ice plants mix well with other succulents either as a filler in containers or as a ground cover around succulent beds. Use as a ground cover among spring- and winter-flowering bulbs. Ice plants are excellent planted in containers or planters providing a brilliant splash of color to patios, seating areas, or around a pool. Use to fill in barren spots in a dry garden or in areas that receive minimal care.

Did You Know?

The name "ice plant" comes from the small crystals of salts that are secreted from the leaves. These crystals gleam in the sun and look like ice.

While ice plants suitable for the low zones are selected for their tolerance to the blazing summers, there is a group of ice plants that is more frost-hardy and better suited to the cooler summers of the intermediate and high zones of the state. The trailing pink-flowered form is Drosanthemum floribundum. *The deeper purple forms are generally* D. hispidum *but are often sold as* D. speciosum. *Plants of this type grow over rock walls and raised beds in the intermediate zones. As is typical of all ice plants, these forms have tiny, pill-shaped green leaves with minute glands that gleam like ice crystals. They bloom for a long time through late winter and early spring, many lasting through summer. All are at least semidormant during the hottest part of summer.*

Bloom Period and Seasonal Color

November to April, occasionally through summer; pink and purple.

Mature Height × Spread

1 to 4 feet × 3 to 6 feet

Zones

3, 4, 5
Hardy to about 15 degrees Fahrenheit, perhaps lower.

Mexican Evening Primrose
Oenothera speciosa

To some a savage weed, to others a welcome wanderer, the Mexican evening primrose is equally at home in cool, high zone gardens or in the low desert. Delicate pink or white flowers with prominent veining open in the late evening. The most commonly sold variety with deep pink flowers is 'Rosea'. The dark green, gently serrated leaves are tinged with red. Plants grow vigorously in fall and winter in the low zones and are deciduous through summer. In higher zones, it grows through summer and is deciduous in winter. This delightful ground cover is native throughout the southwestern United States and adjacent areas of Mexico. It spreads by rhizomes as well as by reseeding and can be invasive if given too much water. The Mexican evening primrose is also referred to as Oenothera berlandieri.

Bloom Period and Seasonal Color
Spring to summer; pale pink to white, fading to deeper pink.

Mature Height × Spread
4 to 12 inches × 2 to 3 feet

Zones
All
Root hardy to at least 0 degrees Fahrenheit.

When, Where, and How to Plant
Plant in fall or spring in full sun or partial shade. Mexican evening primrose grows aggressively in well-drained, fertile soil, but grows well and is not as invasive in rocky, unamended native soil. Dig a hole that is two to three times wider than the container and as deep. Soil amendments are not necessary although a thin layer of compost or mulch can be mixed with the backfill and added to the hole. Fill the hole, pressing the soil gently to remove air pockets. Water immediately, then water every two to four days for the first month.

Growing Tips
Apply fertilizer sparingly; it merely encourages rampant growth. Water established plants every two weeks while they are growing and blooming, monthly or less when plants are dormant. In all zones, established plants grow well on natural rainfall alone.

Care
Mexican evening primrose can take any amount of pruning when it is actively growing. Prune to within 2 inches of the ground in fall just after the leaves begin to grow. Where plants are very thick, use a scythe, lawnmower, or string cutter to cut the plants back. Cut-leaf or flea beetles often leave holes in the foliage but cause only cosmetic damage. Otherwise, this species is not susceptible to pests or disease.

Companion Planting and Design
Use where its aggressive growth is useful, in barren or bald spots in the garden. In intermediate or high zones, it is useful for erosion control. Plant thickly to create an informal border along walkways, near pools or patios, or in contained beds where it will not escape to other parts of the garden. Some low and intermediate zone gardeners use Mexican evening primrose as a flowering lawn that is lush and colorful in the winter but dormant in the summer.

Did You Know?
Ground covers reduce heat buildup on the surface of the soil, which in turn reduces evaporation of soil moisture. They also absorb and deflect heat from the ground that bounces onto adjacent walls or buildings.

Moss Verbena
Verbena pulchella

When, Where, and How to Plant

Plant in fall or spring in full sun or partial shade. Moss verbena is tolerant of well-drained fertile soil or rocky, native soil but does not thrive in wet or heavy clay soil. Dig a hole that is two to three times wider than the container and as deep. Soil amendments are not necessary although a thin layer of compost or mulch can be mixed with the backfill and added to the hole. Fill the hole, pressing the soil gently to remove air pockets. Water immediately, and then water every two to four days for the first month.

Growing Tips

Moss verbena requires no supplemental fertilizer. Water established plants every ten days to two weeks when the plants are actively growing and blooming. Water every three to four weeks in summer in the low zones. Moss verbena is a vigorous reseeder in the garden, but plants do not relocate well so keep the ones that come up in the desired locations and pull out the rest.

Care

Prune to reduce size or reinvigorate any time while plants are actively growing. In low zones, clean out dead plants and cut back rank growth in early fall. Moss verbena is not susceptible to pests or disease.

Companion Planting and Design

Moss verbena is an effortless ground cover for areas of the garden that receive intermittent or irregular watering. Plant generously to create an informal border, line a drive or walkway, or fill in gaps or barren spots in a newly planted garden. This species is useful for erosion control on rocky banks, although in low zones it is generally dormant and unsightly in the summer. Moss verbena makes a fine ground cover for succulent gardens or also in large containers or planters.

Did You Know?

Verbena is an old Latin name for the foliage of European members of the genus that had ancient medicinal and ceremonial use. They were also known as *vervain*, a name you still find in use in France.

Moss verbena grows where most plants fear to set down their roots—among rocks, in compacted desert soils, or in neglected parts of the garden. Spreading from a semiwoody base, the long stems create a lacy carpet of the finely cut, dark green leaves. The flowers are tiny and held in tight, round heads, but blooming is prolific throughout winter and spring. Most plants either die or go dormant in summer in the low zones, although those in the shade or near water bloom intermittently through summer. It is frequently grown as a summer annual in cold winter areas. Sandpaper verbena (Verbena rigida) has larger, rough leaves and elongated heads of purple flowers in spring. This species is not reliable through summer in Zones 1 and 2.

Bloom Period and Seasonal Color
From late fall to early summer, summer only in cold winter areas; purple, occasionally white.

Mature Height × Spread
4 to 8 inches × 2 to 5 feet

Zones
1, 2, 3
Hardy to about 25 degrees Fahrenheit.

Prairie Zinnia
Zinnia grandiflora

Native from the Rocky Mountains south into Mexico, prairie zinnia is a low growing, slightly mounded perennial that is a reliable, low care choice for the intermediate and high zones of Arizona. Fine, needlelike leaves give the short plants a light, airy appearance. Prairie zinnias need to be planted closely together to provide uninterrupted ground cover. Flowers have four or five yellow rays and raised golden disc flowers and are long-lived and prolific from spring through fall. Prairie zinnia can be difficult to grow and maintain as a perennial in the low zones with the intense summer heat, and hot, moist soils. Desert zinnia (Zinnia acerosa) has light green foliage and white flowers that fade to parchment tan color as they age.

Other Common Names
Rocky Mountain zinnia, Desert zinnia

Bloom Period and Seasonal Color
Late spring to fall; yellow, daisylike flowers with an orange eye.

Mature Height × Spread
6 to 12 inches × 12 inches

Zones
All
Hardy to 0 degrees Fahrenheit.

When, Where, and How to Plant
Plant in fall or spring in low zones, or in spring once the soil has warmed in high zones. Place in full sun in all but low zones where afternoon shade is necessary. The prairie zinnia needs extremely well-drained soil, although it is tolerant of a well-drained fertile soil if watering is minimal. Dig a hole that is two to three times wider than the container and as deep. Soil amendments are not necessary. Fill the hole, pressing the soil gently to remove air pockets. Water immediately, then water every two to four days for the first month.

Growing Tips
Apply slow-release or organic fertilizer annually in spring. Water established plants sparingly. In all but the low zones, established plants need irrigation only during extended hot or dry spells. In Zones 1 and 2, water every two weeks in summer but be sure that the soil is very well drained. In all zones, rely on natural rainfall in winter.

Care
Prune severely in early spring to remove dead leaves and debris. Although the prairie zinnia is not susceptible to pests or disease, it may quickly develop root rot in soils with poor drainage or soils that remain too wet when the weather is hot. Overhead watering can cause mildew and rotting. Symptoms include blackened leaves and sudden wilting and death of all or a large portion of the plant. Prevention is the key.

Companion Planting and Design
In intermediate and high zones, this is a colorful but sturdy choice for erosion control. Plant closely together to form a ground cover or plant in front of a large bed of ornamental grasses, native perennials, or shrubs. Prairie zinnia mixes well with succulents such as agaves, sedums, or yuccas. Prairie zinnia does well in containers or planters as long as it is not overwatered.

Did You Know?
The genus was named for Johann Gottlieb Zinn, who died in 1759. Zinn was a noted botanist and anatomist of his time and even has a tendon named for him.

When, Where, and How to Plant

Plant sundrops in fall or early spring. Sundrops will grow in well-drained, fertile soil or rocky, unamended native soil, but do not tolerate wet or heavy clay soil. Place in full sun or partial shade. Dig a hole that is two to three times wider than the container and as deep. Soil amendments are not necessary, although a thin layer of mulch or compost can be incorporated into the backfill. Set the plant in the hole slightly higher than the soil line. Fill the hole pressing down the soil gently to remove air pockets. Water immediately and water every two to four days for the first month.

Growing Tips

Apply slow-release or organic fertilizer in spring and fall while plants are young. Established plants need no supplemental fertilizer. Water established plants every two weeks in summer, more often if it is very hot and dry. Water monthly in winter.

Care

Sundrops grow naturally into a tidy shape and do not require consistent pruning for shape. Prune back in early spring to remove winter-damaged stems or reinvigorate the plant. Since plants are often semidormant and briefly deciduous in summer, resist pruning at this time. Sundrops are not susceptible to pests or disease. Plants often die out after five or six years in the ground seemingly for no reason. It is thought by many horticulturists that they are just short-lived and die from old age.

Companion Planting and Design

Sundrops look marvelous when planted in combination with blue-flowering black dalea or Texas sages. This is a rugged and reliable ground cover for hot, dry areas of the garden. It is useful as an informal border, along drives or walkways, or near a pool or patio where reflected heat is intense.

Did You Know?

Boyce Thompson Southwestern Arboretum near Superior, Arizona performed tests on sun tolerance and low water use on a number of potential ground covers for south Arizona gardens. One of the star performers of those tests was sundrops.

Sundrops are trailing plants with thin, light green leaves that are somewhat sparse on the plant, but the magnificent flowers more than make up for it. Plants bloom prolifically in spring and fall with large, paper-thin, yellow flowers that open during the evening. Sundrops grow quickly with minimal watering and are not as invasive as many other ground covers. The closely related Calyophus drummondiana has darker green, needlelike leaves and small, bright yellow flowers in late spring and summer but grows best in Zones 2 and 3. Saltillo evening primrose (Oenothera stubbei) is a spring blooming species with yellow flowers and also does best in Zones 2 and 3. Ozark sundrops (O. macrocarpa) is a lovely, yellow flowered ground cover for all zones but requires shade in the low zones.

Bloom Period and Seasonal Color
Spring and fall; clear yellow.

Mature Height × Spread
1 to 2 feet × 1 to 3 feet

Zones
1, 2, 3, 4
Hardy to about 20 degrees Fahrenheit.

Trailing Indigo Bush

Dalea greggii

Trailing indigo bush is an attractive, low-growing perennial with tiny, soft, gray leaves. Although solitary plants provide soft color contrast to bright perennial plantings, this species is most often called upon to serve as a ground cover. There are numerous fine stems on each plant that cascade from the center and root along the ground as they grow. Over a short time, these rooted stems create a dense cover and if the plants are spaced closely enough, they completely cover the surface of the soil. Lustrous, deep purple flowers cover the plant in spring. Dalea capitata has minute, deep green leaves and yellow flowers through spring and summer. D. capitata does best in light shade in Zones 1 and 2, but tolerates full sun in Zones 3 and 4.

Other Common Name
Creeping dalea

Bloom Period and Seasonal Color
Spring through summer; indigo to purple.

Mature Height × Spread
1 to 2 feet × 2 to 4 feet

Zones
1, 2, 3, 4
Hardy to 15 degrees Fahrenheit.

When, Where, and How to Plant
Plant in fall or spring in full sun. To use as a ground cover, space plants about 3 feet apart. Trailing indigo bush is tolerant of a wide range of soils including well-drained, fertile soil, and rocky, native soil. Dig a hole that is two to three times wider than the container and as deep. Soil amendments are not necessary although a thin layer of compost or mulch can be mixed with the backfill. Fill the hole pressing the soil gently to remove air pockets. Water immediately following planting, then water every two to four days for the first month. It may take up to two years for plants to become fully established.

Growing Tips
Apply slow release or organic fertilizer annually in fall to young plants; established plants need no supplemental fertilizer. Water established plants every two to three weeks in summer, less in winter.

Care
Prune in early spring to maintain form and remove dead or damaged stems. Maintain the gentle form of this plant by pruning stems at varying lengths. Removing rooted stem sections can also reduce the size. Old plants frequently die out in the middle, especially when they have been overwatered or grown in the shade. Trailing indigo bush is not susceptible to pests or disease.

Companion Planting and Design
Trailing indigo bush is an excellent choice for slope stabilization or erosion control. Plant closely together to form a continuous ground cover for large, hot areas. This species also works well as an informal hedge or border, along drives or walkways, or against walls or buildings where reflected heat is intense. The soft silvery foliage provides a backdrop or serves as a contrast plant in beds of colorful perennials or succulent gardens.

Did You Know?
The genus was named in honor of Thomas Dale and the species in honor of 18th century botanist Josiah Gregg, who died in 1805. Dale was a famous American naturalist, physician, and plant collector who traveled and collected plants in Mexico and California in the mid 19th century.

Trailing Lantana
Lantana montevidensis

When, Where, and How to Plant

Plant in spring after all danger of frost is past. Trailing lantana is tolerant of almost any soil condition from well-drained, fertile soil to rocky, native soil and even heavy clay. Trailing lantana has its best form and blooms most prolifically in full sun, but tolerates light shade well. Dig a hole that is two to three times wider than the container and as deep. Soil amendments are not necessary. Fill the hole pressing the soil gently to remove air pockets. Water immediately following planting then water every two to four days for the first month.

Growing Tips

Apply slow-release or organic fertilizer in spring and once during the growing season. Water established plants weekly in summer, monthly in winter. Monitor watering carefully in late summer; plants usually need less water when the humidity is higher. Leaves may yellow between the veins (called "chlorosis") when plants are overwatered.

Care

Plants are less vigorous in winter, although they rarely lose all their leaves. Prune in early spring to remove frost-damaged stems, or to reinvigorate the plant. Trailing lantana may be lightly pruned through summer to maintain a desired size. It is not susceptible to disease, although it can be a magnet for whiteflies in late summer. Spray leaves with insecticidal soap to keep light infestations under control; there is no remedy for heavy infestations.

Companion Planting and Design

Plant closely to provide a continuous ground cover. Plant trailing lantana under large shrubs such as hibiscus, red bird of paradise, or yellowbells. Create an informal border around patios, pools, or areas where reflected heat is intense. Trailing lantana is also useful to stabilize a slope or as erosion control. This lantana grows well in containers or hanging baskets either alone or mixed with other winter-flowering perennials.

Did You Know?

Lantana comes from an old Latin name for a European species, *Viburnum lantanum,* that has similar flowers but is not related. The word *montevidensis* refers to the Argentine city of Montevideo.

This reliable South American native is immune to heat, tolerates almost any soil condition, and is remarkably drought-tolerant once established. The best performers are the original forms with small, lance-shaped, dark green leaves and small heads of purple or white flowers. Trailing lantana has a delicacy that is completely at odds with its toughness, and it is one of the most effective ground covers for softening a hot location. 'Lavender Swirl' has both purple and white flowers on one plant. There are numerous hybrids between this species and the shrubby Lantana camara in a bewildering array of colors and sizes. Hybrids 'New Gold' and 'Gold Trailing' are widely used and are a light buttery yellow and a bright gold, respectively.

Other Common Name
Weeping lantana

Bloom Period and Seasonal Color
Summer to fall; lavender, purple, white, gold, and yellow.

Mature Height × Spread
1 to 2 feet × 2 to 6 feet

Zones
1, 2, 3
Hardy to 25 degrees Fahrenheit but may be root hardy to 20 degrees Fahrenheit.

Palms *for Arizona*

Palms engender high feeling in the low zones of Arizona. Many people consider them a sign of high water use, indicative of an inappropriate gardening style, or just too "undesert." For others their dramatic forms and tropical appearance help define the warm, sunny climate that has attracted so many residents and visitors alike. Whether you care for them or not, most of the ones commonly found in southern Arizona are natives of deserts or semiarid regions, which greatly accounts for their tremendous success in the lower zones.

Picking the Right One

In nature, most desert species are found in canyons or along fault lines where water seeps up or remains just below the surface. The palms have an almost permanent source of water. But in the garden, mature desert palms are amazingly drought tolerant, performing extremely well on a lean water diet. Like any large family of plants, there are species for almost any taste and style of garden. The only trick is picking the right one.

Pygmy Date Palm

Jelly Palm

Many palms, including some of the best-known, like California fan palm and Canary Island date palm, are tall—too tall for a small suburban lot. After a couple of decades, you are looking at the middle of the trunk with the crown rising far above your head. The soaring height of some species works well when planted intentionally for shade or where there is plenty of room to allow for the full impact of the plants, but it can look ridiculous in small gardens.

There are many species of palms that are small enough to fit comfortably in suburban lots. The bamboo palms in the genus *Chamaedorea* fit comfortably in shaded courtyards, the desert species of *Livistona* from Australia, and closer to home the marvelous Sonoran native palms in the genus *Sabal* are small enough and drought tolerant for most low zone gardens.

Cutting Your Own Hair

Palms are clean plants on the whole and are, therefore, particularly useful in patios, courtyards, or near a pool. They have huge blooming stalks that should be removed entirely each year if either the flowers or the fruit are a problem. They do not shed their leaves annually; in fact, some do not shed them at all but build up long skirts of their leaves.

Pruning leaves, living or dead, from palms is a minor industry in southern Arizona, but it is both poorly practiced and poorly understood most of the time. Palms do not need annual pruning; it is just a custom that has arisen for no particular reason. Like all plants, they retain leaves in a number sufficient to provide the energy to maintain the plant. The plant maintains a fine balance between the number needed to provide the energy needs of the plant, but not much extra, which is why the oldest leaves continually die off in favor of the ever newer ones. Old leaves also provide the props that hold up the newer leaves before the petioles harden off. The size, shape, and flexibility of the entire head of leaves are what give the plants their fabled wind resistance. For all these reasons, it is stressful to the plant to have half or more of its living leaves continually removed, not to mention unnecessary. And frankly to me, they do not look better with half a head of leaves, but rather look like a kid who tried to cut his own hair.

Palms are wonderful plants that blend the lush, exotic feel of tropical regions with a rugged tolerance for the heat and aridity of Arizona. As you look through the pages that follow, take note of the palm species that are in scale with your garden and that will suit its ambience and style.

Blue Hesper Palm
Brahea armata

This Sonoran Desert native palm is an outstanding choice for a moderate-sized palm that provides low and intermediate zone gardeners with great beauty and drama as well as superb heat and drought tolerance. Large waxy, fan-shaped, blue-gray leaves are calming in the fierce summer sun. Slow growing and solitary, blue hesper palm is striking in the garden regardless of its size or maturity. Two closely related, but less common species, also make excellent garden choices. Guadalupe Island palm (Brahea edulis) has bright green leaves growing to 30 feet tall. It is the perfect substitute for the much larger California fan palm in smaller gardens. San Jose hesper palm (B. brandegeei) has a slender trunk topped with leaves that are green above and whitish below.

Bloom Period and Seasonal Color
Summer; long blooming stalks hang below the leaves and down the trunk; flowers are pale cream.

Mature Height × Spread
20 to 40 feet × 10 to 20 feet

Zones
1, 2, 3, 4
Hardy to 15 degrees Fahrenheit.

When, Where, and How to Plant
Plant in late spring or summer, when soils are warm. Blue hesper palm is tolerant of a wide range of soil from very dry and rocky to well-drained, fertile soil. However, it does poorly in heavy clay or soil with poor drainage. Plant in full sun. Dig a hole that is two to three times the width of the container or rootball and only as deep. Mix a thin layer of mulch or compost with the backfill. Fill the hole pressing the soil gently around the roots to remove air pockets. Water thoroughly. Water every three to four days for a month. Water every seven to ten days for the first summer.

Growing Tips
Fertilize young plants annually with a slow-release or organic fertilizer. Mature plants need no supplemental fertilizer. Established plants are extremely drought tolerant, but will grow more quickly if watered every two to three weeks in summer. Reduce watering to once every month or two in winter.

Care
Prune dead leaves or spent blooming stalks anytime. Do not prune living leaves unless they present a danger to people or are damaged. Blue hesper palm is not susceptible to pests or disease.

Companion Planting and Design
The large leaves and cool blue color are calming when blue hesper palm is planted against a south or west facing wall or building, or other locations where reflected heat is intense. Excellent when used near a pool or patio where the soft blue leaves provide a cooling backdrop. Blue hesper palm is particularly effective when planted in groups to fill a barren spot in the garden, or create a dramatic hedgelike planting. This palm is excellent when mixed with desert shrubs or succulents where it will eventually provide gentle, light shade. The plant is slow growing but provide vertically for its eventual height.

Did You Know?
Plants are often named to honor friends or associates. The genus *Brahea* was named for the Danish astronomer, Tyco Brahe.

California Fan Palm

Washingtonia filifera

When, Where, and How to Plant

Plant when soils warm, in late spring or summer, in full sun. California fan palms tolerate a wide range of soils from very dry and rocky, to well-drained, fertile soil and even those that are nearly saturated. Dig a hole two to three times the width of the container or rootball and only as deep. Mix a thin layer of compost or mulch with the backfill. Fill the hole pressing the soil gently around the roots of the plant to remove air pockets. Water thoroughly; then, every two to three days for a month. Water weekly the first summer.

Growing Tips

Apply slow-release or organic fertilizer annually, especially when plants are young or less than 6 feet tall. Water established plants, those that have been in the ground more than two years, every ten to fourteen days in summer; monthly in winter. The drought tolerance of California fan palms increases as they mature.

Care

Prune dead leaves or blooming stalks anytime. Never prune living leaves unless they are in the way or are damaged. Remove leaf bases carefully by pulling off those that can be pulled away easily in your hand rather than cutting. Most plants are self-cleaning and shed dead leaves and old leaf bases in high winds. California fan palm is not susceptible to pests or disease.

Companion Planting and Design

California fan palm is excellent in gardens that have the scale for it. Plant in groups of three to enhance the shade and create a naturalistic grove effect. Birds nest in the leaves, so place where they will not be a problem. California fan palm is dramatic when planted as a street tree, along the boundary of a large property, or as part of a mixed border planting. This species, like many palms, is marvelous in hilly gardens when planted so the crowns are at eye level.

Did You Know?

Although palms are often called trees, the fibrous stems of palms aren't true wood. They are made up of tightly packed fibers and stiffened vascular tissue enclosed by the dead leaf bases.

California fan palms are large, stately plants with full, rounded crowns and a smooth, light brown trunk. Leaves are fan-shaped, light green and up to six feet long. Planted abundantly in the low zones, especially in Phoenix and Yuma, it is a common plant for street-side plantings and public rights of way. Native to canyons in southern Arizona and southern California, this plant needs plenty of vertical space. The small dark fruit is edible but usually enjoyed only by birds. The closely related Mexican fan palm (Washingtonia robusta) has a thinner trunk and smaller head of dark green leaves and old plants are over 80 feet tall. Hybrids are common and are routinely sold by either of these species names.

Other Common Name
Desert fan palm

Bloom Period and Seasonal Color
Summer; cream-colored flowers on long stalks that extend outward from the crown.

Mature Height × Spread
40 to 50 feet × 20 to 25 feet

Zones
1, 2, 3, 4
Hardy to 20 degrees Fahrenheit.

Date Palm
Phoenix species

The tall, graceful edible date palm (Phoenix dactylifera) has fed, clothed, and sheltered desert peoples since the dawn of recorded history in its long association with the people of the North African deserts. The fruit, both fresh and dried, is prized throughout the world, and the relics of old commercial groves are still seen in Phoenix today. Date palms are beautiful plants with straight, grayish trunks that are marked by a diamond pattern of old leaf bases and are crowned by 12-foot dusky, blue-gray feathery leaves. The Canary Island date palm (P. canariensis) has a thick, dark brown trunk, and stiff, dark green 20-foot leaves. The diminutive pygmy date palm (P. roebelenii) grows a mere 8 feet tall and its 4-foot-long leaves curve gracefully from the trunk.

Bloom Period and Seasonal Color
Summer, long-blooming stalks hang below the leaves; flowers are cream to yellow; male and female flowers are separate plants.

Mature Height × Spread
6 to 50 feet × 5 to 40 feet

Zones
1, 2, 3
Hardiness varies by species but ranges from 15 degrees Fahrenheit to 25 degrees Fahrenheit.

When, Where, and How to Plant
Plant in late spring or summer, when soils are warm. Date palms can handle any soils from very dry and rocky to those that are almost wet. Plant in full sun in a location that allows plenty of room for the mature crown. Prepare a hole as deep as the rootball and two to three times as wide. Mix a thin layer of compost or mulch with the backfill. Fill the hole, pressing the soil gently to remove air pockets. Water thoroughly at planting; then, water every two to three days for a month. Water weekly the first summer.

Growing Tips
Pygmy date palms tolerate any amount of heat and sun if the roots are kept cool and well watered. Water established plants every two weeks in summer, once a week for pygmy date palms. The large date palms become increasingly drought tolerant as they age. By the time they are in the ground five years they can thrive on monthly watering. Reduce watering to every other month in winter. Apply slow-release or organic fertilizer annually in early summer.

Care
Prune dead leaves or blooming stalks anytime. Never prune living leaves unless they are a danger or damaged. Leaf bases are firmly attached and cannot be removed without damaging the plant. Date palms are not susceptible to pests or disease, although deeply stressed plants can show wilting leaves and sudden leaf death symptomatic of crown rot. Crown rot is poorly understood in palms; prevention is the best approach.

Companion Planting and Design
Larger plants require plenty of vertical space. They are outstanding in groves or groups for light, filtered shade. These species are excellent where a lusher, more tropical look is desired. Date palms mix well with summer flowering subtropical shrubs like hibiscus, red bird of paradise, and yellowbells. Smaller species grow well in large containers.

Did You Know?
One of the largest collections of edible date palm varieties has been assembled at Arizona State University in Tempe.

When, Where, and How to Plant

Plant in late spring or summer, when soils are warm, in full sun or partial shade. Jelly palm grows best in well-drained, fertile soil although it tolerates a wide range. Plant where there is plenty of room for the mature crown of leaves. Dig a hole two to three times the width of the container or rootball and as deep. Mix a thin layer of compost or mulch with the backfill. Fill the hole pressing the soil gently around the roots to remove air pockets. Water thoroughly. Water every two to three days for a month. Water every week for the first summer.

Growing Tips

Apply slow-release or organic fertilizer monthly during warm weather. Water established plants, those that have been in ground at least two years, weekly in summer, every two to three weeks in winter.

Care

Prune dead leaves and spent blooming stalks anytime. Removing living leaves decreases the vigor of the plant. Leaf bases are sturdy and persistent and should be cut, *not pulled* off the plant. Jelly palm is not susceptible to pests or disease but may develop pale or yellowed leaves indicative of chlorosis when planted in rocky, dry soil or if watered too shallowly. Water deeply and apply iron chelate to alleviate this condition.

Companion Planting and Design

The graceful arching leaves of jelly palm make it an excellent specimen or focal plant. It combines well with other tropical plants to provide an exotic look to plantings around pools or patios. It can also be used to fill a corner or barren spot, or as part of a mixed planting of other palms. Plant generously to line drives, walkways, or along a border. Jelly palm grows well in a lawn but should be deep-watered in addition to the lawn watering.

Did You Know?

Its juicy fruit gives the plant its common name. The fruit is edible right off the plant or it can be cooked and strained to make jelly. It is also fermented into wine.

Jelly palm is a short, vase-shaped solitary palm that grows well in the low and intermediate zones of Arizona. The blue-green, feather-shaped leaves rise in a stiff arch from the crown and fall back in a graceful curve toward the trunk. The trunk is stout and covered with the hefty, persistent, gray leaf bases. Pruning the old leaves regularly exposes the regular rows of leaf bases and is an attractive feature of mature plants. The inflorescence is generally three feet long and the yellow to reddish flowers result in round, bright orange to yellow fruit. Jelly palm hybridizes freely with many other species, but a cross between jelly palm and queen palm has long been recognized. It has the size of the queen palm and the thin, stiff leaflets of this species.

Bloom Period and Color
Summer; yellow to reddish.

Mature Height × Spread
6 to 15 feet × 8 to 12 feet

Zones
1, 2, 3, 4
Hardy to 15 degrees Fahrenheit.

Mediterranean Fan Palm
Chamaerops humilis

I used to live in New Orleans and I am still startled when I see plants growing well in the desert cities that were equally successful along the banks of the Mississippi. The Mediterranean fan palm is part of that amazing group and is reliable in all but the coldest zones. Individual stems are covered with old leaf bases. The leaves are dark green, fan-shaped, and very stiff. When left to its own devices, this palm grows many stems from the base, which crowds the stems and the crowns into a living sphere. More often, all but a few stems are pruned out, creating an elegant, formal plant with multiple curving stems. Slow growing, this Mediterranean native is a dependable choice for southern Arizona gardens where a smaller palm is needed.

Bloom Period and Seasonal Color
Summer; small, inconspicuous flowers; male and female flowers on separate plants.

Mature Height × Spread
10 to 20 feet × 10 to 20 feet

Zones
1, 2, 3, 4
Hardy to 5 degrees Fahrenheit.

When, Where, and How to Plant
Plant in late spring or summer when soils are warm. Mediterranean fan palm handles a wide range of soils from very dry and rocky, to well-drained, fertile soil. Site the palm in full sun. Dig a hole two to three times the width of the container or rootball and only as deep. Mix a thin layer of compost or mulch with the backfill. Gently press the soil around the roots to remove air pockets as you fill the hole. Water thoroughly. Water every two to three days for a month. Water every week for the first summer.

Growing Tips
Apply slow-release or organic fertilizer annually in spring. Water established plants every two weeks in summer, every three to four weeks in winter in low zones. Water established plants every two to three weeks in summer, every month or two in winter in high zones.

Care
Prune dead leaves and spent blooming stalks anytime. Mediterranean fan palm is naturally multitrunked but regular pruning of undesired stems in the summer can train it to be a single trunked plant or one with a selected number of stems. Do not remove living leaves from a stem that is being maintained; it decreases the vigor of the plant. Mediterranean fan palm is not susceptible to pests or disease.

Companion Planting and Design
Spectacular when grown with an asymmetrical number of selected stems and used as a specimen or accent plant. Plants that are not routinely pruned are nearly round and are equally dramatic. Mediterranean fan palm grows well in a lawn but should be deep-watered according to the schedule above in addition to the lawn watering. This palm has great elegance and formality and fits well into highly structured or Oriental style gardens.

Did You Know?
This is the only palm that is native to Europe. All other palms come from the tropical and subtropical regions of the world.

Mexican Fan Palm
Washingtonia robusta

When, Where, and How to Plant
Plant in late spring or summer when soils are warm. Mexican fan palm is very versatile because it is tolerant of a wide range of soils from very dry and rocky to well-drained, fertile soil, including soils that are very wet. Plant in full sun. Dig a hole that is two to three times the width of the container or rootball and only as deep. Mix a thin layer of compost or mulch with the backfill. Fill the hole pressing the soil gently around the roots to remove air pockets. Water thoroughly. Water every two to three days for a month. Water every week for the first summer.

Growing Tips
Apply slow-release or organic fertilizer annually, especially when plants are young. Water established plants every ten to fourteen days in summer; every month or two in winter. This palm increases its drought tolerance as it matures.

Care
Remove leaf bases carefully by pulling those that can be pulled away easily with your hand instead of cutting them. Most individuals are self-cleaning and will drop dead leaves and leaf bases in high winds. Never prune living leaves unless they are in the way or are damaged although you may prune dead leaves or blooming stalks anytime. Mexican fan palm is not susceptible to pests or disease.

Companion Planting and Design
Mexican fan palm is lovely when planted in trios or small groves to enhance the shade and create a grove effect. Birds nest in the leaves, so place where that will not be a problem. Mexican fan palm makes a dramatic street tree, boundary planting, or as part of a large, mixed border planting. In hilly gardens place where the crowns are at viewing level.

Did You Know?
Wild groves of desert palms are cool, shaded places and serve as havens for birds and other wildlife. Groves are located either where water has seeped out of the ground along a fault line or in the canyons of desert mountain ranges.

Mexican fan palms have tall, thin, trunks that rarely stand straight up but weave and curl delightfully as they mature. This species and the closely related California fan palm (Washingtonia filifera) account for most of the palms planted in the low elevation zone cities of Yuma and Phoenix. The bright green leaves are fan shaped and held in a tightly formed head that makes the crown look round. The reddish brown leaf bases cling to the trunk in young trees, but as the plants mature the leaf bases are shed, revealing the smooth, gray trunk. Birds that also use the crowns as favored nesting and roosting sites enjoy the small dark fruit. Hybrids are common between Mexican fan palm and California fan palm and may be sold under either name.

Other Common Name
Skyduster

Bloom Period and Seasonal Color
Summer; cream-colored on long stalks that extend outward from the crown in summer.

Mature Height × Spread
40 to 80 feet × 10 to 15 feet

Zones
1, 2, 3
Hardy to 18 degrees Fahrenheit.

Queen Palm
Syagrus romanzoffiana

Queen palms represent one of the constant puzzles of gardening. That is, they are plants that are sold and used in astronomical numbers but do poorly in the area. Everything about the low zones is hard on queen palms—the soils are too alkaline and lacking in magnesium, the summers are too long and too hot, and there is not nearly enough moisture to sustain them properly. When well grown, queen palms are graceful plants with smooth gray trunks ringed with scars of old leaves. Huge, feather-shaped, deep-green leaves fall gracefully from the crown. They do best in deep, rich soils, with regular watering and where summers are much less rigorous than the Phoenix area. Consequently, queen palms are short-lived in Zones 1 and 2 and seem to grow better in Zone 3.

Bloom Period and Seasonal Color
Summer; cream on long stalks with male and female flowers on separate parts of the stalk.

Mature Height × Spread
30 to 50 feet × 15 to 25 feet

Zones
1, 2, 3
Hardy to 22 degrees Fahrenheit.

When, Where, and How to Plant
Plant in late spring or summer, when soils are warm. Soil drainage is critical. Queen palms grow best in deep, well-drained, fertile soil and do poorly in rocky, dry soil or soils that have poor drainage. Plant in partial shade or full sun. Dig a hole that is two to three times the width of the container or rootball and only as deep. Mix a thin layer of compost or mulch with the backfill. Fill the hole pressing the soil gently around the roots to remove air pockets. Water thoroughly. Water every two to three days for a month. Water every week for the first summer.

Growing Tips
Annually apply a slow-release palm fertilizer that includes micronutrients. This palm requires the micronutrients found in a good palm fertilizer. Monthly applications of chelated iron and magnesium through the growing season help prevent severe leaf yellowing (chlorosis). Water established plants deeply, once a week during summer, monthly in winter.

Care
Prune dead leaves or blooming stalks anytime. Do not prune living leaves unless they are damaged or present a danger. Queen palms are highly susceptible to various crown fungus infections, which cause leaves to wither and look shredded before they are fully developed or cause the leaves to wilt and die quickly. Plants stressed from excess heat or from mineral deficiencies in desert soils are especially susceptible.

Companion Planting and Design
Queen palms are lovely when planted in groups to provide shade and create a grove effect. Use around seating areas to provide light, tall shade, and a tropical, lush look. They grow well in lawns but should be watered deeply in addition to the lawn watering. Queen palms mix well with summer-flowering shrubs such as hibiscus, lantana, and red bird of paradise.

Did You Know?
There are two great divisions of the plant kingdom—monocots, which have only one cotyledon when they germinate, and dicots, which have two. Palms are monocots as are grasses, bulbs, agaves, and yuccas.

When, Where, and How to Plant

Windmill palm grows best in well-drained, fertile soil. Plant in partial shade in low zones, full sun elsewhere, in late spring or summer when soils are warm. Dig a hole that is two to three times the width of the container or rootball and only as deep. Mix a thin layer of compost or mulch with the backfill. Fill the hole pressing the soil gently around the roots to remove air pockets. Water thoroughly. Water every two to three days for a month. Water every week for the first summer.

Growing Tips

Apply slow-release or organic fertilizer annually in spring. Water established plants every week or two during summer in low zones; every month in intermediate and high zones. Reduce watering to once every month or two in winter or rely on natural rainfall.

Care

Prune dead leaves or spent blooming stalks anytime. Do not prune living leaves unless they present a danger or are damaged. Windmill palm is not susceptible to pests or disease and does not get the characteristic leaf yellowing (chlorosis) between the veins when planted in the alkaline soils of the low zones.

Companion Planting and Design

Windmill palm makes a superb specimen or accent plant in small gardens or courtyards. Use this palm to provide contrast to large perennial plantings or as part of a large, mixed hedge or boundary planting. The spare form and the firm, deep green leaves of this species make it particularly effective in very formal or Oriental style gardens. Windmill palm blends well with succulents, particularly in the intermediate and high zones. Plant it in groups to create a dramatic effect around pools, seating areas, or patios. Windmill palm grows well in large containers or planters.

Did You Know?

Windmill palms are the most cold tolerant of all palms but even more startling is their tolerance for wet, cold winters. They are grown throughout the world and old specimens are common in gardens in western Canada and Scotland.

Out of the mountains of China comes one of the sturdiest palms for both low and high zone gardens in Arizona. The windmill palm is a modest-sized plant. The solitary trunk of the windmill palm is densely covered with persistent, tough leaf bases. Inside all the leaf bases are dense mats of dark brown fiber giving the plant a shaggy look. Birds are enormously fond of this matting for nesting material and routinely raid old plants. The deep green, fan-shaped leaves are relatively short and nearly round. They are held on long, thin petioles and are widely spaced, making the head look open and spare and account for the common name. Plants grow slowly and are perhaps the most cold tolerant palm in the world.

Bloom Period and Seasonal Color
Summer; cream-colored flowers.

Mature Height × Spread
20 to 30 feet × 10 to 15 feet

Zones
All
Hardy to 5 degrees Fahrenheit.

Perennials *for Arizona*

In the early years of the 19th century, gardening traditions were much different from those we know today. Important public gardens and large private gardens relied heavily on evergreen trees, long vistas with meadows, clipped hedges and trimmed bushes near the house, and if there were flowers, roses. Vegetables grown for the house were securely tucked into various corners and harvested when they were needed. People who lived in the country and were of more modest means, just let things grow up all around the house, willy-nilly, finding their own way with random and gaudy color combinations. Later, as England gained wealth from its worldwide trade, public and formal gardens began to use color in the form of huge expanses of bedding plants laid out in astounding numbers and changed seasonally with all the perfection a nearly limitless labor force could provide.

The Perennial Revolution

A revolution was ready to happen and it did. Through the writings and efforts of two famous English gardeners, William Robinson and Gertrude Jekyll, a less formal style began to take shape, one that owed much to the informal plantings of flowers, roses, and shrubs in country gardens. This new style relied heavily on the planting of flowering perennials—they were less work than the bedding plants, and they came back every year without undue fuss. The effect was big and showy, and it could be done on any scale and with any budget. Gardeners have never looked back.

Perennials are still the favorite plant for almost any garden in every zone. Their advantages still resonate with gardeners today as they did over 150 years ago. Well-chosen perennials live a long time in the garden, repeat the show annually, and do not demand excessive work on our part. Low zone gardeners in particular should remember that planting a perennial garden is a style and does not have to be a stringent duplication of the plant lists offered in the countless books on perennial gardens. There is a wealth of plants that tolerate the rigorous growing conditions of Arizona that can be used to make glorious perennial gardens regardless of the zone in which you live. In cold climates, well-chosen perennials—whether native or just those well adapted to the area—live through the winter but bloom only seasonally. In the lower zones, perennials are generally evergreen and by choosing carefully, it is possible to keep a perennial planting blooming throughout the year.

Purple Coneflower

96

Successful Perennials

The term, "perennial," is misleading. It actually refers to plants that live and bloom over more than one season. However, it is a gardener's term used to mean any herbaceous plant—not a grass, bulb, woody plant, or succulent (even though they are technically perennial)— that is generally less than four feet tall and has colorful flowers. Many perennials are our favorite plants for attracting a wide variety of birds, such as hummingbirds, and butterflies into the garden. The plants described in this chapter are just a few of the many perennial flowers.

Desert Marigold

In other parts of the country, perennials are often planted either in large beds or along the edges of the lawn as a border. Some are elaborately laid out to move through the color spectrum or create vivid color combinations. Others are set out to bloom for a long time with one area gently blending into another as they bloom. These planting styles come to us from England, but are rarely used in Arizona. I can imagine that these long borders or fanciful color schemes would be just as successful with the native and low water use perennials that characterize Arizona gardens—it only waits for some enterprising gardener to try them out.

Yarrow

Angelita Daisy

Hymenoxys acaulis

Angelita daisy is a relative newcomer to the horticultural scene in the low zones of the state, and it is rapidly becoming a great favorite. This member of the sunflower family blooms almost year-round with small, bright yellow or gold daisylike flowers held high above the foliage on straight, thin stems. The dark green, thin leaves are crowded around swollen stems to create a small mound of a plant, looking somewhat like a living rock. Angelita daisy thrives in dry, hot locations, but also withstands the hot, moist soils of the summer thunderstorm season. This happy combination makes it useful in both public plantings like medians as well as in home gardens. Angelita daisy spreads readily from trailing stems to cover an area of about a foot square.

Bloom Period and Seasonal Color
Year-round but heaviest in spring; yellow and gold.

Mature Height × Spread
12 inches × 12 inches

Zones
1, 2, 3, 4, 5
Hardy to 10 degrees Fahrenheit at least, perhaps lower.

When, Where, and How to Plant
Plant in fall or spring in full sun. Angelita daisy grows best in fast draining soils that are not too fertile. Dig a hole that is two to three times wider than the container and only as deep. Soil amendments are not necessary although a thin layer of compost or mulch may be added to the backfill. Set the plant in the hole slightly higher than the soil line. Fill the hole, pressing the soil gently around the roots to remove air pockets. Water thoroughly, then water every two to four days for two to three weeks. Water every four to seven days until plants are established.

Growing Tips
Angelita daisy does not need supplemental fertilizer. Water established plants every week or two in summer, once a month in winter. Avoid overhead watering; it encourages die back in the center of the plant.

Care
Prune in fall or early spring to remove spent flowers, damaged stems, or to rejuvenate the plant. Cut spent flower stalks anytime. Angelita daisy is not susceptible to pests or disease. However, it may suddenly wilt and die or exhibit patches of blackened leaves that are the result of root rots when grown with too much shade, overhead water, or in soils with poor drainage. Rabbits will eat them, so protect your plants if these animals are a problem.

Companion Planting and Design
Plant Angelita daisies close together to form a ground cover or a low border for a large bed. Its tight, rounded form makes it a natural for a rock garden or interplanted with similarly sized succulents. It mixes well with winter-flowering, summer dormant bulbs, and Mediterranean perennials such as rosemary and lavender. Use against a hot wall or building or other locations where reflected heat is intense. Excellent in containers either planted alone or in a mixed planting.

Did You Know?
The common name comes from the Angelita River in eastern Texas. However, this species does not occur there, although other members of the genus do.

Autumn Sage
Salvia greggii

When, Where, and How to Plant

In the low zones, plant in fall or very early spring; in higher zones plant when the soil is warm and the danger of frost is past. In low zones, salvias grow best in filtered shade in well-drained, fertile soil. In high zones, plant in full sun or filtered shade in well-drained, fertile soil. Dig a hole that is two to three times wider than the container and only as deep. Add a thin layer of compost or mulch to the backfill. Set the plant in the hole slightly higher than the soil line. Fill the hole, pressing the soil gently around the roots to remove air pockets. Water thoroughly then water every two to four days for two to three weeks. Water every four to seven days until established.

Growing Tips

Apply slow-release or organic fertilizer annually in spring. Mulch roots during the growing season to keep the soil from drying out. In low zones, water every four to six days in summer, every seven to ten days in winter. In high zones, water weekly in summer, every three to four weeks in winter.

Care

Prune severely in early spring to remove damaged stems and reinvigorate the plant. Keep spent flowering stalks cut—it encourages continued flowering. Autumn sage is not susceptible to pests or disease.

Companion Planting and Design

Mix autumn sage with other perennials such as lantana, justicia, Russian sage, phlox, and plumbago. Use autumn sage as the background for low annuals. Plant generously to form informal borders, create a mass planting, or to line drives and walkways. Use generously near patios, seating areas, and pools, or in large containers and planters. Hummingbirds are strongly attracted to autumn sage; site plants where these visitors can be enjoyed.

Did You Know?

Josiah Gregg was a frontier trader who traveled throughout the Border States and who found and collected many types of salvia in Texas in the mid-19th century.

Autumn sage is a perennial salvia that is popular in gardens throughout the state. Autumn sage is poorly named, as it actually blooms from late spring through summer. The short, semiwoody stems are brittle. They are thinly covered with smooth, deep green leaves. Flowers are tubular, with a prominent lip, and are incredibly variable in size and color. The most common colors are rose to magenta and reds. 'Furman's Red' has profuse, dark red flowers with a hint of purple. 'Purple Haze' has small but deep violet flowers and 'Cherry Red' is a bright clear red. Salvia × jamesii is an array of naturally occurring hybrids between this species and S. microphylla of which 'Desert Red' with its oversized, velvet red flowers is one of the most striking.

Bloom Period and Seasonal Color
Late spring through summer; purple, red, rose, pink, and white.

Mature Height × Spread
2 to 3 feet × 3 to 4 feet

Zones
All
Hardy to at least 15 degrees Fahrenheit, maybe lower.

Blue Salvia

Salvia azurea var. grandiflora

Long ago I bought a small plant of blue salvia on a whim. All the other blue flowered salvias I knew bloomed in spring or fall. Through the years, blue salvia has thrived and proved itself a reliable addition to the summer garden even in low zones. Often sold as Salvia pitcheri, blue salvia is a low growing, soft leaved plant. The delicate, sky-blue flowers are held above the foliage in long spikes. Mexican sage (S. leucantha) is a short-lived perennial with tall spikes of fuzzy, indigo flowers rising over wide, gray leaves. It blooms in fall in low and intermediate zones. The aromatic S. clevelandii is a large, bushy plant with dark blue flowers collected in whorls up tall stalks in the spring in low and intermediate zone gardens.

Bloom Period and Seasonal Color
Spring and summer; light to dark blue.

Mature Height × Spread
1 to 2 feet × 2 feet

Zones
1, 2, 3, 4
Hardy to 10 degrees Fahrenheit, perhaps lower.

When, Where, and How to Plant
In the low elevation zones, plant in fall or very early spring; in higher elevation zones, plant when the soil is warm and all danger of frost is past. In low elevation zones, blue salvia grows best in filtered shade and well-drained, fertile soil, but in high elevation zones, plant it in either full sun or filtered shade in well-drained, fertile soil. Dig a hole that is two to three times wider than the container and only as deep. Mix a thin layer of compost or mulch with the backfill. Set the plant in the hole slightly higher than the soil line. Fill the hole, pressing the soil gently around the roots to remove air pockets. Water thoroughly. Water every two to four days for two to three weeks, then every four to seven days until established.

Growing Tips
Apply slow-release or organic fertilizer annually in spring. Mulch the roots to prevent the soil from drying out. In low elevation zones, water every four to six days in summer, every seven to ten days in winter. In high elevation zones, water every week in summer, intermittently in winter.

Care
Prune to within a few inches of the ground every spring to remove spent, flowering stalks, damaged stems, and reinvigorate the plant. Keep flowering stalks cut to encourage continued flowering. Blue salvia is not susceptible to pests or disease.

Companion Planting and Design
Use blue salvia with rock penstemons, phlox, wine cups, justicias, or other summer-flowering perennials. Plant generously to form a low border for large beds or to line drives and walkways. Plants are spare and thin, so use generously to form a solid planting to fill in barren spots in a new garden or provide color in a shady location.

Did You Know?
The culinary sage (*Salvia officinalis*) has been cultivated since medieval times in Europe and was brought to America in the 17th century. Could there have been sage in the dressing at the first Thanksgiving?

Brittlebush

Encelia farinosa

When, Where, and How to Plant

Plant in fall in any well-drained but not excessively fertile soil. Brittlebush grows especially well in rocky, native soil. Plant in full sun as even light shade reduces the white caste of the leaves. Dig a hole that is two to three times wider than the container and only as deep. Soil amendments are not necessary. Set the plant in the hole slightly higher than the soil line. Backfill, pressing the soil gently around the roots to remove air pockets. Water thoroughly. Water every two to four days for two to three weeks, then every four to seven days until established.

Growing Tips

Brittlebush needs no supplemental fertilization. In fact, conditions that are too rich may encourage root rots and other problems. Water weekly in fall and spring, but reduce watering to once a month in summer. Water sparingly in winter; monthly if the weather is particularly hot or dry.

Care

Prune plants severely in fall to remove summer-damaged stems and to reinvigorate. Remove spent, blooming stalks anytime during the growing season. Brittlebush is not susceptible to pests or disease. Although many desert bees and insects use the plants as a gathering spot, they rarely cause any harm.

Companion Planting and Design

Brittlebush mixes well with other desert perennials such as ruellia, globemallow, and penstemons. Bright yellow flowers and crisp, white foliage are particularly effective with the green leaves and blue to purple flowers of dalea and Texas ranger. Plant in groups or in mass to fill barren spots or use in areas of the garden that receive minimal care. Mix with succulents such as ocotillo, desert spoon, and agaves for a naturalistic look. Plant anywhere that reflected heat is intense.

Did You Know?

A resin exuded by the stem of brittlebush was chewed by native peoples of the region. Spanish priests burned the same resin as an incense in their churches and gave the plant its Mexican common name, *incienso*.

Brittlebush is one of the most common plants in the rocky hills of southern Arizona. Entire hillsides erupt in spring with the splashy, bright yellow flowers of this rugged perennial. Brittlebush is an outstanding addition to low zone gardens, regardless of their style. Bushes need only minimal care to look their best and grow beautifully on natural rainfall with minimal irrigation during extended dry spells. The 3-foot tall plants have gray-green leaves that form in clusters up the stems. They are coated with a thick mat of minute, soft white hairs. As the plants become water-stressed, leaves become whiter. Flowers are yellow discs with bright yellow rays, which are held on branched stalks high above the foliage.

Bloom Period and Seasonal Color

November to May; bright yellow on long stalks above the foliage.

Mature Height × Spread

3 to 4 feet × 3 to 4 feet

Zones

1, 2, 3, 4
Hardy to 5 degrees Fahrenheit if drainage is excellent and grown dry, but it is difficult to grow where summers are cool, or wet.

Bush Morning Glory

Convolvulus cneorum

This native to the Mediterranean region of Europe is a durable and delightful perennial in the low zones of the state. The low-growing plants form a soft mound of gray-green leaves that are liberally covered with white hairs giving the plant a silvery sheen. The flowers, which are similar to those of morning glory, bloom profusely from late spring to early summer and can hide the foliage completely. From a distance the flowers appear pure white, but on closer inspection the buds and the outer petals are tinged in pink. Like many Mediterranean plants, bush morning glory is perfectly suited to the hottest, driest, and most difficult spot in the garden. It is often used in roadside medians or other terribly hot places.

Bloom Period and Seasonal Color
March to November, heaviest in spring; white, tinged with light pink.

Mature Height × Spread
2 to 4 feet × 2 to 4 feet

Zones
1, 2, 3, 4
Hardy to about 20 degrees Fahrenheit.

When, Where, and How to Plant
Plant in fall or spring in fast-draining soils that are not too enriched, including rocky, native soil. Plant in full sun for best form and bloom but bush morning glory also tolerates filtered shade. Dig a hole that is two to three times wider than the container and only as deep. Soil amendments are not necessary. Set the plant in the hole slightly higher than the soil line. Backfill, pressing the soil gently around the roots to remove air pockets. Water thoroughly. Water every two to four days for two to three weeks, then every four to seven days until established.

Growing Tips
Apply slow-release or organic fertilizer annually in fall. Plants that are fertilized too much or too often become floppy and weak. Water established plants sparingly; every week or two in summer, once a month or less in winter.

Care
Prune lightly in fall if the plant has become leggy or overgrown. Bush morning glory has a highly symmetrical form and does not need regular pruning. Plants that are overwatered, especially in summer, or receive overhead watering become floppy and unsightly. They may show blackened leaves, sudden wilting, and death that are results of root rots and fungal disease. Prevention is the best remedy. Otherwise, bush morning glory is not susceptible to pests or disease.

Companion Planting and Design
Plant closely to create a low border for larger shrub plantings or to fill in a small space. It is an excellent choice to relieve the reflected heat around pools, patios, courtyards, or against hot walls or buildings. Plant generously to line a drive or walkway, particularly one that is used at night; the silvery foliage and white flowers glow in dim light. Bush morning glory is drought and heat tolerant enough to use in areas that receive minimal care. Mix with salvia, justicia, globemallow, or verbena for good contrast.

Did You Know?
The name, *cneorum*, comes from the Greek word, *kneorum*, and refers to a short, olivelike shrub that this plant resembles.

California Fuschia
Zauschneria californica

When, Where, and How to Plant

Plant in fall or spring in well-drained, fertile soil. Locate in full morning sun or filtered shade. Dig a hole that is two to three times wider than the container and only as deep. Set the plant in the hole slightly higher than the soil line. Add a thin layer of compost or mulch to the back fill. Fill the hole, pressing the soil gently around the roots to remove air pockets. Water thoroughly. Water every two to four days for two to three weeks, then every four to seven days until established.

Growing Tips

Apply slow-release or organic fertilizer once in spring and again in fall. In low zones, water established plants weekly during summer, every ten to fourteen days in winter. In high zones, water every seven to ten days in summer, intermittently in winter.

Care

Prune severely to within a few inches of the ground in late winter in low zones and then again in early spring just as leaves begin to emerge in high zones to remove damaged, spent stems and rejuvenate the plant. California fuschia stems are brittle and break off easily, but plants recover quickly. It is not susceptible to pests or disease, although it can develop symptoms of fungal disease such as blackened leaves and the sudden wilting and death of many stems when grown in heavy, poorly drained soils or from overhead watering.

Companion Planting and Design

Plant generously to create an informal border or to line a drive or walkway. California fuschia will quickly spread to fill a barren spot in a newly planted garden, a difficult corner, or create a mass planting under light green palo verdes. Plant near patios, in courtyards, and around pools and seating areas both for the long, brilliant blooms, and the hummingbirds that are regular visitors.

Did You Know?

The genus was named for Johann Baptista Zauschner, who was a Czech professor of medicine and botany. Many plants were given the epithet *californica* if they were originally described in the West, but this one truly came from collections in California.

Every fall one corner of my garden explodes with the bright, orange-red trumpets of California fuschia. It marks the change of the seasons better than a calendar in the low desert. Once it has begun to bloom you know that fall is nearly here. In higher zones, or where summer temperatures are more moderate, it often blooms throughout summer. The leaves are a soft, dusky green and are held on loose stems that trail along the ground, increasing the size of the plant year after year. Flowers are tubular with a flared end and the stamens and pistils extend well beyond the petal. The less commonly found Zauschneria cana is a more upright plant with needlelike, gray foliage and thin, orange-red flowers with a green tip.

Other Common Name
Hummingbird bush

Bloom Period and Seasonal Color
Summer to fall; orange to orange-red, rarely white.

Mature Height × Spread
1 to 2 feet × 2 to 3 feet

Zones
1, 2, 3, 4, 5
Hardy to 10 degrees Fahrenheit, perhaps lower.

Chocolate Flower
Berlandiera lyrata

When I first encountered chocolate flower, I was skeptical. It seemed unlikely that a flower could replicate the sweet, seductive smell of real chocolate. I was wrong! This small perennial reeks of the real thing, and it is a must for serious chocolate lovers. Chocolate flower is also a lovely garden plant with long, lobed leaves that rarely grow more than a few inches above the ground. The flowers are held high above the foliage with deep, yellow ray flowers and a flat, dark brown disc. After the bloom is spent, the petals fall off revealing the light green receptacle framed by rows of green bracts, all of which are as ornamental as the flowers. These receptacles are excellent in dried arrangements.

Bloom Period and Seasonal Color
Spring through summer, heaviest in spring; yellow ray flowers and dark brown to maroon disc flowers.

Mature Height × Spread
1 to 2 feet × 1 to 2 feet

Zones
1, 2, 3, 4
Hardy to about 20 degrees Fahrenheit.

When, Where, and How to Plant
Plant in fall or early spring in full morning sun or filtered shade. Chocolate flower grows in a wide range of soils from well-drained, fertile soil to rocky, native soil. Dig a hole that is two to three times wider than the container and only as deep. Add a thin layer of compost or mulch to the backfill. Set the plant in the hole slightly higher than the soil line. Fill the hole, pressing the soil gently around the roots to remove air pockets. Water thoroughly. Water every two to four days for two to three weeks, then every four to seven days until established.

Growing Tips
Apply slow-release or organic fertilizer annually in spring. Mulch the roots well to keep the soil from drying out. In low zones, water established plants every four to seven days in summer, monthly in winter. In intermediate zones, established plants thrive on natural rainfall with supplemental irrigation needed only when the weather is exceptionally hot or dry. Water every month or two in winter.

Care
Prune spent flowers regularly to encourage repeat blooming. Chocolate flower is not susceptible to pests or disease although it is often short-lived in low zone gardens. Plants reseed freely in most gardens and can be left to grow where they germinate, or they can be moved to other locations in late fall and winter.

Companion Planting and Design
Mix chocolate flower with other small perennials such as verbena, wine cups, and gaillardia. Plant generously to create a showy display or to form an informal border at the edge of the bed. Plant several near a seating area, patio, or pool to enjoy the aroma of chocolate in the evening and early morning. Chocolate flower is a good container plant and can be either planted alone or in a mixed planting.

Did You Know?
Native people in the Southwest used this plant as a flavoring long before they knew about cocoa.

Chuparosa
Justicia californica

When, Where, and How to Plant

Plant in fall or spring in any fast-draining soil including fertile soil, sandy soil, or rocky, native soil. Chuparosa does not tolerate heavy clay or consistently wet areas. Plant in full sun or filtered shade. Dig a hole that is two to three times wider than the container and only as deep. Soil amendments are not necessary although a thin layer of compost or mulch can be added to the backfill. Set the plant in the hole slightly higher than the soil line. Fill the hole, pressing the soil gently around the roots to remove air pockets. Water thoroughly. Water every two to four days for two to three weeks, then every four to seven days until established.

Growing Tips

Chuparosa does not need supplemental fertilizer. Water established plants every two to three weeks in winter when they are actively growing; water monthly or just often enough to prevent wilting in summer.

Care

Prune in spring to remove winter-damaged stems or to rejuvenate the plant. Chuparosa has excellent natural form and does not need to be pruned regularly to shape it. Chuparosa is often frustratingly slow to become established, but is long-lived once it is well established. It is not susceptible to pests or disease.

Companion Planting and Design

Mix chuparosa with other native perennials such as brittlebush, penstemons, and globemallow in a naturalistic garden. In good conditions, plants may grow large and can be used as a specimen or focal plant. Plant generously around large succulents such as ocotillo and organ pipe cactus to provide color and contrast. Plant several to create informal borders, line drives and walkways, or to soften the edges of patios, seating areas, and around pools. The vivid winter blooms are irresistible to hummingbirds.

Did You Know?

Hummingbirds aren't the only ones to enjoy these flowers. The flowers taste like cucumber and are delicious when added to salads or eaten on their own, but make sure they have not been sprayed with pesticides before you eat them.

Chuparosa blooms through the long mild winter of the low zones providing arresting color in a dry garden and a feast for the hummingbirds that visit it. Thin, pale green stems twine and twist forming a loose, rounded form. The dusky, gray-green leaves are slightly pointed and thick and occur sparingly on the stems. The thin, tubular scarlet-red flowers are prolific on the plant in winter. Pale yellow flowered forms are offered occasionally. Two of the best yellow selections are the infrequently seen 'Tecate Gold', which is a gold and copper bicolor, and 'Tilden', which is bright yellow. Native to the washes and drainages of southern Arizona, chuparosa is one of the most important food sources for hummingbirds during winter.

Bloom Period and Seasonal Color

November to March; scarlet red to red-orange and bright yellow.

Mature Height × Spread

2 to 3 feet × 4 to 6 feet

Zones

1, 2, 3
Hardy to 28 degrees Fahrenheit, root hardy to about 23 degrees Fahrenheit.

Daylily
Hemerocallis species

Daylilies are effortless summer-flowering perennials for the intermediate and high zones of Arizona. The long, strap-shaped, light green leaves form a flowing rosette from the base of the plant. Plants multiply from their tuberous roots and quickly form into large clumps. The flowers are large and showy on branched stems held high above the foliage with wide, open, and flared petals. Each trumpet-shaped flower is open for only one day. 'Stella d'Oro' has large, bright yellow flowers and is the most commonly sold variety. Breeders have created a phenomenal range of colors from mauve to orange, pink to yellow, and there are also evergreen, deciduous, and dwarf selections. Daylilies are difficult to grow in low zones and only do well in yards that have cool, moist, and deeply irrigated and fertile soils.

Bloom Period and Seasonal Color
Spring through summer; yellow, orange, red, maroon, bicolors, mixed colors in single and double forms with smooth or ruffled petals.

Mature Height × Spread
2 to 4 feet × 2 to 3 feet

Zones
3, 4, 5, 6
Deciduous varieties are hardy to 35 degrees Fahrenheit, evergreen varieties generally are hardy to 20 degrees Fahrenheit.

When, Where, and How to Plant
Plant in spring or summer in full sun for best flowering, although daylilies will tolerate partial shade. Daylilies prefer moist, well-drained, fertile soil that does not dry out quickly. Dig a hole that is two to three times wider than the container and only as deep. Add a thin layer of compost or mulch to the backfill. Set the plant in the hole slightly higher than the soil line. Fill the hole, pressing the soil gently around the roots to remove air pockets. Water thoroughly. Water every two to four days for two to three weeks, then every four to seven days until established.

Growing Tips
Apply slow-release or organic fertilizer annually in spring and again in midsummer. Mulch the plants generously to keep the roots cool and help retain soil moisture. Water established plants every seven to ten days in summer; water both evergreen and deciduous varieties monthly or less in winter.

Care
Prune blooming stalks when all flowers are spent to keep the plant tidy and maintain continuous bloom. Divide crowded clumps in fall about every three or four years to keep the plant vigorous. Daylilies are susceptible to daylily rust, a serious problem in the eastern United States, but that has not become common in the West. Rust appears as reddish brown spots or lesions on the leaves. Buy rust-free stock from reliable dealers because treatment is not successful. Some leaf-chewing insects mar the foliage but cause no permanent harm.

Companion Planting and Design
Plant daylilies to form a loose informal border in front of evergreens or large shrubs. Mix with other summer-flowering perennials or use them to line lawns, walkways, or soften the edges of a patio or pool area. Dwarf forms are particularly well suited for containers either singly or in mixed plantings.

Did You Know?
The genus name comes from the Greek word, *hemeral*, meaning "a day" and *kallos*, meaning "beauty." It refers to the lovely flowers that remain open only for one day.

Desert Marigold
Baileya multiradiata

When, Where, and How to Plant
Sow seed or set out transplants in fall. Desert marigold grows well in any type of soil that is sharply drained including well-drained, fertile soil. To sow seed, apply a thin layer of slow-release or organic fertilizer to the bed and rake to turn the soil. Broadcast seed evenly and cover lightly, pressing the soil with a rake to firm the surface and prevent seed from washing away. Water every two to three days until seed germinate, then water every three to four days until there are five leaves. To set out transplants, dig a hole that is two to three times wider than the container and only as deep. Soil amendments are not necessary. Fill the hole, pressing the soil gently around the roots to remove air pockets. Water thoroughly. Water every two to four days for two to three weeks, then every four to seven days until established.

Growing Tips
Desert marigold needs no supplemental fertilizer. Water weekly in fall and spring, but reduce watering to once a month in summer. Established plants usually do not need supplemental irrigation in winter unless the weather is exceptionally hot or dry.

Care
Prune plants to a few inches above the ground in fall to remove summer-damaged stems and rejuvenate. Cut off spent flowering stalks anytime; it helps maintain continuous bloom. Desert marigold is not susceptible to pests or disease.

Companion Planting and Design
Desert marigold is outstanding when planted in mass and is particularly useful in areas of the garden that receive minimal care. It also mixes well with annual spring-flowering wildflowers, desert perennials such as globemallow, penstemons, or dicliptera, or mixed with succulents. Plant generously at the base of a wall or building, or near a pool or patio where reflected heat is intense.

Did You Know?
The genus was named for Jacob Whitman Bailey, an early American microscopist. The epithet, *multiradiata*, refers to the numerous ray flowers in the blooming head.

Nothing speaks of the low desert spring as effectively as the rambunctious bloom of desert marigold. Brilliant yellow flowers are held high above the velvet-soft, gray-white basal leaves. In good growing conditions, the leaves form a clump at the base of the plant and send up dozens of blooming stalks. These desert natives can be fickle about where they thrive; in some gardens desert marigold is nearly a weed; in others it is barely able to find a foothold. This is particularly true when planted from seed, so try using the more reliable transplants if you have had trouble getting it established. Plants are short-lived but reseed generously in most dry gardens, coming up in surprising places, usually in summer.

Bloom Period and Seasonal Color
Throughout the year, heaviest bloom from November to April; bright yellow rays with yellow discs.

Mature Height × Spread
1 foot × 1 foot

Zones
1, 2, 3, 4
Hardy to the mid 20s, perhaps lower.

Desert Milkweed
Asclepias subulata

Desert milkweed is a classy desert perennial native to the hot deserts of the American Southwest. It has numerous thin, gray-green stems that are coated with a white, waxy coating giving it an elegant, refined look. The tiny, threadlike leaves occur intermittently in the spring and fall but are mostly absent during this time. Despite all this refinement and elegance, desert milkweed is a tough native that can grow almost without attention in low zone gardens. The creamy white flowers that look like a vase crowned with a coronet are in dense heads at the top of the stems through the warm season. Butterflies find the flowers irresistible. The similar Asclepias albicans grows nearly 6 feet tall, with finger-thick, bright white stems and nearly identical flowers.

Bloom Period and Seasonal Color
Intermittently from spring to fall, heaviest in spring; creamy white.

Mature Height × Spread
4 feet × 2 feet

Zones
1, 2, 3
Hardy to 25 degrees Fahrenheit.

When, Where, and How to Plant
Plant in fall or spring in full sun. Desert milkweed grows best in rocky, native soil, but will tolerate other soil types as long as the drainage is spectacular. Dig a hole that is two to three times wider than the container and only as deep. Soil amendments are not necessary although a thin layer of compost or mulch can be added to the backfill. Set the plant in the hole slightly higher than the soil line. Fill the hole, pressing the soil gently around the roots to remove air pockets. Water thoroughly. Water every two to four days for two to three weeks, then every seven days until established.

Growing Tips
Desert milkweed needs no supplemental fertilizer. Water established plants monthly in summer; rely on natural rainfall in winter. Overwatered plants become floppy and unsightly and are subject to rot. Prune affected stems to the ground, but prevention is the best remedy.

Care
Prune individual stems down to the base in summer if they have fallen over or have become damaged from wind, traffic, or as a result of overwatering. Aphids often crowd the stems in late spring and can be sprayed off with strong jets of water or removed by hand. They inflict only minor cosmetic damage. Many native bees and insects use the plants to rest or congregate but they are not harmful.

Companion Planting and Design
Desert milkweed is dramatic when used in mass plantings to fill narrow beds, line drives or walkways, or create a delicate backdrop for low perennial or succulent plantings. Use any place where reflected heat is intense. Desert milkweed mixes well with other desert perennials such as black dalea, globemallow, and penstemons.

Did You Know?
The flat, black seeds of milkweeds carry a silky white plume and are crammed into a pair of horn-shaped pods. When ripe, the pods split, and the seeds float out carried away on their delicate parachutes to find a place to grow.

Dicliptera
Dicliptera resupinata

When, Where, and How to Plant
Plant in fall or spring in partial shade or full sun. Dicliptera tolerates a wide range of soils, from well-drained, fertile soil to rocky, native soil. Dig a hole that is two to three times wider than the container and only as deep. Add a thin layer of compost or mulch to the backfill. Set the plant in the hole slightly higher than the soil line. Fill the hole, pressing the soil gently around the roots to remove air pockets. Water thoroughly. Water every two to four days for two to three weeks, then every four to seven days until established.

Growing Tips
Dicliptera does not need supplemental fertilizer. Water established plants every seven to ten days in summer, once a month or less in winter.

Care
Stems will die back in summer if the plant becomes too dry. Prune in early fall to remove summer-damaged stems and again in early spring to remove spent flowers or winter damage. Dicliptera is not susceptible to pests or disease.

Companion Planting and Design
Their purple flowers and striking foliage mix especially well with yellow flowering plants such as desert marigold and sundrops. Mix dicliptera with other spring-flowering desert plants such as globemallow, penstemons, and chuparosa. The loose form of dicliptera makes it more effective when planted in groups to maximize the effect of the bloom. Dicliptera provides a good filler for barren spots in a newly planted garden or for areas of the garden that receive minimal care. Mix with cactus, creosote bush, agaves, or use as a perennial in native gardens. Plant generously around a patio or pool.

Did You Know?
The local office of the University of Arizona Extension Service in Phoenix has compiled a list of plants less susceptible to rabbit damage, and dicliptera is noted as one of the most resistant. I have found this to be true in my own garden where rabbits are a continual nuisance.

This low-growing perennial with numerous, intertwining wiry stems is native to the slopes and washes of southeastern Arizona, southwestern New Mexico, and on into Mexico. The dusky green, heart-shaped leaves are rimmed with purple. The purple caste is more pronounced in winter. Flowers are prolific up and down the stems and are formed into deep tubes that end in flared petals. Dicliptera blooms are deep purple and last for months through late winter and spring. Hummingbirds find the nectar at the base of the petals irresistible. Following the flowers are heart-shaped, tan pods that hold the seed. This delicate-looking perennial is actually a rugged desert plant that can take extremes of heat and drought right in stride.

Bloom Period and Seasonal Color
From May to October; deep purple to rose-purple.

Mature Height × Spread
2 to 3 feet × 2 to 3 feet

Zones
1, 2, 3, 4
Hardy to 30 degrees Fahrenheit, but root hardy to 20 degrees Fahrenheit.

Firewheel
Gaillardia aristata

I am deeply impressed by this low-growing perennial; it is almost never out of bloom in my low zone garden. Even when one of these short-lived plants dies out, there is always a seedling ready to take its place. The flowers are stunning, up to 4 inches across with rays that range from pure yellow to yellow-banded with reddish-brown and all blends in between. Discs are dark and can be flat or gently rounded. Plants are low and sprawling and if left to spread would form a ground cover. Gaillardia × grandiflora is a hybrid between this species and the annual G. pulchella and has produced many cultivars including the compact 'Goblin' group. Nearly all gaillardias sold as transplants are part of this hybrid group.

Other Common Names
Blanket flower, Indian blanket

Bloom Period and Seasonal Color
Year-round, heaviest in spring and summer; yellow to reddish-brown.

Mature Height × Spread
1 to 2 feet × 1 to 2 feet

Zones
All
Hardy to 10 degrees Fahrenheit, perhaps more.

When, Where, and How to Plant
Plant in low zones in fall or early spring or in spring in high zones. Plant in well-drained, fertile soil in full sun or filtered shade. To sow, work in a thin layer of slow-release or organic fertilizer to the bed. Broadcast seed evenly and rake to cover lightly. Water every one or two days for two to three weeks or until seedlings appear. Water seedlings every three to five days until there are five leaves. To transplant, dig a hole that is two to three times wider than the container and only as deep. Add a thin layer of compost or mulch. Set the plant in the hole slightly higher than the soil line. Fill the hole, pressing the soil gently around the roots to remove air pockets. Water thoroughly. Water every two to four days for two or three weeks, then every four to seven days until established.

Growing Tips
Apply slow-release or organic fertilizer annually in spring. Mulch lightly to maintain soil moisture. Water established plants every one to two weeks in summer. In winter, water every ten to fourteen days in low elevation zones, intermittently elsewhere.

Care
Prune to the basal leaves in early spring. Divide in spring every two or three years by digging up and discarding the oldest plants and replanting the newest ones to keep plants tidy and vigorous. Divide more often if clumps become large and messy. Prune spent flowers to encourage reblooming. Firewheel is not susceptible to pests or disease.

Companion Planting and Design
Mix firewheel with summer-flowering perennials and shrubs such as salvias, lantana, yellow bells, or flame anisacanthus. Firewheel blends well in annual or wildflower plantings. Plant closely together to create showier blooms or to serve as an informal ground cover. Plant generously to create a low informal border, to fill in barren spots in newly planted beds, or to fill a difficult corner. Firewheel grows well in a large container or planter.

Did You Know?
The genus was named in honor of Gaillard de Charentonneau, an 18th century French magistrate who was a patron of botanical exploration.

When, Where, and How to Plant

Sow seed in spring after all danger of frost is past. Sow in well-drained, fertile soil, although four o'clock appears to do well in any soil with good drainage. Place four o'clock where it will receive morning sun, filtered, or deep shade. It is not necessary to prepare a bed, just press seed into the ground about an inch below the surface. Cover and press down the soil gently. Water thoroughly. Water every two to four days until plants germinate, then water weekly.

Growing Tips

Four o'clock does not require supplemental fertilizer. A light mulch around the roots keeps the soil from drying out and protects roots in winter. Established plants need minimal watering, every week or two in summer is enough. Plants grown in more sun may require watering every seven to ten days. Plants are dormant in winter and natural rainfall is sufficient.

Care

Prune stems to the ground in fall. Four o'clocks reseed throughout the garden and small plants can be moved in early spring. Four o'clocks are not susceptible to pests or disease. In intermediate zones, the large root may be dug, placed in a bucket with sawdust or sand, and stored in a cool, dry location to overwinter.

Companion Planting and Design

Plant in mass groups for dramatic effect and to brighten a shady bed. Place in areas that are too shady for other summer-flowering plants. Use four o'clocks generously near seating areas, porches, patios, or pools where the night flowering and delicate scent can be readily enjoyed. Four o'clock mixes well with other summer-flowering perennials such as salvia, red justicia, plumbago, and blue mist.

Did You Know?

The story goes that these charming natives of Peru acquired their common name because you could set the clock by the opening of their flowers. If you want to keep one particular color, remove all plants but those that bloom in "your" color. If you keep doing that during successive years, you will eventually create a pure color strain.

When I relocated to the desert, lots of plants had to be left behind or released to the care of friends and relatives. But I could not part with a pure white form of four o'clock that I received from the garden of a beloved neighbor. This old-fashioned plant has thrived in the desert, fulfilling one of the toughest assignments in low zone gardens by blooming in the dry shade. Four o'clock is a perennial that is commonly grown as an annual in high zones. Fortified by a huge, swollen root, each plant sends up a sturdy, pale green stem from which numerous branches with dark green leaves grow throughout summer. In the hottest part of the summer, the flat button-shaped flowers open every evening, filling the garden with their sweet, delicate fragrance.

Other Common Name
Marvel of Peru

Bloom Period and Seasonal Color
Summer to fall; purple, yellow, red, magenta, and white.

Mature Height × Spread
3 to 4 feet × 1 to 2 feet

Zones
1, 2, 3, 4
Hardy to 30 degrees Fahrenheit.

Gaura
Gaura lindheimeri

Gaura starts out as a low set of deep green basal leaves. In most forms, the leaves are tinged with maroon or reddish hues. But in late spring, long, branched blooming stalks begin to rise over the plant and this modest little plant is transformed. Small, starlike white flowers emerge from pink buds and continue through most of summer. The stalks are so airy and the flowers so delicate the effect is of a cloud floating over the garden. To complete the illusion, as the flowers fade they return to a pale, ethereal pink. The selection 'Siskiyou Pink' has dark pink buds with flowers that open white but quickly change to pink for the rest of the season. The flowers of 'Whirling Butterflies' are white throughout the blooming season.

Bloom Period and Seasonal Color
June to September; pink buds, white flowers which fade to pink.

Mature Height × Spread
2 to 4 feet × 2 to 3 feet

Zones
All
Hardy to 5 degrees Fahrenheit, perhaps lower.

When, Where, and How to Plant
Plant in fall or early spring in filtered shade or in full sun in the high elevation zones. Locate gaura in well-drained, fertile soil although it grows almost as well in rocky, native soil as long as it receives adequate watering. Dig a hole that is two to three times wider than the container and only as deep. Add a layer of compost or mulch to the backfill. Set the plant in the hole slightly higher than the soil line. Fill the hole, pressing the soil gently around the roots to remove air pockets. Water thoroughly. Water every two to four days for two to three weeks, then every four to seven days until established.

Growing Tips
Gaura needs minimal supplemental fertilizer; in fact, too much fertilizer shortens the plant's life. Mulch the roots well in summer to keep soil evenly moist. In low elevation zones, water weekly in summer, more often if temperatures are extreme. Water every month or two in winter while plants are dormant. In high elevation zones, water every ten to fourteen days in summer and rely on natural rainfall in winter.

Care
Prune gaura in spring to remove winter damage, reduce size, and reinvigorate. Prune spent flowering stalks anytime. Gaura is not susceptible to pests or disease although it can be short-lived if grown in soils that are too rich or in full sun in low zones.

Companion Planting and Design
Plant in groups for best effect; solitary plants often fail to show up in mixed plantings. Plant to form a low border, line walkways or drives, or as a filler for barren spots in a newly planted garden. Gaura combines well with spring-flowering bulbs and perennials such as Angelita daisy or verbena or against a dark green hedge to highlight the delicate flowers.

Did You Know?
Ferdinand J. Lindheimer lived in New Braunsfels, Texas, in the middle of the 19th century. He was a newspaper publisher and avid collector and student of Texas plants, many of which are named for him.

Globemallow
Sphaeralcea ambigua

When, Where, and How to Plant
Plant in fall or spring in full sun or partial shade. Globemallow grows in a wide range of soils from heavy, clay soil to well-drained, fertile soil, but perhaps grows best in rocky, native soil. Dig a hole that is two to three times wider than the container and only as deep. Add a thin layer of compost or mulch to the backfill. Set the plant in the hole slightly higher than the soil line. Fill the hole, pressing the soil gently around the roots to remove air pockets. Water thoroughly. Water every two to four days for two to three weeks, then every four to seven days until established.

Growing Tips
Globemallow does not need supplemental fertilizer. Water every three to four weeks in summer, every two to three weeks while the plants are growing and blooming. Overwatered plants become overgrown and floppy.

Care
Prune to within a foot of the ground in early fall to reinvigorate the plant. After the first bloom of spring is finished, prune off the flowering heads and water generously. Globemallow will rebloom with this treatment at least once, sometimes twice. In rocky soils, globemallow reseeds readily and seedlings can be relocated in November. Globemallow is not susceptible to pests or disease.

Companion Planting and Design
Globemallow blends well with other desert perennials such as penstemon, ruellia, and justicia. Use globemallow in naturalistic gardens, or at the edge of gardens where care is minimal. Plant generously against a hot wall or building, around a pool, or other areas where reflected heat is intense. Globemallow's great heat and drought tolerance makes it compatible with native succulents such as ocotillo, saguaro, and prickly pear, as well as agaves and yuccas.

Did You Know?
Early settlers knew this plant as sore eye poppy, which is undoubtedly a translation of the Mexican name for the plant, *mal de ojo*. Indian peoples of the area used a concoction made from this plant to treat eye diseases.

In spring the roadsides of southern Arizona are smothered with the lively bloom of globemallow. Most bloom in shades of orange but there are populations that bloom pink, coral, purple, white, blue, and occasionally red. Nurserymen have been selecting and growing these color forms and it is now wise to buy the plants in bloom to be sure you get the color you want. The gray-green leaves are small, halberd-shaped, and crinkled both on the surface and around the edge, and laced with fine hairs. Plants grow quickly to 3 or 4 feet tall with dozens of long-blooming stalks. Regardless of the color, globemallow is one of the most reliable spring-flowering perennials in low zone garden, combining great beauty and astounding drought tolerance.

Other Common Names
Desert mallow, Sore eyes

Bloom Period and Seasonal Color
February to May; orange, red, purple, lavender, and white. Intermittent bloom in summer, often blooms again in fall.

Mature Height × Spread
3 to 4 feet by 4 to 5 feet

Zones
1, 2, 3, 4
Hardy to about 20 degrees Fahrenheit.

Golden Columbine
Aquilegia chrysantha

Columbines have long been favored by gardeners for their spectacular displays of graceful, spurred flowers, and reliable blooming over a long season. In the low zones of Arizona, golden columbine is the only columbine gardeners can really count on, but it is equally at home in summer gardens in the high zones. This Arizona native forms a spherical base of dusky green, fern-shaped leaves from a central crown. Tall, branched flowering stalks arise in late spring or summer depending on the zone. Dozens of pure yellow or gold, three- to four-inch spurred flowers open over the six-week blooming period. The plants are biennial, but reseed freely and within a couple of years there are blooming individuals every season.

Bloom Period and Seasonal Color
March to September; bright yellow with spurs nearly as long as the petals.

Mature Height × Spread
3 to 4 feet × 1 to 2 feet

Zones
All
Hardy to 10 degrees Fahrenheit, perhaps lower.

When, Where, and How to Plant
Plant in fall in the low zones, in early spring as soon as soil can be worked in higher zones. In the low zones, golden columbine will grow in full sun if the roots are kept moist and cool in a well-drained, fertile soil, but it thrives and blooms equally well in deep shade. In higher zones, plant in full sun or filtered sun in moist, cool, fertile soil. Dig a hole that is two to three times wider than the container and only as deep. Add generous amounts of compost or mulch to the backfill. Set the plant in the hole slightly higher than the soil line. Fill the hole, pressing the soil gently around the roots to remove air pockets. Water thoroughly. Water every two to four days for two to three weeks, then every four to seven days until established. Columbine may also be grown from seed sown directly in the ground in fall.

Growing Tips
Golden columbine needs no supplemental fertilizer. Water established plants weekly when they are blooming, monthly or less when out of bloom. Mulch plants heavily, especially if they are grown in full sun, to keep roots moist and cool.

Care
Cut back blooming stalks after blooms are spent. Plants reseed freely and seedlings can be relocated in November in low zones or in early spring in high zones. Golden columbine is not susceptible to pests or disease.

Companion Planting and Design
Combine golden columbine with other spring-flowering annuals or spring-flowering bulbs. This species mixes well with other shade-loving perennials such as manfredas, four o'clocks, and salvias. Suitable for containers or planters either in mass or in mixed plantings. Use in mass for extraordinary effect near patios or along walkways for a burst of seasonal color.

Did You Know?
This species has one of the largest elevation ranges in the entire flora of Arizona. Plants are found growing from 3,000 to 11,000 feet above sea level.

Jerusalem Sage
Phlomis fruticosa

When, Where, and How to Plant

Plant in fall or early spring in full sun or filtered shade. Jerusalem sage grows equally well in well-drained, fertile soil or rocky, native soil but does not tolerate heavy soil or poorly drained ones. Dig a hole that is two to three times wider than the container and only as deep. Add a thin layer of compost or mulch to the backfill. Set the plant in the hole slightly higher than the soil line. Fill the hole, pressing the soil gently around the roots to remove air pockets. Water thoroughly. Water every two to four days for two to three weeks, then every four to seven days until established.

Growing Tips

Jerusalem sage does not need supplemental fertilizer. Mulch the roots through summer to maintain even soil moisture and keep the roots cool. Water every one to two weeks in summer, every two to three weeks in winter.

Care

Like many salvias, Jerusalem sage grows long stems that bloom in spring and decline after blooming. Prune old stems and dead wood to the base in fall; new blooming stems will arise from the young shoots at the base. Remove flowering stalks back to the first set of five leaves as soon as they are spent to encourage repeat blooming. Jerusalem sage is not susceptible to pests or disease although it develops the characteristic blackened leaves and sudden wilting indicative of root rots when grown in heavy soil with poor drainage.

Companion Planting and Design

Mix Jerusalem sage with salvia, penstemon, or lantana, as well as succulents such as small yuccas and agaves. The large, gray leaves and dramatic blooms blend well with other Mediterranean perennials such as lavender, oregano, and rosemary. Plant generously to form an informal border or background for smaller perennials or annuals. In small gardens, use as a seasonal specimen or focal plant.

Did You Know?

Phlomis is the Greek name for the plant. The epithet, *fruticosa*, refers to a plant that is shrubby or semiwoody.

Jerusalem sage is a charming shrublike plant with large, gray-green, fuzzy leaves. Leaves are numerous and plants grow into soft rounded forms. Like many salvias, stems that have ceased blooming start to decline and become woody with new stems forming at the base of the plant. Bright, lemon-yellow flowers are clustered together at intervals around the tall blooming stalks. Jerusalem sage is a spring-flowering perennial in low zones and a summer-flowering perennial or annual in high zones. The striking flowers of this Mediterranean native make a bold addition to flower arrangements and are excellent when dried. The related Phlomis lanata *has rounder leaves that are white underneath and is generally a shorter plant. Flowers of this cold tender species are purple in the summer.*

Bloom Period and Seasonal Color
Spring and summer; deep yellow.

Mature Height × Spread
3 to 4 feet × 3 to 4 feet

Zones
1, 2, 3, 4
Hardy to about 10 degrees Fahrenheit.

Lantana

Lantana camara hybrids

Lantana is one of the most reliable plants in the low and intermediate zones for summer color regardless of the growing conditions. Lantana has dark green, prickly leaves that emerge early in spring and last until the first frost of autumn. The tiny flowers are crammed into round heads at the ends of the stem. Almost all lantana offered by nurseries are hybrids crossed between the large, shrubby Lantana camara *and the low trailing* L. montevidensis. *These forms provide a vivid color range from the magenta and yellow of 'Irene', deep pink of 'Christine', the blend of yellow, pink, and purple in 'Confetti', or the rich orange-red of 'Radiation'. Lantana bloom for such a long time that they are often grown as annuals for their spectacular bloom in high zone gardens.*

Bloom Period and Seasonal Color
Summer; yellow, orange, gold, white, red, pink, or magenta.

Mature Height × Spread
1 to 5 feet × 3 to 5 feet

Zones
1, 2, 3, 4
Hardy to 25 degrees Fahrenheit.

When, Where, and How to Plant
Plant in spring after all danger of frost has passed. Lantana grows best in well-drained, fertile soil in full sun or filtered shade. Dig a hole that is two to three times wider than the container and only as deep. Add a generous amount of compost or mulch to the backfill. Set the plant in the hole slightly higher than the soil line. Fill the hole, pressing the soil gently around the roots to remove air pockets. Water thoroughly. Water every two to four days for two to three weeks, then every four to seven days until established.

Growing Tips
Apply slow-release or organic fertilizer in early spring and late summer. Water established plants every three to seven days in summer. Lantana plants are semidormant in the coldest part of winter and should receive only minimal watering at that time.

Care
Prune lightly throughout summer to shape and keep plants from becoming overgrown or leggy. Prune severely to within a foot of ground in spring as the leaves emerge to remove dead or winter-damaged wood. Plants often appear to decline in late summer; prune lightly and fertilize, and bloom will resume until cold weather. Lantana is susceptible to leaf yellowing, drying, and loss from heavy infestations of whiteflies. Spraying with insecticidal soap helps minimize whitefly damage.

Companion Planting and Design
Plant lantana generously to create informal hedges or borders. Mix with summer-flowering shrubs such as red bird of paradise and yellowbells. Interplant lantana with scarlet flax, Shirley poppies, or spring-flowering bulbs to mask their bare stems when dormant. Use lantana around pools, against hot walls, or other areas where reflected heat is intense. Lantana grows extremely well in containers and is a favorite food of numerous species of butterflies.

Did You Know?
Thomas Jefferson imported seed of *Lantana camara* from the Caribbean for his garden at Monticello. He grew them in pots so he could move them in for the winter. Although the seeds are toxic to people and should not be eaten, birds find them irresistible.

Mexican Hat

Ratibida columnifera

When, Where, and How to Plant

Plant from seed or transplants in fall or early spring. Mexican hat grows best in full sun (higher elevation zones) or filtered shade (low elevation zones) in well-drained, fertile soil. To sow seed, work in a thin layer of slow-release or organic fertilizer to the bed. Broadcast seed evenly and cover lightly. Water every other day for two to three weeks or until seedlings appear. Water every three to five days until there are five leaves. Dig a hole two to three times wider than the container and only as deep. Add a thin layer of compost or mulch to the backfill. Set the plant in the hole slightly higher than the soil line. Fill the hole, pressing the soil gently around the roots to remove air pockets. Water thoroughly. Water every two to four days for two or three weeks, then every four to seven days until established.

Growing Tips

Apply slow-release or organic fertilizer annually in spring. In low elevation zones, water every three to four days in spring; reduce to once a week in summer, every other week in winter. In higher elevation zones, water weekly in summer, rely on natural rainfall in winter.

Care

Cut stems down to the basal leaves once bloom is finished. Mexican hat produces numerous seedlings that can be relocated in late fall or winter in the low elevation zones or early spring elsewhere. Mexican hat is not susceptible to pests or disease.

Companion Planting and Design

Mix Mexican hat with gaillardia, zinnia, scarlet flax, and coreopsis. Use generously to fill in barren spots in newly planted beds or to hide winter dormant plants. Mexican hat makes an effective backdrop for low-growing perennials or as a casual border. Mexican hat blooms later than most spring annuals in low elevation zones. This makes it particularly useful to extend the season around seating areas.

Did You Know?

Cheyenne Indians made a tea from the Mexican hat leaves to draw out rattlesnake poison and relieve symptoms of poison ivy.

This willowy, North American native enhances beds of annual wildflowers as well as traditional perennial plantings. Plants begin as a basal set of finely lobed, apple-green leaves. Plants grow to nearly a foot tall and in late spring, send up the strong-branched flowering stems. The flowers are fanciful and their unusual shape accounts for the common name. The dark brown disc flowers are jammed into a tall, fingerlike receptacle. The wide ray flowers ring the base of receptacle, draping like a flashy skirt in combinations of yellow, maroon, and brown. The entire flower looks like a thimble with a skirt. Mexican hat reseeds freely, so keep the ones you want and pull out the rest. I find that the seedlings often have unusual flower forms and color combinations.

Bloom Period and Seasonal Color
Spring through summer; yellow, red-orange, brownish red with dark brown discs.

Mature Height × Spread
2 to 3 feet × 2 feet

Zones
All
Hardy to 0 degrees Fahrenheit.

Mexican Oregano
Poliomintha maderensis

We tend to value plants mostly for their visual appeal, good color, nice contrast, and great form. But one touch of Mexican oregano leaves, which have a spicy, sweet, pungent, and tantalizing smell reminiscent of a Mexican kitchen, makes it apparent that plants can delight all our senses. There are numerous plants called oregano in Mexico, but the flavor of this species is more delicate than most oreganos. The small, deep green leaves are crowded on long, arching stems. The tubular purple to lavender flowers that fade to white are tightly congested at the leaf bases along the ends of the stems. Flowering begins in May and continues through summer. It isn't just people who enjoy Mexican oregano; hummingbirds feast on the nectar in the flowers.

Bloom Period and Seasonal Color
May to September; purple or lavender, fading to white.

Mature Height × Spread
2 to 3 feet × 3 to 4 feet

Zones
1, 2, 3
Hardy to about 25 degrees Fahrenheit.

When, Where, and How to Plant
Plant in fall or early spring in full morning sun or filtered shade. Mexican oregano grows best in any type of well-drained soil but will quickly rot in heavy clay or consistently wet soil. To plant seedlings, dig a hole that is two to three times wider than the container and only as deep. Add generous amounts of compost or mulch to the backfill. Set the plant in the hole slightly higher than the soil line. Fill the hole, pressing the soil gently around the roots to remove air pockets. Water thoroughly. Water every two to four days for two to three weeks, then every four to seven days until established.

Growing Tips
Mexican oregano does not need supplemental fertilizer. Mulch the roots through summer to keep the soil from drying out completely. Water established plants once a week in summer, more often if the weather is exceptionally hot or dry and every two to three weeks in winter.

Care
Prune plants to within a foot or two of the ground in fall after blooming is complete or in early spring before its first flush of growth. Prune the oldest stems to the ground every two or three years to reinvigorate the plant. Mexican oregano is not susceptible to pests or disease.

Companion Planting and Design
Mexican oregano is an excellent perennial to use near a patio, pool, or walkway where the delicate fragrance of the leaves can be enjoyed. It mixes well with other perennials such as gaillardia, Mount Lemmon marigold, and red justicia, or use at the base of yellowbells to provide good color contrast. Hummingbirds are strongly attracted to this species, so site plants where they can be viewed and admired.

Did You Know?
The oregano most commonly used in cooking is actually from Europe and the Middle East and is in the genus *Origanum*; it is usually called Syrian oregano or Greek oregano. The flavor is musky, deep, and savory. The commercially available Mexican oregano is *Aloysia lycioides* and it has a sharp, pungent, clean taste.

Mount Lemmon Marigold
Tagetes lemmonii

When, Where, and How to Plant
Plant in fall or early spring in filtered shade or full sun. Although Mount Lemmon marigold tolerates native, rocky soil, it usually grows larger and blooms more prolifically in well-drained, fertile soil. Dig a hole that is two to three times wider than the container and only as deep. Add a thin layer of compost or mulch to the backfill. Set the plant in the hole slightly higher than the soil line. Fill the hole, pressing the soil gently around the roots to remove air pockets. Water thoroughly. Water every two to four days for two to three weeks, then every four to seven days until established.

Growing Tips
Apply a slow-release or organic fertilizer annually in spring. Water established plants every four to seven days in summer in low elevation zones, weekly in all other zones. Water once every month or two in winter when plants are virtually dormant. Resume regular watering when leaves emerge in spring.

Care
Prune to within a foot or two of the ground in spring to remove winter-damaged or dead stems and to reinvigorate the plant. Prune lightly in spring to encourage bushier growth and more bloom, but do not prune in summer. Mount Lemmon marigold is not susceptible to pests or disease.

Companion Planting and Design
Mix Mount Lemmon marigold with summer-flowering perennials such as red bird of paradise, yellowbells, Texas rangers, or hibiscus to extend the blooming season. Plant generously to create informal hedges, fill in barren corners, or blank spots in newly planted gardens. Plant as a border for driveways, walkways, or around seating areas and patios. Mount Lemmon marigold grows well in large containers or planters either singly or in mixed plantings.

Did You Know?
While this species smells strongly of anise, it is the closely related Mexican tarragon that has a long culinary history. It was used by the Aztecs to flavor their foamy, cocoa-based drink they called *chocolatl*.

The Arizona native Mount Lemmon marigold is a spectacular, late season perennial for low and intermediate zone gardens. The aromatic, light green leaves are finely cut and widely spaced enough on the plant to give it an open and airy look. Mount Lemmon marigold flowers late in summer through fall with flowers held high above the foliage. Flowers have dark gold to yellow-gold rays in a tight circle around yellow disc flowers. The closely related Mexican tarragon (Tagetes lucida) has thin, dark green leaves that are congested on short stems. It, too, is fall-flowering with dark yellow rays and yellow discs. With a strong anise flavor to the foliage, Mexican tarragon is used to make soothing teas and serve as a tarragon substitute as well as an ornamental.

Bloom Period and Seasonal Color
October to November; yellow-gold to gold.

Mature Height × Spread
3 to 4 feet × 2 to 4 feet

Zones
1, 2, 3, 4
Hardy to 20 degrees Fahrenheit, perhaps lower.

Penstemon
Penstemon species

With over 500 penstemon species, it is hardly an exaggeration to state that there are penstemons for every garden. In low elevation zones in spring, the reliable Parry's penstemon (Penstemon parryi) sends up 3-foot-tall stalks with pink flowers, as does the stunning red-flowered firecracker penstemon (P. eatonii). The summer blooming rock penstemon (P. baccharifolius) provides low and intermediate elevation gardens with slim red flowers above the deeply-serrated leaves all summer. The dark rose of P. triflorus, the large, round pink to white flowers of P. cobaea, and the native Palmer's penstemon (P. palmeri) with 5-foot stalks of fragrant, pale pink flowers are just a few of the other penstemons for low and intermediate elevations. In the high elevation zones, the intense purple flowers of P. strictus bloom throughout the mountain summer.

Other Common Name
Beard tongue

Bloom Period and Seasonal Color
Spring or summer; red, magenta, pink, white, and purple.

Mature Height × Spread
2 to 6 feet × 1 to 2 feet

Zones
All
Hardiness varies by species.

When, Where, and How to Plant
Plant in fall or spring in full sun or filtered shade. Penstemons accept a wide range of growing conditions depending on the species. Low zone natives prefer rocky, native soil; most others grow in any sharply drained soil. Dig a hole that is two to three times wider than the container and only as deep. Apply a thin layer of compost or mulch to the backfill. Place the plant in the hole slightly higher than the soil line. Fill the hole, pressing the soil gently around the roots to remove air pockets. Water thoroughly. Water every two to four days for two to three weeks, then every four to seven days until established.

Growing Tips
Penstemons resent too much fertilizer; it causes excessive leaf growth and inhibits flowering. Water established low zone native plants every one to two weeks in summer, water other species weekly in summer. Water established plants in low zones every seven to ten days while the plants are growing and blooming. Water penstemon weekly while they're growing and blooming in high zones, rely on natural rainfall in winter.

Care
Prune spent blooming stalks anytime. Pruning spent stalks of rock penstemon encourages repeat blooming. Penstemons, especially in Zone 1, are susceptible to sudden death from root rots when grown in too much shade or with too much summer water. Otherwise, penstemons are not susceptible to pests or disease.

Companion Planting and Design
Mix desert penstemons with annual wildflowers such as Mexican gold poppy or desert bluebells for a stunning spring color display. Plant generously to cover bare areas, fill in tree wells, and to line driveways, walkways, patios, and pool areas. Native penstemons do well in areas that receive minimal care. Hummingbirds are strongly attracted to penstemons, so plant them where you can enjoy these delightful visitors.

Did You Know?
Penstemon parryi grows readily from seed sown by gardeners in fall and treated just as annual wildflowers. Natural reseeding occurs in the warm days of late spring through summer.

Pineleaf Milkweed
Asclepias linaria

When, Where, and How to Plant

Plant in fall or spring in full sun or partial shade. Pineleaf milkweed grows best in rocky, native soil but will tolerate almost any type of soil as long it is very well drained. Dig a hole that is two to three times wider than the container and only as deep. Add a thin layer of compost or mulch to the backfill. Set the plant in the hole slightly higher than the soil line. Fill the hole, pressing the soil gently around the roots to remove air pockets. Water thoroughly. Water every two to four days for two to three weeks, then every seven days until established.

Growing Tips

Desert milkweed needs no supplemental fertilizer. Water established plants weekly in summer, every two to three weeks in winter. Plants that get too much water become floppy and unsightly and are subject to root rots.

Care

Prune individual stems to the base in spring or summer if they fall over or are damaged. Aphids sometimes crowd the stems in late spring and can be sprayed off with strong jets of water or removed by hand. They inflict only minor cosmetic damage.

Companion Planting and Design

Pineleaf milkweed mixes well with perennials such as penstemon, salvia, or globemallow. Plant generously to create a mass of summer bloom in front of dark evergreen shrubs or to fill in a barren spot in a newly planted garden. Use against hot walls or buildings, near a pool, or other areas where reflected heat is intense. Plant pineleaf milkweed in areas that receive minimal care. Plant generously near patios or seating areas to enjoy the constant stream of butterflies which visit the plants.

Did You Know?

The genus was named after the Greek god of medicine, *Asklepios*. The leaves and flowers of this species are a preferred food for the caterpillars of the Queen butterfly, and the nectar of the flowers is prized by the adult butterfly.

Pineleaf milkweed is one of a number of desert perennials that appear to be more delicate than they really are. I am partial to plants like this—they are chameleons in the garden; delicate, restful reminders of the calming nature of a garden, but rugged enough to withstand the brutal, desert summers without much care. Pineleaf milkweed has dark green, needlelike leaves that spiral up the numerous stems. Bright, white flowers with the odd vase-shape of all milkweeds are crammed into large heads at the ends of the stems. Butterflies are drawn to the plant for its nectar, but I am drawn by its combination of delicate beauty, terrific drought and heat tolerance, and its year-round bloom. It is almost too good to be true.

Bloom Period and Seasonal Color
March to October, intermittently otherwise; white.

Mature Height × Spread
2 to 3 feet × 2 to 3 feet

Zones
1, 2, 3, 4
Hardy to 25 degrees Fahrenheit.

Purple Coneflower
Echinacea purpurea

Tall and stately purple coneflowers grace summer perennial plantings throughout the intermediate and high zones of Arizona. The coarse, bristly leaves form low-growing clumps through spring. The dark green of the oblong leaves is accented by smooth reddish stems. As summer proceeds, flowering stalks up to 4 feet tall emerge topped by the remarkable flowers. The ray flowers have long, downward purple petals. The discs are upright, rounded, and usually dark brown. The entire effect of the flowers ought to be bizarre, but they are strangely graceful. This reliable perennial spreads gently in the garden from the roots forming large stands over the years. Low zone gardens find purple coneflower difficult to maintain as a perennial because of the heat.

Bloom Period and Seasonal Color
Spring and summer; deep purple rays with raised dark brown disc flowers.

Mature Height × Spread
3 to 4 feet × 2 to 3 feet

Zones
3, 4, 5, 6
Hardy to 0 degrees Fahrenheit.

When, Where, and How to Plant
Plant in spring after all danger of frost is past. Purple coneflower grows best in full sun or light shade in well-drained, fertile soil. Dig a hole two to three times wider than the container and only as deep. Add a thin layer of compost or mulch to backfill. Set the plant in the hole slightly higher than the soil line. Fill the hole, pressing the soil gently around the roots to remove air pockets. Water thoroughly. Water every two to four days for two to three weeks, then every four to seven days until established.

Growing Tips
Keep beds well mulched during the summer to prevent the soil from drying out. Apply slow-release or organic fertilizer annually in late spring. Water established plants every one to two weeks, more often if temperatures are extreme. Plants are dormant in winter and need only minimal watering.

Care
Regular removal of spent flowering stalks promotes continuous bloom. Purple coneflower spreads slowly from underground stems. Thin clumps by cutting out a few stems each year to maintain good airflow and prevent infestations of powdery mildew. Lift and divide clumps every three to four years to promote vigorous growth and blooming. Other than powdery mildew in overgrown clumps, purple coneflower is not susceptible to pests or disease.

Companion Planting and Design
The large, bold flowers and coarse foliage of purple coneflower make it a good contrasting plant and companion to more delicate perennials such as yarrow, blue mist, and salvias. Use as a background for small perennials or annuals or interplant with roses and other flowering shrubs. Allow clumps to spread to form impressive massed displays, or to line drives, walkways, or patios. Purple coneflower is highly regarded as a cut flower because the flowers are long lasting.

Did You Know?
This species, along with *Echinacea angustifolia* and *E. pallida*, was used extensively by Plains Indians to cure a wide range of illnesses and heal wounds. Modern practitioners recognize many of this plant's healing properties, particularly its effectiveness in minimizing viral infections.

Red-hot Poker
Kniphofia species

When, Where, and How to Plant
Plant as soon as the soil can be worked in spring. Red-hot poker grows best in full sun in well-drained, moist, fertile soil. Dig a hole that is two to three times wider than the container and only as deep. Add generous amounts of compost or mulch to the backfill. Set the plant in the hole slightly higher than the soil line. Fill the hole, pressing the soil gently around the roots to remove air pockets. Water thoroughly. Water every two to four days for two to three weeks, then every four to seven days until established.

Growing Tips
Mulch plants regularly to prevent the soil from drying out. Apply slow-release or organic fertilizer annually in spring. Water established plants once or twice a week summer, never letting them dry out completely. Water enough in winter to prevent plants from drying out.

Care
Clear out dead or damaged leaves by cutting near the base or pulling them out in fall. Remove flowering stalks as soon as they are spent. Protect the crown in winter by mulching heavily or tying the leaves over the crown. Red-hot poker is not susceptible to pests or disease.

Companion Planting and Design
Mix with daylilies, phlox, and salvias for contrast offered by the spiky bloom and the graceful, grasslike foliage. Red-hot poker is useful as an informal border in front of large beds or can fill a barren spot in the garden. The flowers are spectacular and make an impressive focal or specimen plant. Use generously around patios or walkways where visiting hummingbirds can be enjoyed.

Did You Know?
Botanists have long used the family Liliaceae as a massive collection of most of the monocots that were not a grass or a palm. Recent research has split this huge family into twenty-nine families and the genus *Kniphofia* now finds itself in Asphodelaceae along with *Aloe, Bulbine, Gasteria,* and *Haworthia.*

This beautiful South African perennial is known for its dense stands of grasslike leaves and tall, congested flowering heads reminiscent of aloe blooms. Although Kniphofia uvaria is how most are offered, most plants sold are actually hybrids between this species and many others. Pure K. uvaria has a 3-foot head of coral flowers marked with yellow, while most garden forms of the plant have brilliant red to red-orange flowering heads marked with yellow. The dark blue-green leaves are folded toward the middle and are generally serrated along the edge. Red-hot poker does not tolerate the extreme summer heat of the low zones. It is best grown in the coolest parts of the intermediate zone and throughout the high zones where it is a long-lived effortless perennial.

Other Common Name
Torch lily

Bloom Period and Seasonal Color
Summer; yellow, red, or bicolored.

Mature Height × Spread
2 to 6 feet × 2 to 3 feet

Zones
3, 4, 5, 6
Root hardy to 0 degrees Fahrenheit.

Red Justicia
Justicia candicans

Whenever anyone asks for a reliable plant that isn't fussy, blooms most of the year, and is attractive to humming-birds, my first thought is red justicia. Red justicia has abundant thin, upright stems that are crowded with soft, pale green leaves. Tucked among the leaves near the tips of the stems, the flowers emerge from enlarged green bracts. The thin, tubular red to red-orange flowers end in three flared petals and are irresistible to hummingbirds. Mexican honeysuckle (Justicia spicigera) has yellow-green leaves and bright orange flowers virtually year-round. J. sonorae is a low growing perennial with thin, dusky green leaves and purple or dark blue tubular flowers. The shrublike J. adhatoda has large, congested heads of pure white one-inch flowers.

Bloom Period and Seasonal Color
October to May, intermittent in summer; red to red-orange.

Mature Height × Spread
3 to 4 feet × 3 to 4 feet

Zones
1, 2, 3, 4
Hardy to 20 degrees Fahrenheit.

When, Where, and How to Plant
Plant in fall or spring in full sun or filtered shade. Red justicia grows and blooms best in well-drained, fertile soil but will tolerate any well-drained soil. Dig a hole that is two to three times wider than the container and only as deep. Add a thin layer of compost or mulch to the backfill. Set the plant in the hole slightly higher than the soil line. Fill the hole, pressing the soil gently around the roots to remove air pockets. Water thoroughly. Water every two to four days for two to three weeks, then every four to seven days until established.

Growing Tips
Apply two or three inches of mulch in summer to keep the soil from drying out. Provide slow-release or organic fertilizer annually in fall to young plants; older plants do not need supplemental fertilizer and become floppy and weak when grown too richly. Water weekly in summer, every other week in winter.

Care
Prune red justicia to within a foot or two of the ground in early fall or early spring to reduce size, remove dead or damaged stems, and to reinvigo-rate the plant. Plants can also be shaped by selectively pruning overgrown stems to the base. Red justicia is not susceptible to pests or disease.

Companion Planting and Design
Mix red justicia with perennials such as brittle-bush, penstemons, plumbago, lantana, and salvia. Plant generously to create an informal border or hedge. Red justicia also serves as a background for small perennial or annual plantings, or fills in barren spots in a newly planted garden. Use red justicia against a hot wall, near a pool, or along drives, walkways, or patios where reflected heat is intense. Red justicia makes an attractive long-blooming container plant and is attractive to hummingbirds.

Did You Know?
The genus was named in honor of James Justice, a noted 18th-century Scottish horticulturist who died in 1763. The epithet, *candicans*, means "shiny" or "woolly white," and refers to the leaves.

When, Where, and How to Plant

Plant in fall or early spring in full sun or filtered shade. Ruellia will grow in almost any well-drained soil but does best in well-drained, fertile soil. Dig a hole that is two to three times wider than the container and only as deep. Add a thin layer of compost or mulch to the backfill. Set the plant in the hole slightly higher than the soil line. Fill the hole, pressing the soil gently around the roots to remove air pockets. Water thoroughly. Water every two to four days for two to three weeks, then every four or five days until established.

Growing Tips

Ruellia needs no supplemental fertilizer. When grown with too much fertilizer or too much water, it can spread rapidly and become a nuisance. Water every five to seven days in summer, monthly or less in winter.

Care

Ruellia has good natural form and rarely needs pruning to maintain its shape. To reduce size or remove winter damage, prune selected stems to the ground in spring. Badly overgrown clumps can be pruned to within inches of the ground in spring to rejuvenate the plant. Plants grown in deep shade become floppy and often fail to bloom. Divide crowded clumps and relocate seedlings in winter. Ruellia is not susceptible to pests or disease.

Companion Planting and Design

Ruellia makes an excellent informal border or hedge to line a driveway, walkway, or patio. Use ruellia generously near a pool, against a hot wall, or other areas where reflected heat is intense. Dwarf forms make excellent edging along walkways or paths, in front of larger perennials or shrub plantings. Ruellia makes a good container plant, and this is a good way to control its spread in a small garden.

Did You Know?

The genus was named in honor of Jean Ruel, a French herbalist who died in 1537. The epithet honors the famous pair of botanists, Elizabeth Knight Britton, one of the founders of the New York Botanical Garden and her husband Nathaniel, the first director of that garden.

Ruellia is deceptive; the thin, dark green leaves arranged along the numerous thin stems look tender and ready to wilt. In fact, it is one of the most drought and heat tolerant perennials for low zone gardens. Ruellia spreads rapidly from underground stems making it a nuisance in gardens with too much water, but the parade of paper-thin purple flowers makes it a splendid choice for summer color in drier locations. The selection 'Chi Chi' has pink flowers, and a white flowered form carries no name. The popular dwarf form 'Katie' has dark purple flowers, is no more than 12 inches tall, and spreads less aggressively. Two other dwarf forms, the pink-flowered 'Colobe Pink' and an unnamed white are just becoming available.

Bloom Period and Seasonal Color
April to October; purple, lavender, pink, and white.

Mature Height × Spread
1 to 3 feet × 2 to 4 feet

Zones
1, 2, 3, 4
Hardy to 25 degrees Fahrenheit, perhaps slightly lower.

Russian Sage

Perovskia atriplicifolia

Russian sage is remarkably durable in all zones of the state. The delicate, finely cut, pale gray to white leaves are widely spaced on the stems. The plant looks translucent, like a blue haze in the garden and is especially cooling in a low zone garden. Flowers range from a light, sky blue to intense indigo and are held in long spikes at the ends of the stems from spring through summer. The combination of the waving blue flowers and the light, ghostly foliage gives the plant an ethereal quality that is entirely at odds with its tolerance of hot, dry conditions as well as the rigors of a mountain in the winter. 'Blue Spire' has deep blue flowers and 'Blue Mist' has pale blue flowers.

Bloom Period and Seasonal Color
Spring and summer; light blue to deep indigo.

Mature Height × Spread
3 to 4 feet × 3 to 4 feet

Zones
All
Hardy to 0 degrees Fahrenheit, possibly lower.

When, Where, and How to Plant
Plant in fall or spring in full sun or filtered shade. Although tolerant of a wide range of soils as long as drainage is very sharp, Russian sage grows best in well-drained, fertile soil. Dig a hole that is two to three times wider than the container and only as deep. Add a generous layer of compost or mulch to the backfill. Set the plant in the hole slightly higher than the soil line. Fill the hole, pressing the soil gently around the roots to remove air pockets. Water thoroughly. Water every two to four days for two to three weeks, then every four to seven days until established.

Growing Tips
Fertilize annually in early fall (low elevation zones) and late spring (high elevation zones) with slow-release or organic fertilizer. Mulch the roots generously through summer to keep soil from drying out completely. Water weekly in summer; every ten to fourteen days in winter in low zones. Russian sage is dormant in winter in high zones; rely on natural watering during that time.

Care
Prune to within a foot or two of the ground in early spring to remove winter-damaged stems or reinvigorate the plant. Cut spent blooms regularly through the growing season; it helps prolong the blooming period. Russian sage is not susceptible to pests or disease.

Companion Planting and Design
Mix Russian sage with perennials such as plumbago, salvias, or phlox. Plant generously to maximize the lovely foliage and bloom and to create a loose informal border or fill a barren spot in the garden in front of a deep green hedge. Russian sage is particularly effective planted around structures like a statue or fountain.

Did You Know?
Botanists believe that this plant may be misnamed—that what we are growing in our gardens is actually a hybrid between *Perovskia atriplicifolia* and *P. abrotanoides*. It also isn't especially Russian but is native to Pakistan, Turkestan, and Iran.

Sacred Datura

Datura wrightii

When, Where, and How to Plant

Plant in spring in full sun or partial shade. Datura grows in almost any type of soil that is well drained, including rocky, native soil. Dig a hole that is two to three times wider than the container and only as deep. Soil amendments are not necessary. Set the plant in the hole with the roots well below the soil line. Fill the hole, pressing the soil gently around the roots to remove air pockets. Water thoroughly. Water every two to four days for two to three weeks or until established.

Growing Tips

Sacred datura needs no supplemental fertilizer. Established plants survive on natural rainfall even in low elevation zones, but watering twice a month in summer increases the vigor and bloom. Rely on natural rainfall in winter when the plant is dormant.

Care

As leaves begin to yellow in fall, cut the plant to the ground. Plants may be pruned anytime during the growing season if they become too large or leggy. Prune using gloves; all parts of the plant are poisonous if ingested, and some people are allergic to contact with the leaves or sap. Sacred datura is not susceptible to pests or disease.

Companion Planting and Design

The spectacular summer-flowering of sacred datura makes it a great choice near seating areas, patios, or pools. Sacred datura thrives in tree wells, surrounding the tree with a living groundcover. Interplant with winter-flowering bulbs, spring-flowering annuals, or penstemons to cover the barren area left by the deciduous leaves. Use in a dark area of the garden, or along a drive or walkway where the dramatic night flowering will be most effective.

Did You Know?

The remarkable fruit of sacred datura looks like a Medieval weapon—it is a golf ball sized, round pod covered with sharp prickles. I am continually amazed to find seedlings hundreds of feet from the main plant and cannot imagine who is brave enough to move them around.

Sacred datura should always be planted where you will see it first thing in the morning. It is wonderful to be greeted on a summer morning by dozens of huge, white trumpets, and inhale their delicate, sweet perfume. This glorious bloom doesn't last long; as soon as the sun touches the flowers, they fold, wilt, and die. Some populations have lavender or purple flowers, and there are dark purple forms available. The triangular, dusky green leaves cover the thick, fleshy trailing stems profusely, and large, old plants function as an oversized ground cover throughout the summer. The plant is deciduous in winter, with only the swollen, underground root living beneath the soil. All parts of the plant are poisonous if eaten, and some people are allergic to the leaves. The botanical name is sometimes listed as Datura meteliodes.

Other Common Names

Jimson weed, Angel's trumpet

Bloom Period and Seasonal Color

May to October, heaviest in summer; white, lavender, or purple.

Mature Height × Spread

3 to 4 feet × 5 to 6 feet

Zones

All
Hardy to 0 degrees Fahrenheit.

Summer Phlox
Phlox paniculata

Summer phlox reminds me so much of the casual, blowsy summer gardens that one of my grandmothers maintained. It was a garden where the plants were free to set the design and big, bold plants like fragrant shrubby roses, huge hollyhocks, and summer phlox dominated. Today they are just as delightful, although now there are many newer varieties and colors. Growing from a basal set of dark green leaves, the tall, congested flowering stalks are resplendent with the fragrant blooms throughout summer. This is a plant of the intermediate and high zones of Arizona. Some of the old varieties, like those in my grandmother's garden, can only be found in old gardens to be passed along from gardener to gardener.

Bloom Period and Seasonal Color
Summer; pink, red, white, lavender, and purple including bicolors.

Mature Height × Spread
3 to 5 feet × 1 to 2 feet

Zones
3, 4, 5, 6
Hardy to 0 degrees Fahrenheit.

When, Where, and How to Plant
Plant in spring as soon as the soil is warm enough to work. Although summer phlox grows easily from seed, it is best to use transplants because the colors are not consistent when grown from seed. Place in full sun or partial shade in well-drained, fertile soil. Dig a hole that is two to three times wider than the container and only as deep. Add a thin layer of compost or mulch to the backfill. Set the plant in the hole slightly higher than the soil line. Fill the hole, pressing the soil gently around the roots to remove air pockets. Water thoroughly. Water every two to four days for two to three weeks, then every four to seven days until established.

Growing Tips
Apply slow-release fertilizer or organic fertilizer annually in spring as plants begin to grow. Water established plants weekly in summer and intermittently in winter. Resist overhead watering; it encourages mildew infestations and the fragile stems with their heavy heads of flowers are prone to falling over from the pressure of the water.

Care
Remove dead stems and spent blooming stalks in fall to keep plants tidy. Mulch the roots heavily to protect them from freezing in winter. Plants spread by rhizomes (underground stems) as well as reseed freely and make large clumps over the years. Plants that are too congested are frequently susceptible to mildew infestations. Keep clumps thinned by removing some plants every year or two to minimize the problem.

Companion Planting and Design
Mix summer phlox with tall perennials such as yarrow, roses, or Russian sage for a colorful summer bed. Plant generously as background for smaller perennials or annual wildflower beds. Dwarf varieties are especially well-suited for use as a low border lining a walkway or seating area.

Did You Know?
The name of the genus comes from the Greek word for flame. The word also refers to plants with flame-colored flowers. The epithet, *paniculata*, means having a panicle which is an inflorescence with a central stalk and flowers held on branches.

Tufted Evening Primrose
Oenothera caespitosa

When, Where, and How to Plant

Plant in fall or spring in low elevation zones; in spring as soon as the soil can be worked in high elevation zones. Tufted evening primrose grows well in almost any fast-draining soil from well-drained, fertile soil to rocky, native soil, but does poorly in heavy soil. Dig a hole that is two to three times wider than the container and only as deep. Add a thin layer of compost or mulch to the back-fill. Set the plant in the hole slightly higher than the soil line. Fill the hole, pressing the soil gently around the roots to remove air pockets. Water thoroughly. Water every two to four days for two to three weeks, then every four to seven days until established.

Growing Tips

Apply slow-release or organic fertilizer annually in spring. Water established plants once a week in summer in low elevation zones, every ten to fourteen days in high elevation zones. Water once a month or less in winter in low elevation zones; rely on natural rainfall when the plant is dormant in high elevation zones.

Care

Prune or pull off dead or winter-damaged leaves in early spring. Tufted evening primrose is not susceptible to pests or disease.

Companion Planting and Design

Tufted evening primrose is beautiful in mixed perennial plantings with salvias, penstemons, and sundrops. Although the flowers open at night, they remain open through the morning hours. Plant generously to form a low border along a patio, walkway, drive, or around a pool. In the high elevation zones, tufted evening primrose can be used in the hot, dry parts of the garden that receive minimal care. Mix with spring-flowering annuals such as tidy tips or farewell-to-spring, and perennials such as desert marigold.

Did You Know?

The name of the genus comes from the Greek word for the European species *Oenothera biennis*, *oinotheras*. The epithet *caespitosa* refers to the habit of growing in tufts or dense clumps.

Night-blooming plants are one of the specialties of arid gardens and tufted evening primrose is one of the showiest for all Arizona gardens. Perched on a short stem, the paper-thin, 3-inch white flowers are backed by pinkish bracts and open for one night only. Spent flowers turn a delicate, faded pink. As an important nectar source for a host of night insects including the striking hawk moth, tufted evening primrose is pollinated by these nocturnal visitors. Dusky green leaves are 4 to 6 inches long, and deeply lobed with fine soft hairs. Numerous small plants crowd the stem creating a small mound of plants and their blooms. Tufted evening primrose reseeds freely, which is fortunate because the life of individual plants can be short. In cold winter regions, the plants are deciduous.

Bloom Period and Seasonal Color

Spring and early summer; white with pink bracts.

Mature Height × Spread

1 to 2 feet × 1 to 2 feet

Zones

All
Hardy to 10 degrees Fahrenheit.

Western Mugwort
Artemisia ludoviciana

In the rocky walls and canyon sides of central and eastern Arizona, alert hikers notice a burst of the graceful gray to white foliage of western mugwort. Removed to England over one hundred years ago and grown there for decades as an ornamental plant, it has returned to American gardens as the cultivars 'Silver Queen' and 'Silver King'. But Arizona gardeners can still find the shorter, spreading forms that rule the natural world. Flowers hardly count in this species; it is grown for the irregularly dissected, aromatic, pale foliage. In the garden, western mugwort provides a calming presence; the gentle foliage lights up dark corners and provides excellent contrast when used in colorful perennial plantings. 'Valerie Finnis' is a compact form with larger than usual foliage.

Other Common Names
White sage, Artemesia, Wormwood

Bloom Period and Seasonal Color
July to October; yellowish white terminal clusters.

Mature Height × Spread
2 to 4 feet × 3 to 5 feet

Zones
All
Hardy at least to -5 degrees Fahrenheit; perhaps lower.

When, Where, and How to Plant
Plant in early spring in almost any well-drained, alkaline soil including rocky, native soil. Plant in full sun or filtered shade. Dig a hole that is two to three times wider than the container and only as deep. Soil amendments are not necessary. Set the plant in the hole slightly higher than the soil line. Fill the hole, pressing the soil gently around the roots to remove air pockets. Water thoroughly. Water every two to four days for two to three weeks, then every four to seven days until established.

Growing Tips
Western mugwort needs no supplemental fertilizer. Water weekly in summer, although established plants can grow on much less. Western mugwort gets floppy and leggy in deep shade or when over-watered. Plants are dormant in winter; reduce watering to once a month, or rely natural rainfall.

Care
Prune to remove winter-damaged stems and reinvigorate in early spring. Western mugwort is not susceptible to pests or disease. Overwatered plants, or those growing with poor drainage, may develop blackened leaves, soft stems, and sudden wilting that indicate root rot. This species spreads by rhizomes that form 2- to 3-feet wide clumps. Divide in early spring by digging up the plant and discarding the oldest sections and replanting the newer ones if the plant becomes too large.

Companion Planting and Design
Western mugwort mixes well with plumbago, salvias, red justicia, and globemallow providing both color and textural contrast. Western mugwort's full sun tolerance, ability to grow in rocky soils, and minimal watering requirements make it ideal for succulent gardens, or outer areas of the garden that receive minimal care. Its spreading habit makes it a good choice for erosion control on steep slopes.

Did You Know?
The name mugwort almost defies description. The "mug" part is generally thought to have derived from a long line of Old English, Germanic, and French words meaning "fly" or "midge." The "wort" part means "a plant." The whole thing was originally ascribed to a European member of the genus, *Artemesia vulgaris*, that was used extensively to repel insects and cure a wide variety of diseases.

When, Where, and How to Plant

Plant from early spring to midsummer in low elevation zones; in early spring in higher elevation zones. Site in full sun or filtered shade. Wine cups grows best in well-drained, fertile, but alkaline, soil. Dig a hole that is two to three times wider than the container and only as deep. Add a thin layer of compost or mulch to the backfill. Set plants in the hole slightly higher than the soil line. Fill the hole, pressing the soil gently around the roots to remove air pockets. Water thoroughly. Water every two to four days for two to three weeks, then every four to seven days until established. Wine cups may also be planted from seed sown in fall.

Growing Tips

Wine cups needs no supplemental fertilizer. Mulch the roots in summer in low elevation zones to keep the soil from drying out and in winter in high elevation zones to protect the crown. Water established plants weekly in summer in low elevation zones; every seven to ten days in high elevation zones.

Care

Remove spent flowers anytime. Plants increase by runners and can be divided in the spring if they become crowded or messy. Wine cups is not susceptible to pests or disease, although in low elevation zones it may be short-lived, possibly due to the heat.

Companion Planting and Design

Wine cups is lovely when mixed with low growing, summer-flowering perennials such as gaillardia, chocolate flower, and blue salvia. Plant generously to use as a border in front of larger perennials or shrubs, or to fill barren gaps in the garden. Wine cups mixes well with annual plantings of lupines, California poppies, and scarlet flax. Wine cups grows well in containers or planters either singly or in mixed plantings. In high elevation zones, it may be used for erosion control on steep slopes.

Did You Know?

Callirhoe was the daughter of Achelous of Greek mythology. The epithet, *involucrata*, refers to the whorl of bracts that are beneath the flower known as an involucre.

Throughout central Texas, the spring wildflower displays are astounding. Rolling hills dotted with evergreen oaks and juniper trees and the gentle pastureland between them are carpeted in uninterrupted swaths of color. While the bluebonnet is the most famous of the Texas wildflowers, wine cups is perhaps the most commonly grown outside of that state. These low flat plants have parsley-like leaves that rise on thin stems from a central crown. Two-inch wide flowers arise from the same crown in rich magenta or purple. These reliable perennials grow and bloom equally well in all zones of Arizona gardens and are sustained by a large, fleshy root. Wine cups are summer-flowering in both high and low zone gardens in late spring and summer.

Other Common Name
Poppy mallow

Bloom Period and Seasonal Color
Spring through fall; deep purple to magenta, occasionally white.

Mature Height × Spread
2 feet × 2 feet

Zones
All
Hardy to 0 degrees Fahrenheit.

Yarrow
Achillea millefolium

Yarrow are glorious perennials in the summer gardens of the intermediate and high zones of Arizona. Plants are usually tall, although dwarf forms have been developed, with airy, dill-like foliage. The tiny flowers are held above the foliage in large, flat heads consisting of hundreds of flowers. Yarrow comes in a rainbow of colors, and many begin one color early in the season and change colors as they age. Established plants spread by runners and some forms self-seed freely. Alert gardeners often find new color variations from among those seedlings. The strain 'Garden Pastels' is just that, and the 'Galaxy' strain has darker tones. 'Debutante' is white with red accents, and 'Moonshine' has silver foliage and lemon-yellow flowers.

Other Common Name
Milfoil

Bloom Period and Seasonal Color
Summer to fall; yellow, white, orange, pink, and red.

Mature Height × Spread
2 to 3 feet × 2 to 3 feet

Zones
3, 4, 5, 6
Hardy to 0 degrees Fahrenheit.

When, Where, and How to Plant
Plant seed in spring as soon as the ground can be worked or transplant early in spring. Yarrow grows best in well-drained, fertile soil in full sun. Prepare beds for seed by adding slow-release or organic fertilizer to the bed and working it in gently with a rake or fork. Broadcast seed evenly and cover lightly, pressing the soil with a rake to prevent seeds from washing away. Water every day or two until seeds germinate, then water every four to seven days until established. To set in transplants, dig a hole that is two to three times wider than the container and only as deep. Backfill, pressing the soil gently around the roots to remove air pockets. Water thoroughly. Water every two to four days for two to three weeks, then every four to seven days until established.

Growing Tips
Yarrow needs no supplemental fertilizer. Apply generous amounts of mulch in summer to prevent the soil from drying out. Water established plants weekly in summer, monthly or less in winter.

Care
Cut spent flowering heads anytime; they are excellent in dried arrangements. Cut back to the ground in fall after bloom is complete. Yarrow spreads from runners and can be divided every two or three years to keep the plant from becoming overgrown. Yarrow is not susceptible to pests or disease.

Companion Planting and Design
Use yarrow as background for plantings of phlox, blue mist, Russian sage, and salvias. Plant generously to create drifts or fill in barren spots in the garden. Mix yarrow with succulents such as yuccas and agaves for contrast and color. Deep-colored varieties are especially effective with ornamental grasses.

Did You Know?
Yarrow has a long association with divination and numerous sayings and verses refer to the plant. Stalks of yarrow are traditionally used when consulting the *I Ching* or *Chinese Book of Changes*.

Roses *for Arizona*

It is hard to imagine gardens without roses; they have been a part of our gardening history for centuries. Chinese and European gardeners brought them in from the wild hundreds, if not thousands, of years ago. Bred, hybridized, selected, and transformed, there are thousands of varieties offered today in a host of styles and forms. The delicate layered petals that open generously and copiously against the deep, green foliage commands our attention and admiration. The unlikely contrast of the thorny stems and the gentle flowers has inspired poets and dreamers since ancient times. But the most memorable and evocative part of growing roses is their aroma, that heady, sweet, unmistakable scent, often with spicy accents, that adds immeasurably both to the mystique and the pleasure of roses in the garden. Like many people, the first thing I do when I see a rose is lean over and smell it, and those without scent are just a tiny bit disappointing.

Nothing to Fear

Gardeners in the low zones of Arizona often turn away from roses, assuming that they do not fit in or that the environmental conditions are too difficult to grow them well. Perhaps they have been daunted by the specter of their diminished plants in the summer. But even in the hottest areas of the state, with the combination of careful selection and attention to the details of their cultivation, roses can be glorious garden plants. Whether you grow them in dedicated beds and care for them like doting parents, or choose to blend them into a more diverse planting, if you want a rose, there is one out there to suit your taste and your needs. I like roses best when they are mingled with other perennials or placed where they become a colorful part of the garden. Large uniform rose beds are best reserved for demonstration and teaching gardens; at home, I want a lot more diversity and interest.

Tougher Than They Look

I am especially drawn to the so-called heirloom or old garden roses and am amazed at how many varieties thrive in the withering heat of the desert summer, as well as the cold winters of the high zones. Many of these varieties are very old, with lineages of up to 200 years or more. Others are of entirely unknown parentage. They have been found in old gardens

'Double Delight'

Climber Rose

among the bulbs and perennials or have been handed down in a family, one generation after another; some have come to us from cemeteries. They share a heritage of toughness and endurance after living so long with minimal care or in abandoned gardens. These roses have found their own way, growing in neglected conditions and without the tender care of a gardener and this has tempered them into rugged, carefree plants in the garden. Many are exuberant bushes much larger and less refined than their modern hybrid kin.

Most modern hybrid roses in the low zones are a labor of love and a testament to undying hope. But many heirloom varieties bloom well into the summer and remain fit and full of leaves, continuing to bloom through the blazing summer heat. Gardeners in the cooler zones may not have to work so hard at growing roses, and the profusion of varieties and classes attests to the bounty of roses in these climates.

Modern hybrid roses are generally sold without soil (bare root). This is a great way to buy roses and get them established in the garden. But bare-root roses are sensitive to drying out and care must taken to prevent it. When you select bare-root roses, have the nursery swaddle them with moss or soil and encase them in plastic for the ride home. Once you are home, plunge the rose in a bucket of water that covers the entire root system and as much of the stems as possible. Leave it in the shade for a day or two. This treatment helps rehydrate the plant after shipping and greatly decreases transplant shock. Opinions vary on whether or not to put in fertilizer or other soluble treatments in the water - some growers swear by it, others disdain it as unnecessary.

Not a Shrinking Violet

Care of roses can be as complicated or straightforward as you care to make it depending on the varieties you are growing and the zone in which it is grown. Always select rose varieties that are well suited to your zone. There are rose societies throughout the state; consult with their members, attend a meeting, or visit a demonstration garden if there is one in your area to find out the most appropriate roses for your location. Choosing the proper variety solves most of the difficulties that gardeners face in growing healthy, vigorously blooming roses.

Roses grow best in rich, fertile soil that is kept evenly watered throughout the year and never dries out completely. Although most rose growers also provide a steady program of fertilization for their roses, a rich soil is vital for the plant to receive and absorb the nutrients that it needs. Fertilizers are supplements, provided at intervals to keep plants growing quickly or bloom more prolifically, but the soil provides the steady diet of water, nutrients, and minerals roses require.

Fertilizers for roses are as varied as the roses themselves. They can be dry or water soluble, specially blended specifically for roses, or as individual mineral components, derived from inorganic or organic sources; the choices can quickly become overwhelming. Choose a type of fertilizer that is easy for you to use and that provides a gentle, steady fertilizer regimen for the plants rather than a monumental jolt once in a while. All purpose, well balanced fertilizers provide a good fertilizer for roses, as do organic amendments such as compost, mulch and alfalfa meal. Mulching roses is strongly recommended in all zones because it cuts down on soil evaporation and enhances the fertility of the soil over time. Mulch is especially important in the hot areas of the state.

Pruning is an art form that is best learned by doing. In the hottest parts of the state, roses are pruned lightly in late summer or early fall to encourage a fall flush of growth and bloom. They are then pruned hard in the winter—January or February—

'Carefree Delight' Shrub Rose

for shape and to foster vigorous spring growth and bloom. In cooler areas, each of these prunings takes place a little earlier (summer) and a little later (winter) but is still highly recommended for most modern hybrid forms. Shrub roses rarely need such aggressive pruning; it is better to keep gently pruning and pinching them through the summer to keep them tidy and remove dead wood. Most rose societies provide free pruning demonstrations; take advantage of the offer and learn how to prune properly from the pros in your area.

The enduring appeal of roses and their surprising sturdiness to conditions throughout the state make roses a wonderful part of any garden. Look deeply into the vast selection of roses to choose varieties and styles that will enhance your garden for years to come.

Climber Rose
Rosa species and hybrids

I find climbing roses irresistible and romantic. Strolling, or better yet, lunching, under an arch loaded with fragrant blooms makes me feel as if I have walked back to a more graceful, leisurely age. Most climbers bloom over a long season and grow quickly to cover the wall or trellis that supports them. Some varieties are large-flowered natural climbers and others are sports of hybrid teas and floribundas with the long, fast growing stems of a climber. 'Fourth of July' has red and white striped petals and brilliant yellow stamens. 'Altissima' has fragrant, velvet red flowers held in clusters while 'America' has a spicy scent and its flowers are a blend of orange and pink. In higher zones, 'Don Juan', with its lacquer red, single blooms against shiny, green foliage, is a reliable choice.

Bloom Period and Seasonal Color
Spring and summer; a variety of colors.

Mature Height × Spread
6 to 15 feet × 6 to 15 feet

Zones
All
Hardiness depends on variety.

When, Where, and How to Plant
In low zones plant bare-root roses in winter, container-grown roses from January to March. In higher zones, bare-root roses are planted early in spring, container-grown ones throughout spring. Roses grow best in full sun in well-drained, fertile soil. Dig a hole that is three to four times wider than the container and just as deep. Add generous amounts of compost to the soil and work it in thoroughly. Set the rose in the hole with the bud union well above the soil line. Fill the hole, pressing the soil gently to remove air pockets. Mulch the root zones of the plant but do not allow mulch to touch the bark. Water every two to three days for three weeks.

Growing Tips
Apply balanced, slow-release, or organic fertilizer every month when roses are actively growing. Do not fertilize in summer or from November to January in the low zones. Do not fertilize in winter in the higher zones. In low zones, water deeply two to three times a week in summer, every ten days in winter. In higher zones, water weekly in summer, every other week the rest of the year.

Care
In low zones, prune to remove dead wood and summer-damaged stems in September; perform heavy pruning in January. In higher zones, prune heavily in March. For climbers and shrubs, leave the large, framing canes unpruned until they are as long as you want them. Annually prune the secondary canes of these types to create the desired growth pattern.

Companion Planting and Design
Use climber roses against a wall or trellis to create a dramatic focal point. Allow them to climb over an arch or trellis to form an entry to a building or areas of the garden.

Did You Know?
Settlers on the *Mayflower* reported "the shore was fragrant like the smell of a rose garden." It turned out that the local Indian tribes routinely planted native shrub roses to beautify their camps.

Floribunda Rose

Rosa hybrids

When, Where, and How to Plant

In low elevation zones, plant bare-root roses in winter and container-grown roses from January to March. In higher elevation zones, plant bare-root roses in early spring; wait until summer to plant container-grown ones. Grow roses in full sun in well-drained, fertile soil. Dig a hole three to four times wider than the container and just as deep. Add generous amounts of compost and work it in thoroughly before planting. Set the rose in the hole with the bud union above the soil line. Fill the hole, pressing the soil gently to remove air pockets. Mulch the root zone but do not allow mulch to touch the bark. Water thoroughly after planting and every two to three days for three weeks.

Growing Tips

Apply balanced, slow-release, or organic fertilizer every month while roses are actively growing. Do not fertilize in summer or from November to January in the low zones. Do not fertilize in winter in the higher zones. In low elevation zones, water deeply two to three times a week in summer, once a week in fall and spring, every ten days in winter. In higher elevation zones, water weekly in summer, every other week the rest of the year.

Care

In low elevation zones, prune to remove dead or damaged wood in September and prune heavily again in January, removing up to a third of the bush and leaving only eight to twelve healthy canes. Prune heavily in March in higher elevation zones. Roses are susceptible to powdery mildew, cane borers, and aphids.

Companion Planting and Design

Mix roses with perennials such as salvias, summer phlox, and daylilies. Roses are stunning when grown in mass plantings. Plant generously around walkways, seating areas, courtyards, or patios.

Did You Know?

President Woodrow Wilson's wife, Edith, originally planted the Rose Garden at the White House in 1913. It was renovated in 1961 under the direction of Jacqueline Kennedy.

I once saw a garden that had gone mad for a white rose. It was a very formal place with clipped hedges of evergreen shrubs and linear paths. But thousands of blooms of the floribunda 'Iceberg' were encased in the beds and it was a breathtaking effect. 'Iceberg' has the short, shrubby habit, and clustered flowers that bloom over a long season that is typical of the class. Floribundas have great disease tolerance and grow well in the low and intermediate zones of the state. 'Europeana' has deep red flowers while 'Betty Boop' has creamy white petals edged in red. 'French Lace', with its delicate apricot flowers, and 'Singin' in the Rain', with its apricot to gold flowers, are well suited to the higher zones.

Bloom Period and Seasonal Color
Spring and summer; a variety of colors.

Mature Height × Spread
6 to 15 feet × 6 to 15 feet

Zones
All
Hardiness depends on variety.

Grandiflora Rose
Rosa hybrids

The classification of roses can be confusing; there are numerous systems worldwide to keep them all organized. But the class called grandiflora is more confusing than most. It was developed in the 1950s to pair the flower style and long stems of hybrid teas and the hardiness and long bloom of floribundas. The first grandiflora was 'Queen Elizabeth', and it is still the standard for the class with its upright, shrubby growth habit and full-headed clusters of pink flowers. It is an outstanding rose for the low and intermediate zones of Arizona. Other grandifloras include 'Tournament of Roses', 'Caribbean' (an apricot blend), the full red 'Crimson Bouquet', and the new 'Glowing Peace' (an orange pink blend). In higher zones, 'Fame!', with deep pink flowers, is recommended.

Bloom Period and Seasonal Color
Spring and summer; a variety of colors.

Mature Height × Spread
4 to 8 feet × 3 to 5 feet

Zones
All
Hardiness depends on variety.

When, Where, and How to Plant
In low zones plant bare-root roses in winter; container-grown roses from January to March. In higher zones, bare-root roses are planted early in spring, container-grown ones throughout spring and into early summer. Roses grow best in full sun in well-drained, fertile soil. Dig a hole that is three to four times wider than the container and just as deep. Add generous amounts of compost to the soil and work it in thoroughly before planting. Set the rose in the hole with the bud union well above the soil line. Fill the hole, pressing the soil gently to remove air pockets. Mulch the root zones of the plant but do not allow mulch to touch the bark. Water thoroughly. Water every two to three days for three weeks.

Growing Tips
Apply balanced, slow-release, or organic fertilizer every month while plants are actively growing. Do not fertilize in summer or from November to January in the low zones. Do not fertilize in winter in the higher zones. In low zones, water deeply two to three times a week in summer, once a week in fall and spring, every ten days in winter. In higher zones, water weekly in summer, every other week the rest of the year.

Care
In low zones, prune to remove dead wood and summer-damaged stems in September. Prune heavily in January removing up to half the bush, and leaving four to eight healthy canes. At this time, strip off the leaves. Prune heavily in March in higher zones. Roses are susceptible to powdery mildew, cane borers, and aphids.

Companion Planting and Design
Mix roses with perennials such as salvias, summer phlox, and daylilies. Roses are stunning when grown in mass groups or in containers. Plant generously around walkways, seating areas, and courtyards, or use container-grown plants throughout patios to enjoy the long and often fragrant blooms.

Did You Know?
The Empress Josephine had over 250 rose varieties in her garden at Malmaison.

When, Where, and How to Plant

In low zones, plant heirloom roses from January to May. In higher zones, plant from early spring to early summer. Roses grow best in full sun in well-drained, fertile soil. Dig a hole that is three to four times wider than the container and just as deep. Add generous amounts of compost to the soil and work it in thoroughly before planting. Set the rose in the hole and fill the hole with the bud union well above the soil line, pressing the soil gently to remove air pockets. Mulch the root zones of the plant but do not allow mulch to touch the bark. Water thoroughly. Water every two to three days for three weeks.

Growing Tips

Apply balanced, slow-release or organic fertilizer every month when plants are actively growing. Do not fertilize in summer or from November to January in the low zones. Do not fertilize in winter in the higher zones. In low zones, water deeply two to three times a week in summer, once a week in fall and spring, every ten days in winter. In higher zones, water weekly in summer, every other week the rest of the year.

Care

Prune heavily in late winter or early spring to remove dead or damaged wood, thin the bush, or reduce the size. Mulch heavily to conserve moisture in summer and protect roots in winter. Most heirloom roses are not susceptible to the common rose pests or disease.

Companion Planting and Design

Smaller varieties mix well with other perennials or shrubs. Plant generously to form informal hedges or border plantings. Use rambling or climbing varieties along a wall or up an arbor or a trellis for added color. They are also useful as a screen. The smaller varieties are excellent as container plants.

Did You Know?

Fossils containing imprints of rose leaves have been dated to be thirty-five to forty million years old.

Heirloom roses are a polyglot group of species—hybrids and cultivars in which there are a bewildering number of classes. Their common bond is that all of the classes were in existence before 1867. Most are prolific bloomers. Although some bloom only once, others are in continuous bloom throughout the warm weather. Some are old roses with new names that have been found in old gardens, cemeteries, or abandoned farmsteads in recent years. 'Mutabilis' flowers open bright yellow, then fade to orange, pink, and finally crimson. It grows in all zones but Zone 6. 'Martha Gonzalez' is a small shrub with flat, crimson flowers. 'Zephirine Drouhin' is a sweetly fragrant, nearly thornless climber that blooms a cerise pink. 'Baronne Prevost', with its fragrant, double pink flowers and 'Hermosa', with its lavender to pink, fragrant flowers, are both very cold hardy.

Bloom Period and Seasonal Color
Spring through summer; a variety of colors.

Mature Height × Spread
3 to 12 feet × 3 to 6 feet

Zones
All
Hardiness depends on variety.

Hybrid Tea Rose
Rosa hybrids

Hybrid teas are crosses between hybrid perpetuals, bourbons, and teas. The class is considered to date from 1867 with the introduction of a rose named 'La-France'. Hybrid teas make outstanding cut flowers and most varieties in the floral trade are in this class. Blooms are solitary on long, sturdy stems and continue for a long season. 'Mr. Lincoln' is a long-time favorite in low and intermediate gardens with its deep red flowers and old rose fragrance. 'Peace', one of most popular roses of all time, has a delightful shifting array of gentle pink, orange, gold, and yellow colors. In higher zones, the rich red 'Olympiad' with its distinctive gray-green foliage and the extremely vigorous coral to pink flowered 'Touch of Class' are good choices.

Bloom Period and Seasonal Color
Spring and summer; a variety of colors.

Mature Height × Spread
3 to 5 feet × 2 to 3 feet

Zones
1, 2, 3, 4
Hardiness depends on variety.

When, Where, and How to Plant
In low zones, plant bare-root roses in winter, container-grown roses from January to March. In higher zones, bare-root roses are planted early in spring, container-grown ones throughout spring. Roses grow best in full sun and in well-drained, fertile soil. Dig a hole that is three to four times wider than the container and just as deep. Add generous amounts of compost to the soil and work it in thoroughly before planting. Set the rose in the hole with the bud union well above the soil line. Fill the hole, pressing the soil gently to remove air pockets. Mulch the root zones of the plant but do not allow mulch to touch the bark. Water thoroughly. Water every two to three days for three weeks.

Growing Tips
Apply balanced, slow-release, or organic fertilizer every month when roses are actively growing. Do not fertilize in summer or from November to January in the low zones. Do not fertilize in winter in the higher zones. In low zones, water deeply two to three times a week in summer, once a week in fall and spring, every ten days in winter. In higher zones, water weekly in summer; every other week the rest of the year.

Care
In low zones, prune to remove dead wood and summer-damaged stems in September. Prune heavily in January removing up to half the bush, and leaving four to eight healthy canes. At this time, strip off the leaves. In higher zones, prune heavily in March. Protect hybrid teas with a thick blanket of mulch where temperatures regularly dip below freezing. Roses are susceptible to powdery mildew, cane borers, and aphids.

Companion Planting and Design
Mix roses with perennials such as salvias, summer phlox, and daylilies. Roses are stunning when grown in groups to maximize the effect of the bloom and the fragrance. Plant generously around walkways, seating areas, courtyards, or patios.

Did You Know?
George Washington hybridized a rose in 1797. He named it 'Martha Washington'.

Lady Banks' Rose

Rosa banksiae

When, Where, and How to Plant

Plant from January to March in full sun, although in the hottest zones, it will grow well with an eastern exposure. Lady Banks' rose grows best in deep, well-drained, fertile soil. Dig a hole that is three to four times wider than the container and just as deep. Add generous amounts of compost to the soil and work it in thoroughly before planting. Set the rose in the hole with the plant slightly above the soil line. Fill the hole, pressing the soil gently to remove air pockets. Mulch the root zones of the plant but do not allow mulch to touch the bark. Water thoroughly. Water every two to three days for three weeks.

Growing Tips

Apply balanced, slow-release, or organic fertilizer every other month when the plants are actively growing but do not fertilizer in summer or from November to January. Water deeply every four to seven days in summer, every ten to fourteen days in winter.

Care

Prune carefully; this rose blooms on old wood. Prune in spring to remove canes that are too long or are growing in the wrong direction by cutting them as close to the base of the plant as possible. Prune secondary branches each spring to train them along the arbor or trellis. Mulch heavily to conserve moisture in summer. Lady Banks' rose is not susceptible to most common rose pests or disease.

Companion Planting and Design

Plant against a trellis, wall, or on an arbor for the dramatic spring flowering. This large, heat-tolerant rose is also useful to cool hot walls or areas where reflected heat is intense. Plant as a hedge or screen where space permits. Use as a focal or specimen plant. Excellent for erosion control where there is sufficient space.

Did You Know?

There is a Lady Banks' rose in Tombstone that was planted in 1885 and has become something of a sensation. Supported by an ever-expanding trellis, it is over nine feet tall and covers an area over 8,000 square feet.

Along the side of my parents' house was a large empty lot. To hide it and provide some privacy, my mother planted a row of Lady Banks' roses. Not only did they hide the view, they tried to hide that entire side of the yard. This old variety, introduced in 1807, sends out long, virtually thornless shoots with dark green leaves. Lady Banks' rose is much more tolerant of the hot and dry conditions of the low zones than most hybrid roses. Left alone, this rose grows naturally into a large, fountainlike shrub, but it is more often grown up a trellis or support, like a climber. The small, yellow flowers occur in dense clusters. 'Lutea' is a scentless, double yellow, and 'White Banksia' is a double white that smells like violets.

Bloom Period and Seasonal Color
April; yellow or white.

Mature Height × Spread
10 to 20 feet × 12 to 20 feet

Zones
1, 2, 3, 4
Hardy to 25 degrees Fahrenheit.

Miniature Rose

Rosa hybrids

Miniature roses are one of the most useful roses in any garden. There are miniature varieties that grow well in any zone in the state. In addition, their diminutive size makes them ideal for growing in containers that can be moved to favorable locations throughout the year. Miniatures are variable in their form, some are shrubby, and some almost climb. Many have hybrid tea form, others look like small floribundas. 'Gourmet Popcorn' is a prolific, long-blooming white, and 'Fairhope', also white, has a light, sweet fragrance. 'Miss Flippins' is red with an exceptionally long blooming season, and 'Black Jade' is velvety red with hybrid tea form. 'Magic Carousel' has white petals with a red edge, and 'Minnie Pearl' is a blended pink with dark, glossy foliage.

Bloom Period and Seasonal Color
Spring and summer; a variety of colors.

Mature Height × Spread
2 to 3 feet × 1 to 2 feet

Zones
All
Hardiness depends on variety.

When, Where, and How to Plant
In low zones plant bare-root roses in winter, container-grown roses from January to March. In higher zones, plant bare-root roses in early spring; do not plant container-grown ones until early summer. Roses grow best in full sun and in well-drained, fertile soil. Dig a hole that is three to four times wider than the container and just as deep. Add generous amounts of compost to the soil and work it in thoroughly before planting. Set the rose in the hole with the bud union well above the soil line. Fill the hole, pressing the soil gently to remove air pockets. Mulch the root zones of the plant but do not allow mulch to touch the bark. Water thoroughly. Water every two to three days for three weeks.

Growing Tips
Apply balanced, slow-release, or organic fertilizer every month when plants are actively growing. Do not fertilize in summer or from November to January in the low zones. Do not fertilize in winter in the higher zones. In low zones, water deeply two to three times a week in summer, once a week in fall and spring, every ten days in winter. In higher zones, water weekly in summer, every other week the rest of the year.

Care
Prune heavily in January removing up to a third of the bush, taking out dead or damaged canes and twiggy growth. Leave eight to twelve healthy canes. In higher zones, prune heavily in March. Mulch roots to retain moisture in summer and protect them during winter.

Companion Planting and Design
Use miniatures generously as the border for a larger rose bed, to fill in barren spots in a newly planted garden, or as a bright flowering hedge. Because miniatures are outstanding even very tender varieties enjoy wide use. Mix with spring- or summer-flowering perennials or annuals to extend the season and provide long-lasting bloom.

Did You Know?
Rosaries were originally formed of beads made of rose buds.

Shrub Rose
Rosa species

When, Where, and How to Plant
Plant bare-root roses as early in spring as the soil can be worked. Container-grown roses can be planted in spring and early summer. Roses grow best in full sun in deep, well-drained, fertile soil, although Wood's rose does well in partial shade. Dig a hole that is three to four times wider than the container and just as deep. Add generous amounts of compost to the soil and work it in thoroughly before planting. Set the rose in the hole with the plant slightly above the soil line. Fill the hole, pressing the soil gently to remove air pockets. Mulch the root zones of the plant but do not allow mulch to touch the bark. Water thoroughly. Water every two to three days for three weeks.

Growing Tips
Apply balanced, slow-release, or organic fertilizer every month when roses are actively growing. Do not fertilize in winter. Water weekly in summer, every two to three weeks the rest of the year.

Care
Prune in the early spring to remove dead or damaged wood, crossing branches, and twiggy growth. Remove up to a third of the bush, leaving eight to twelve healthy canes. Remove spent flowers anytime. Mulch heavily to maintain soil moisture in summer and protect the roots during winter. Shrub roses are very resistant to most rose pests and disease.

Companion Planting and Design
Plant shrubs roses generously to form a hedge or background for perennial or annual plantings. Roses may be used singly or mixed with other shrubs to create an informal hedge. Smaller varieties mix well with other perennials to create a long blooming season. Some larger varieties make excellent specimen or focal points for patios, or around pools or courtyards. Smaller varieties grow well in containers or planters.

Did You Know?
Although there are archaeological records that indicate roses were cultivated in Greece as early as 50 B.C. that is hardly the record. Roses are known to have been in cultivation in China since at least 2500 B.C.

Shrub rose is another class of rose that is hard to pin down. They are descended from a wide variety of types including rugosa, moss, and damask roses. Shrub roses are very cold hardy and show excellent disease resistance and are therefore some of the best choices for high zone gardens in Arizona. 'Sally Holmes' is a robust, white-flowered shrub rose that blooms all summer. 'Rachel Bowes Lyon' has multiple shades of pastel colors and makes a fine hedge or specimen. All the David Austin English shrub roses do well in Arizona high zone gardens. The native Wood's rose (Rosa woodsii) is a small shrub rose with light pink flowers that bloom throughout the summer. Late in summer, bright red fruit, called hips, decorate the plants and are quickly consumed by birds.

Bloom Period and Seasonal Color
Summer; a variety of colors.

Mature Height × Spread
3 to 4 feet × 3 to 4 feet

Zones
4, 5, 6
Hardy to 10 degrees Fahrenheit, some varieties much more.

Shrubs *for Arizona*

Shrubs are the backbone of all our gardens, no matter where we garden or what style of garden we prefer. Shrubs give form and substance to even a minimal gardening effort. Evergreen shrubs in particular are deeply valued both as foundation plants and to form hedges along the edge of the garden. This is probably the oldest use of shrubs—setting the living definition of where one garden ends and another begins.

What More Could You Want?

Shrubs divide large areas into smaller ones providing a visual screen between one section of the garden and another. Even in small gardens, using well-placed shrubs to hide one area from another makes the garden seem larger and more interesting. Shrubs also hide unsightly sheds, fences, buildings, views, or neighbors. They keep out noise, cut down on dust, serve as nest and roost sites for countless birds, and many provide colorful blooms as well. What more could we want from our plants?

In Arizona, shrubs can play an important role in keeping our homes cooled against the heat of summer. When planted close to a hot wall, shrubs absorb and reflect tremendous amounts of heat and radiation from the sun. Deciduous shrubs are especially useful against southern or western windows where the summer leaves keep out the hot sun, and the bare limbs of winter allow the welcome winter sunlight in.

Yellow Bird of Paradise

Prune with a Purpose

Pruning shrubs is not difficult, but it is too often poorly done. Most shrubs have wonderful natural form; indeed, some have astounding symmetry and regularity of form. The first rule of good pruning is to be sure only to prune with a purpose in mind and then only when necessary. The ridiculous and all too common practice of shearing and close pruning on a timetable, rather than for a purpose or effect, would be outlawed in a perfect world. It does not improve the looks of

Fairyduster

the plants, it emphatically diminishes the health and vigor (and sometimes the bloom) of the plants, and it serves no real purpose.

If you must prune to remove unruly or wayward limbs, or reduce the size of a shrub, cut the offending branch back as far into the shrub as possible. Continue this way until the shrub is the size or shape you want. You are, in effect, pruning from the inside out with the intent of keeping the form of the shrub rather than just removing the outer layer of the shrub.

Points to Ponder

Gardeners in Arizona are lucky to have a large variety of shrubs that are not only attractive but can tolerate the dry conditions, and, in some areas, the high heat that are such important gardening considerations here. When choosing a shrub, keep in mind what function you want it to perform in the garden. When shrubs are planted as a border, scale becomes of paramount importance. Massive hedges of oleander or privet have inundated too many small, urban yards. Hedges can provide plenty of privacy without sacrificing scale. Delightful hedges can be composed of a mixed group of shrubs. Blending evergreens with deciduous shrubs, spring-flowering shrubs with summer-blooming ones, or any combination that inspires you, creates a vivid border that adds immeasurably to the interest and vitality of a garden.

While shrubs have many practical uses, be sure to leave room for some that are planted just for their great beauty, long season of bloom, wonderful foliage, or graceful form. Planting any-thing for the sheer beauty and wonder of the plant should always be a considera-tion in any garden no matter how large or how small.

Damianita

Apache Plume
Fallugia paradoxa

Some plants really live up to their names. Apache plume is found throughout the intermediate and high elevation zones of Arizona—a region it shares with the historic homelands of the Apache people. In late summer and fall, the solitary, five-petaled white flowers give way to clusters of tiny fruit, each of which sports a feathery pinkish white appendage which is the plume. The result is arresting, the entire plant looks like a cloud on the ground. To add another spurt of color, the fruit turns from pale green to dark rosy purple in fall. The leaves are small and green to gray-green. Young twigs are coated with gray hairs but as they age, turn a rich, dark brown.

Bloom Period and Seasonal Color
May to September; white.

Mature Height × Spread
5 to 6 feet × 4 to 6 feet

Zones
All
Hardy to 0 degrees Fahrenheit.

When, Where, and How to Plant
Plant in fall or spring in low elevation zones, in spring as soon as the soil can be worked in high elevation zones. Locate Apache plume in full or partial sun. This shrub tolerates a wide range of well-drained soils from fertile, garden soil to rocky, native ones, but does poorly in heavy clay. Dig a hole three to four times wider than the container and just as deep adding a thin layer of compost or mulch to the backfill. Set the plant in the hole slightly higher than the soil line. Fill the hole, pressing the soil gently to remove air pockets. Mulch the roots but do not allow mulch to touch the bark. Water thoroughly. Water every three to four days for two or three weeks, then water every seven to ten days for the first year.

Growing Tips
Apache plume, like most drought-adapted shrubs, requires no, or minimal, supplemental fertilizer. Adding a generous layer of mulch to keep soil from drying out is all the extra fertilizer it will need. In the low elevation zones, water established plants every two to three weeks in summer, every month or two in winter. In intermediate and high elevation zones, rely on natural rainfall for established plants unless the weather is exceptionally hot or dry.

Care
Prune to remove dead or damaged wood in spring. Apache plume has excellent natural form and rarely needs pruning for shape. It is not susceptible to pests or disease.

Companion Planting and Design
Mix Apache plume with shrubs such as sugarbush, barberry, or scrub oak to form an informal hedge or boundary planting. The bloom and subsequent plumed fruit is fascinating enough to use the plant as a specimen or focal plant. Within its native range, use Apache plume in outlying areas of the garden that receive minimal care or as part of a naturalistic garden. It serves as a good background for colorful annual wildflower displays.

Did You Know?
The Hopi Indians of northern Arizona use an infusion of the leaves of this plant to stimulate hair growth.

Arizona Rosewood

Vauquelinia californica

When, Where, and How to Plant

Plant in fall or spring in low elevation zones, in spring as soon as the soil can be worked in intermediate elevation zones. Plant in full or partial sun. Arizona rosewood tolerates any well-drained soil including rocky, native ones. Dig a hole three to four times wider than the container and just as deep. Add a thin layer of compost or mulch to the backfill. Set the plant in the hole slightly higher than the soil line. Fill the hole, pressing the soil gently to remove air pockets. Mulch the roots but do not allow mulch to touch the bark. Water thoroughly. Water every three to four days for two or three weeks, then water every seven to ten days for the first year.

Growing Tips

Arizona rosewood requires no supplemental fertilizer. In the low elevation zones, water established plants every two weeks in summer, every month in winter. In intermediate and high elevation zones, rely on natural rainfall unless the weather is exceptionally hot or dry.

Care

Arizona rosewood can be trained as a small tree by pruning the lowest two or three branches each year in early spring. Do not remove over a quarter of the plant in any year. When grown as a shrub, Arizona rosewood has excellent natural form and rarely needs pruning for shape. Prune in early spring to remove dead or damaged wood; remove spent flowering heads anytime. Arizona rosewood is not susceptible to pests or disease.

Companion Planting and Design

Use Arizona rosewood with hopbush, jojoba, or Texas sage to create an informal hedge, screen, or border planting. The dark green leaves serve as a perfect backdrop for perennial or annual plantings. As a small tree it makes a fine specimen plant for a small garden, courtyard, or patio. It is useful against hot walls or around pools where reflected heat is intense.

Did You Know?

The genus honors the French chemist Nicolas Louis Vauquelin, who died in 1829. The epithet refers to the state of California.

This large, dense native shrub makes an attractive addition to Arizona gardens throughout the state. The long, leathery, dark green leaves and loose, rounded form are reminiscent of oleander from a distance. The naturally rounded form and wide tolerance of growing conditions make this evergreen shrub useful in the low and intermediate elevation zones. In early summer, the plant is resplendent with its tiny, creamy white flowers held in large, showy clusters. Each flower resembles a miniature wild rose—a testament to this shrub's place in the rose family. Chihuahuan rosewood (Vauquelinia corymbosa) is a more cold-hardy species with thin, drooping leaves and much larger, flowering heads. Leaves of both species often take on a bronze caste in cold weather. The variety angustifolia has pencil thin, serrated leaves.

Bloom Period and Seasonal Color
Late spring to summer; white in clusters.

Mature Height × Spread
10 to 25 feet × 5 to 15 feet

Zones
1, 2, 3, 4
Hardy to 15 degrees Fahrenheit.

Baja Fairyduster
Calliandra californica

Baja fairyduster is as charming as its name suggests. These are open, loosely branched shrubs whose tiny, dusky green leaves are crammed together at intervals along the stem. The flowers are breathtaking scarlet puff-balls that appear nearly year-round. Hummingbirds adore them. Practically unknown to gardeners twenty years ago, these gorgeous shrubs have become well regarded in low elevation zone gardens for their long blooming season and tolerance of extreme heat. Some authorities suggest that what is sold as Baja fairyduster is actually Calliandra peninsularis, another Baja native, or hybrids between these two. These are very difficult species to distinguish and for garden use it hardly matters. The much smaller, summer deciduous pink fairyduster (Calliandra eriophylla) limits its pink to white blooms to early spring.

Other Common Name
Red fairyduster

Bloom Period and Seasonal Color
August to May, intermittent in June and July; scarlet red to orange-red.

Mature Height × Spread
4 to 5 feet × 4 to 5 feet

Zones
1, 2, 3
Hardy to 25 degrees Fahrenheit.

When, Where, and How to Plant
Plant in spring in full sun; plants grown in too much shade bloom poorly. Baja fairyduster tolerates any well-drained soil from fertile, garden soil to rocky, native ones, but languishes in heavy clay. Dig a hole three to four times wider than the container and just as deep. Add a thin layer of compost or mulch to the backfill. Set the plant in the hole slightly higher than the soil line. Fill the hole, pressing the soil gently to remove air pockets. Mulch the roots but do not allow mulch to touch the bark. Water thoroughly. Water every three to four days for two or three weeks, then water every seven to ten days for the first summer.

Growing Tips
Baja fairyduster requires no supplemental fertilizer although a generous layer of mulch will keep the soil from drying out too quickly and provide extra nutrients. Water established plants every two weeks in summer, every month or two in winter.

Care
Prune to shape; remove dead wood or damaged branches in spring after all danger of frost is past. If the plant becomes leggy or sparse, prune to within a couple of feet of the ground in early spring. Baja fairyduster is not susceptible to pests or disease.

Companion Planting and Design
Baja fairyduster is outstanding in conjunction with other colorful desert perennials such as globemal-low or brittlebush. Its drought tolerance makes it a good choice to mix with prickly pears, cholla, and agaves. Use against a hot wall, to cover a western window or around a pool where reflected heat is intense. Plant in groups to maximize the effect of the blooms.

Did You Know?
The flowers of this member of the bean family have barely noticeable petals; the extraordinary color comes from the dozens of stamens congested together. There are eight to twelve flowers clustered tightly together resulting in the characteristic puffball look.

Barberry
Berberis species

When, Where, and How to Plant
Plant in fall or spring in low elevation zones; in spring as soon as the soil can be worked in high elevation zones. Plant in full or partial sun. Barberry grows in a wide range of soils from well-drained, fertile soil to rocky, native ones, but does poorly in heavy clay. Dig a hole three to four times wider than the container and just as deep. Add a thin layer of compost or mulch to the backfill. Set the plant in the hole slightly higher than the soil line. Fill the hole, pressing the soil gently to remove air pockets. Mulch the roots but do not allow mulch to touch the bark. Water thoroughly. Water every three to four days for two or three weeks, then water every seven to ten days for the first year.

Growing Tips
Apply slow-release or organic fertilizer in fall to young plants. Established plants need no supplemental fertilizer. Water established plants every two to three weeks in summer in intermediate or high elevation zones, every two weeks in low elevation zones. Rely on natural rainfall in winter in all zones unless the weather is exceptionally hot or dry.

Care
Barberries are naturally multitrunked but can be pruned to a small tree by removing the lowest three or four branches each spring. Avoid removing more than a quarter of the plant in any year. Prune to remove dead or winter-damaged wood in early spring. When grown as a shrub, barberry has a beautiful, natural symmetry and rarely needs pruning for shape. Pests and disease are not a problem.

Companion Planting and Design
Use barberry to form an informal hedge, screen, or boundary planting. The dark green leaves make it a good background for perennial or annual plantings. When pruned to a small tree, use as a specimen in patios, courtyards, or small gardens.

Did You Know?
Berberis is an Arabic word for a species that occurs in the Middle East.

Barberry is the Arizona version of holly. Two species are prevalent in the state, Berberis fremontii *and* B. haematocarpa. B. fremontii *is the species most commonly offered in nurseries and has dark, blue-green, deeply lobed leaves with the characteristic spiky tips. The yellow flowers are profuse in the spring and are quickly followed by bright red berries that are just as quickly devoured by birds. This is a full, evergreen shrub that grows in all zones of the state.* B. haematocarpa *is not as cold tolerant and grows best below 4,500 feet in elevation in intermediate and low elevation zones. The two species are virtually indistinguishable. Agarito (B. trifoliolata) is another cold hardy barberry that grows into a short, erratically branched shrub. The fruit makes outstanding jelly.*

Bloom Period and Seasonal Color
Spring and early summer; bright yellow.

Mature Height × Spread
6 to 10 feet × 5 to 8 feet

Zones
All
Hardiness varies by the species.

Black Dalea
Dalea frutescens

Black dalea belongs to an extraordinary genus of shrubs and perennials that is unfamiliar to most gardeners outside the Southwest but which provides year-round beauty in low and intermediate gardens. Black dalea is a graceful shrub that blends easily with almost any garden style. The evergreen leaves are tiny, usually deep green although some have a silver sheen. Flowers erupt in spring and again in fall in a deep, indigo blue. While each flower is tiny, there is a host of them and the plant appears to change color overnight. Other shrubs in the genus include the mauve to purple flowered Dalea pulchra, *the winter-flowering, pink to purple* D. versicolor, *and the brilliant blue spring- and fall-flowering* D. bicolor.

Bloom Period and Seasonal Color
April and May, September to November; deep indigo to violet.

Mature Height × Spread
3 to 4 feet × 4 to 5 feet

Zones
1, 2, 3, 4
Hardy to 15 degrees Fahrenheit.

When, Where, and How to Plant
Plant this shrub in fall or spring in full or partial sun. Black dalea tolerates any well-drained soil from fertile, garden soil to rocky, native ones, but struggles in heavy clay. Dig a hole three to four times wider than the container and just as deep. Add a thin layer of compost or mulch to the backfill. Set the plant in the hole slightly higher than the soil line. Fill the hole, pressing the soil gently around the roots to remove air pockets. Mulch the roots but do not allow the mulch to touch the bark. Water thoroughly. Water every three to four days for two or three weeks, then water every seven to ten days for the first year.

Growing Tips
Black dalea needs no supplemental fertilizer, but annual applications of mulch help maintain nutrients in the soil. Water established plants every two to three weeks in summer, although it will tolerate more frequent watering when the weather is very hot or dry. Water once a month in winter or rely on natural rainfall.

Care
Older plants often become floppy and tend to die out in the middle. To avoid this, prune the plant severely every two to three years in early spring. Stems root readily if they lay on the ground and can be removed or relocated from November to February. Black dalea is not susceptible to pests or disease.

Companion Planting and Design
Black dalea looks spectacular when mixed with yellow flowering plants such as sundrops or Baja primrose. Plant in mixed perennial beds with globemallow, salvia, or ruellia. Black dalea blends well and offers a soft contrast to succulent plantings and provides vivid color for areas of the garden that receive minimal care. It is extremely heat tolerant and can be used against a hot wall or near a pool where reflected heat is intense.

Did You Know?
The genus was named in honor of the 18th century botanist, Thomas Dale. The epithet *frutescens* refers to the shrubby, almost woody, habit of the plant.

Blue Mist
Caryopteris × clandonensis

When, Where, and How to Plant
Plant in fall or spring in low elevation zones, in spring as soon as the soil can be worked in high elevation zones. Locate in full or partial sun. Blue mist grows best in well-drained, fertile soil but also tolerates rocky soil. Dig a hole three to four times wider than the container and just as deep. Add a thin layer of compost or mulch to the backfill. Set the plant in the hole slightly higher than the soil line. Fill the hole, pressing the soil gently to remove air pockets. Mulch the roots but do not allow mulch to touch the bark. Water thoroughly. Water every three to four days for two or three weeks, then water every seven to ten days for the first year.

Growing Tips
Apply slow-release or organic fertilizer annually in spring. In low elevation zones, water every four to seven days in summer, every two to three weeks in winter. In higher elevation zones, water every week in summer if weather is dry or hot; rely on natural rainfall in winter.

Care
Prune in early spring to remove winter-damaged stems or shape the plant. Prune spent blooms anytime. Not susceptible to pests and disease, although heavy, wet soil may encourage root rots.

Companion Planting and Design
Mix with perennials such as phlox, penstemon, or gaillardia to provide color and texture contrast. Plant blue mist generously to create a casual border or fill in a barren spot in a newly planted garden. The delicate flowers make a stunning color display in a mass planting. Butterflies are strongly attracted to this species so plant it generously near patios, seating areas, or pools where the butterflies, as well as the flowers, can be enjoyed.

Did You Know?
The name of the genus is derived from the Greek words *karyota,* meaning "a nut," and *pteron,* which means "wing." It refers to the shape of the fruit.

Blue mist is a light, airy plant that provides delicate beauty and long-lasting bloom in all zones of Arizona. The pale blue flowers are held high above the foliage in long, gracefully arching stalks throughout summer. The aromatic leaves are gray to white and the combination gives the entire plant an ethereal, almost translucent quality. Tolerant of conditions in all zones, it thrives in Arizona; blooming in spring and again in fall in the low elevation zones, and throughout summer in higher ones. There are many cultivars of this Asian native. 'Heavenly Blue' has dark blue flowers, 'Dark Knight' has dark blue flowers and whiter than usual foliage. The less common 'Worcester Gold' has light lavender flowers and yellowish leaves.

Bloom Period and Seasonal Color
Spring and summer; dark blue to lavender.

Mature Height × Spread
2 to 3 feet × 3 to 4 feet

Zones
All
Hardy to at least 10 degrees Fahrenheit, perhaps lower.

Creosote Bush
Larrea tridentata

Widely regarded as the toughest of all desert plants, creosote bush is the most numerous type of plant in the Mohave, Sonoran, and Chihuahuan Deserts. These plants have a different growth habit and character in each desert with Sonoran plants being among the handsomest. Creosote bush has an open, wispy form with small, hard, dark green leaves. The leaves are covered with a resinlike substance that is the source of the pungent aroma. The bright yellow flowers are profuse in spring and are followed by round fruits that are covered with a soft, white down. Creosote bush is often neglected in the haste to plant shrubs and other desert perennials, but nothing gives the garden the flavor and character of the desert like creosote bush. Gardeners that have mature specimens are extremely fortunate.

Bloom Period and Seasonal Color
Late spring, intermittent in summer; bright yellow.

Mature Height × Spread
4 to 12 feet × 4 to 12 feet

Zones
1, 2, 3, 4, 5
Hardy to 5 degrees Fahrenheit.

When, Where, and How to Plant
Plant in fall in low elevation zones; in spring in higher elevation zones. Site in full sun. Creosote bush grows best in rocky, native soil, but is also tolerant of other well-drained soils. Dig a hole three to four times wider than the container and just as deep. Add a thin layer of compost or mulch to the backfill. Set the plant in the hole slightly higher than the soil line. Fill the hole, pressing the soil gently to remove air pockets. Water thoroughly. Keep newly transplanted creosote from becoming too dry by watering, every three to four days for two or three weeks, then water every seven to ten days during hot weather.

Growing Tips
Creosote bush never needs supplemental fertilizer. Established plants are extraordinarily drought tolerant. However, it can take two to three years for a transplanted individual to match the drought tolerance of naturally growing shrubs. After the first year in the ground, water plants every two to three weeks in summer but rely on natural rainfall in winter.

Care
Pruning old creosote bushes is difficult, the wood is very hard, and the loose shape makes them easy to ruin. It is generally best to prune only dead wood. Some gardeners prune creosote bush nearly to the ground in order to have them fill out with lush, tender shoots. I admit to a strong aversion to this technique. While the plant survives just fine, it has lost all of the special character of creosote bush. Creosote bush resents overhead water, which browns and ultimately kills the leaves. Creosote bush is not susceptible to pests or disease.

Companion Planting and Design
Creosote bush casts an excellent light shade for small succulents or serves as a base for perennials such as globemallow, dicliptera, or penstemons. Use it to lend scale and soften large succulents such as saguaro and ocotillo. Creosote bush makes a good specimen or accent plant, particularly in a small garden.

Did You Know?
Experiments have shown that creosote bush is so drought tolerant it can live for three years without rainfall.

When, Where, and How to Plant

Plant in fall or early spring in full sun to maintain best form and bloom. Damianita grows in almost any type of soil from deep, well-drained, fertile soil to rocky, native soil. Dig a hole three to four times wider than the container and just as deep. Soil amendments and treatments are not necessary. Set the plant in the hole slightly higher than the soil line. Backfill, pressing the soil gently to remove air pockets. Mulch the root zones but do not allow mulch to touch the bark. Water thoroughly. Water every three to four days for two or three weeks, then water every seven to ten days for the first year.

Growing Tips

Damianita needs no supplemental fertilizer. In low elevation zones, water established plants weekly in summer; water monthly or less in winter. In intermediate and high elevation zones, water established plants every three weeks in summer, relying on natural rainfall in winter. In all zones, avoid extensive overhead watering.

Care

Prune to shape; remove dead wood or damaged stems in fall or early spring. Avoid hot weather pruning; it can cause sunburn of the stems. Remove spent flowering heads anytime to continue the bloom. Damianita is not susceptible to pests and disease.

Companion Planting and Design

In intermediate and high elevation zones, use damianita in hot, rocky locations and for erosion control on steep slopes. Plant generously to form informal hedges or borders. It is an excellent choice for areas with strong reflected heat—around pools, near driveways, walkways, or streets. Damianita mixes well both with summer-flowering perennials or succulents. In hot summer areas, it is advisable to provide afternoon shade in the summer for best results.

Did You Know?

The genus comes from the Greek words *chrysos*, meaning "gold," and *aktinos*, meaning a "ray," referring to the flowers. The designation *mexicana* refers to Mexico but was assigned to many plants that were found along the United States and Mexican border.

This relative newcomer to Arizona gardens is quickly making a real hit in Arizona gardens in all zones. Damianita is a dense shrub with small, dark green leaves that are evergreen and highly aromatic. The flowers have bright yellow or gold rays and yellow discs and are prolific on the plant. The flowers are held above the foliage on thin stalks and seem to coat the plant when it's in full bloom. This charming Chihuahuan shrub looks remarkably like the Arizona native turpentine bush (Ericameria laricifolia), which is a larger plant, actually a shrub, with similar flowers that bloom only in fall. Low elevation zone gardeners find that damianita blooms less vigorously in the hottest part of summer, but in intermediate and high elevation zones, it blooms all summer.

Bloom Period and Seasonal Color
April to September; yellow or gold.

Mature Height × Spread
1 to 2 feet × 2 to 3 feet

Zones
All
Hardy to 0 degrees Fahrenheit.

Emu Bush
Eremophila maculata

Emu bush is a member of an Australian genus of shrubs that are fairly new to low elevation zone Arizona gardeners. Emu bush is an effortless evergreen shrub that is virtually immune to heat, alkaline soils, and drought. As an added benefit, the emu bush blooms for a long time in the winter. The tubular, deep red flowers cluster thickly up and down the stem, rising from each leaf base. The blooms turn down, making it hard to see their spotted interiors. 'Pink Beauty' is a large shrub with pink or mauve blooms that is variously described as a cultivar or hybrid of this species. There are unnamed forms that bloom yellow. The selection 'Valentine' is compact with deep magenta blooms and dusky purple-tinged foliage.

Bloom Period and Seasonal Color
December to April; red, rose-pink, magenta, and yellow.

Mature Height × Spread
5 to 10 feet × 5 to 10 feet

Zones
1, 2, 3
Hardy to 25 degrees Fahrenheit, perhaps lower.

When, Where, and How to Plant
Plant in fall for best results although spring planting is possible. The emu bush grows in almost any soil from well-drained, fertile soil to rocky, native soil. However, it does poorly and is short-lived in heavy clay or soils that are consistently moist. Dig a hole three to four times wider than the container and just as deep. Add a thin layer of compost or mulch to the backfill. Set the plant in the hole slightly higher than the soil line. Fill the hole, pressing the soil gently to remove air pockets. Mulch the roots but do not allow mulch to touch the bark. Water thoroughly. Water every three to four days for two or three weeks, then water weekly through the first winter.

Growing Tips
Emu bush requires no supplemental fertilizer but annual applications of mulch help provide needed nutrients. Water established plants every two to three weeks in winter while they are growing and blooming, every month in summer.

Care
Prune in late summer to shape, reduce size, or remove dead or damaged wood. The emu bush has a complicated branching habit making it difficult to prune well. Remove shoots that grow horizontally or toward the ground and cut the branch to a junction well inside the bush. It is not susceptible to pests or disease.

Companion Planting and Design
The evergreen leaves of the emu bush make it an excellent background plant for perennial or annual plantings. Mix with other shrubs such as jojoba, Arizona rosewood, and Texas sage to create an informal hedge, visual screen, or boundary planting. Emu bush is drought tolerant enough to grow in areas that receive minimal care. Plant emu bush to protect a hot wall, or for added color around pools, patios, or other areas where reflected heat is intense.

Did You Know?
The word *eremophila* is derived from the Greek *eremia*, meaning "desert," and *phileo*, meaning "to love." It is a most fitting name for this most xeric genus. The epithet *maculata* refers to the spotted petals.

Fire Bush
Hamelia patens

When, Where, and How to Plant
Plant in spring after all danger of frost is past. Place in full or partial sun in deep, well-drained, fertile soil. Fire bush is tolerant of very alkaline soils. Dig a hole three to four times wider than the container and just as deep. Add a generous layer of compost or mulch to the backfill. Set the plant in the hole slightly higher than the soil line. Fill the hole, pressing the soil gently around the roots to remove air pockets. Mulch the roots but do not allow mulch to touch the bark. Water thoroughly. Water every three to four days for two or three weeks or until the plant is established.

Growing Tips
Apply slow-release or organic fertilizer annually in spring. Keep roots well mulched in summer to prevent the soil from drying out too quickly. Water weekly in summer, more frequently if it is very hot or dry. Water every two to three weeks in winter.

Care
Prune dead or winter-damaged wood in early spring just as the leaves emerge. Prune lightly in summer to shape or remove damaged wood. Fire bush is not susceptible to pests or disease.

Companion Planting and Design
Mix fire bush with summer-flowering perennials and shrubs such as lantana, hibiscus, red bird of paradise, and salvias. Fire bush can be pruned to a small tree shape and used as specimen or focal point for patios, courtyards, or seating areas. Use fire bush near pools or against hot walls where reflected heat is intense. Fire bush grows well in large containers. Hummingbirds visit the flowers all summer and the fruit attracts many birds in fall.

Did You Know?
The genus was named to honor the French botanist and horticultural writer, Henri Louis du Hamel du Monceau, who died in 1781. The epithet means "spreading" and refers to the shrubby habit of the plant.

The first time I saw fire bush, I fell completely under its spell. Although briefly deciduous, fire bush recovers quickly and after setting a quick flush of bright spring growth, the flower buds begin to emerge. Fire bush is a true heat seeker; the thin, orange buds arranged in clusters at the ends of the branches stay closed until the weather turns really hot in late May or early June. Then the flowers begin to burst open and remain like orange sparklers on the plant for the rest of the summer. They are followed in the fall by round, black fruits that are devoured by birds. Then, as the weather cools, the soft, green leaves of summer gradually turn a deep, burnished red for fall.

Other Common Name
Scarlet bush

Bloom Period and Seasonal Color
May to November, red-orange; foliage turns burnt orange November to January.

Mature Height × Spread
3 to 10 feet × 3 to 10 feet

Zones
1, 2, 3
Hardy to 25 degrees Fahrenheit, root hardy to about 20 degrees Fahrenheit.

Firethorn
Pyracantha species

Most gardeners admire firethorn for its fast growth, ease of culture, and the brilliant red to orange cool-season fruit. Pyracantha is most successful in the intermediate and high elevation zones of the state, although many low elevation zone gardeners try it. These shrubs with their complicated branching generally have small, glossy evergreen leaves. The fragrant white flowers bloom in spring and summer. But the real show are the huge falls of red or orange fruit in autumn. Pyracantha coccinea is the most cold hardy species and has orange fruit. 'Lalandei' is tall and upright while 'Lowboy' is a dwarf form. P. fortuneana is a vigorous species with bright red berries. 'Graberi' is tall with glossy, dark green leaves while 'Tiny Tim' is a dwarf form and 'Walderi' spreads as a ground cover.

Bloom Period and Seasonal Color
Spring and summer; white.

Mature Height × Spread
2 to 15 feet × 4 to 6 feet

Zones
All
Hardy to 10 degrees Fahrenheit, but *P. coccinea* is hardy to 0 degrees Fahrenheit.

When, Where, and How to Plant
In low elevation zones, plant in fall; spring plantings may have trouble becoming well established before it gets hot. In high elevation zones, plant in spring as soon as the soil can be worked. Locate in full or partial sun. Pyracantha grows best in well-drained, fertile soil. Dig a hole three to four times wider than the container and just as deep. Add a thin layer of compost or mulch to the backfill. Set the plant in the hole slightly higher than the soil line. Fill the hole, pressing the soil gently to remove air pockets. Mulch the roots but do not allow mulch to touch the bark. Water thoroughly. Water every three to four days for two or three weeks, then water every seven to ten days for the first year.

Growing Tips
Pyracantha needs no supplemental fertilizer, but chelated iron applications in spring and summer help prevent iron chlorosis. Water established plants deeply every two to three weeks in summer; every month or two in winter.

Care
Prune in late winter or early spring to remove dead or damaged wood or reduce size. Pinch the tips throughout the growing season to maintain tight form and control size but be aware that plants bloom on two-year-old wood so maintain enough for bloom and fruit. Pyracantha is susceptible to fire blight—a bacterial infection known for the sudden wilting and death of a branch. Prune out infected branches to control spread; there is no prevention or cure.

Companion Planting and Design
Mix with other shrubs to form an informal hedge or border. Pyracantha is excellent when planted against a wall or building as an espalier or with its natural form. The deep green leaves make this a good choice for a background plant. Dwarf forms are well suited for growing in large containers.

Did You Know?
The word pyracantha comes from the Greek *pyr*, meaning "fire," and *akantha*, meaning "thorn." The common name refers both to its thorny nature and the blazing red of the fruit.

Flame Anisacanthus
Anisacanthus quadrifidus var. *wrightii*

When, Where, and How to Plant
Plant in spring in full or partial sun either in well-drained, fertile soil or rocky, native soil. Dig a hole three to four times wider than the container and just as deep. Add a thin layer of compost or mulch to the backfill. Set the plant in the hole slightly higher than the soil line. Fill the hole, pressing the soil gently to remove air pockets. Mulch the roots but do not allow mulch to touch the bark. Water thoroughly. Water every three to four days for two or three weeks, then water every seven to ten days for the first year.

Growing Tips
Flame anisacanthus needs no supplemental fertilizer but mulching the roots keeps soil from drying out in summer as well as protects roots in winter; mulch also helps provide any needed nutrients. Water established plants weekly in summer in the low elevation zones, less in intermediate or high elevation zones. Rely on natural rainfall in winter.

Care
Prune just as leaves emerge to remove dead or damaged stems and to shape. Every two or three years prune flame anisacanthus to within a foot or two of the ground to reinvigorate the plant. Prune lightly for up to two months after leaves emerge to shape; later pruning sacrifices bloom. Flame anisacanthus is not susceptible to pests or disease.

Companion Planting and Design
Use flame anisacanthus in mixed perennial plantings with other summer-flowering perennials such as salvia, lantana, and California fuschia. It mixes well with shrubs such as yellowbells and little-leaf cordia. Plant generously for spectacular, long-season blooming displays near patios, pools, or seating areas. Locate where you can enjoy the continuous visits by hummingbirds.

Did You Know?
Individual flowers do not remain on the plant for the five or six months the plant blooms, new ones replace them every few weeks. To remove old blooms, give the plant a vigorous shaking and they will fall away cleanly.

I find orange a difficult color to use well in a garden. It is garish, demanding, and blends poorly with other colors. But I would never want to be without the bright orange flowers of flame anisacanthus. This 3-foot tall, deciduous shrub has light green, lance-shaped leaves that are some of the last to arrive in spring. But as the heat intensifies, so does this plant. Throughout summer, it is ablaze with brilliant orange tubular flowers whose tips flare at the end like a star. The color of the flowers seems to shift over the season, beginning as a bright, clear orange and softening to a deep russet in fall. Hummingbirds love it for its nectar; I love it for its toughness and long, brilliant bloom.

Bloom Period and Seasonal Color
May to November; orange to red-orange.

Mature Height × Spread
3 to 4 feet × 3 to 4 feet

Zones
1, 2, 3, 4, 5
Hardy to 5 degrees Fahrenheit.

Four-wing Saltbush
Atriplex canescens

Shrubs have many tasks in the garden—providing a screen to hide ugly areas, forming the backdrop for colorful plantings, or creating the anchor that visually holds an area together. One of the finest choices for any of these uses is four-wing saltbush. A semievergreen shrub with dense, grey-green leaves, the four-wing saltbush grows best in the intermediate elevation zones of the state. The large, tan, winged pods stay on the plant a long time and are excellent for dried arrangements. The related quail bush (Atriplex lentiformis) is much larger, and while nearly as cold hardy, it is a better choice in the heat of the low elevation zones. The amazingly xeric desert holly (A. hymenelytra) is a small shrub from the lower Colorado River area of Arizona with holly-shaped ghostly white leaves.

Other Common Name
Chamiso

Bloom Period and Seasonal Color
March to September; inconspicuous greenish white.

Mature Height × Spread
4 to 8 feet × 5 to 8 feet

Zones
1, 2, 3, 4, 5
Hardy to 5 degrees Fahrenheit and perhaps lower.

When, Where, and How to Plant
Plant in fall or spring in low elevation zones; in spring as soon as the soil can be worked in higher elevation zones. Site in full or partial sun. Four-wing saltbush tolerates almost any well-drained soil, including ones that are salty, very alkaline, or rocky. Dig a hole three to four times wider than the container and just as deep. Soil amendments are not necessary. Set the plant in the hole slightly higher than the soil line. Fill the hole, pressing the soil gently around the roots to remove air pockets. Mulch the roots but do not allow mulch to touch the bark. Water thoroughly. Water every three to four days for two or three weeks, then water every seven to ten days for the first year.

Growing Tips
Four-wing saltbush needs no supplemental fertilizer. All saltbushes grow quickly and become very large with generous watering. Plan watering schedules to achieve the size of plant that is desired. Water established plants monthly in summer and rely on natural rainfall in winter.

Care
Prune to remove unwanted branches; clear out dead, damaged stems in late winter. Plants have excellent natural form and rarely need pruning for shape. Four-wing saltbush is not susceptible to pests or disease.

Companion Planting and Design
Four-wing saltbush is effective as a screen or boundary planting where supplemental irrigation is difficult. It mixes well with other shrubs such as Texas sage, sugarbush, or hopbush to create an informal hedge or background for more colorful perennial or annual plantings. This plant is extremely valuable to a wide range of birds for cover, food, and nesting sites. Four-wing saltbush is resistant to fire and is useful in areas where fires are common.

Did You Know?
The genus comes from the Greek, *aka*, which is the name for the common orache (*Atriplex hortensis*). The epithet *canescens* refers to the fine hairs covering the leaves, which is why the leaves appear white.

Greythorn
Ziziphus obtusifolia

When, Where, and How to Plant
Plant in fall or early spring in full sun. Site in almost any well-drained soil; greythorn does particularly well in rocky, native soil but does not tolerate heavy clay or soils with poor drainage. Dig a hole three to four times wider than the container and just as deep. Soil amendments and treatments are not necessary. Set the plant in the hole slightly higher than the original soil line. Fill the hole, pressing the soil gently to remove air pockets. Water thoroughly. Water every three or four days for two or three weeks, then water every week for the first summer.

Growing Tips
Greythorn does not require supplemental fertilizer. Water established plants every three to four weeks in summer, although mature plants may be grown without supplemental watering. Rely on natural rainfall in winter unless the weather is exceptionally hot or dry.

Care
Pruning is a terrible chore with this thorny plant. Prevention is the best defense. Site the plant well away from driveways, walkways, or seating areas so it can be left to grow undisturbed. If pruning is necessary, use long-handled pruners and leather gloves, cutting away only as much as necessary. Prune in summer or early fall. Greythorn is not susceptible to pest or disease.

Companion Planting and Design
Mix with other shrubs such as hopbush, jojoba, or unpruned mesquites to form a boundary planting or an impenetrable hedge. They are particularly effective when planted to prevent trespass. Use greythorn as a backdrop to greener and more colorful shrubs or perennial plantings. Plant anywhere that reflected heat is intense or in areas of the garden that receive minimal care. Birds love the thorny branches for roosting or nesting, and they will devour the fruit.

Did You Know?
The Native Americans of southern Arizona treated sore eyes with a wash made from the roots. The roots have also been used as a substitute for soap.

When we moved into our present home, there was a large greythorn in the backyard on whose behalf I resisted all efforts to remove it. This grey, thorny jungle gym of a plant intrigues and delights me. Despite its thorns that also have thorns of their own, it is a beautiful, bright shrub for low and intermediate gardens. The small, gray-green leaves drop off during summer leaving the gray-white to bluish thorny stems exposed. Birds delight in it for cover and nesting sites, and they will devour the tiny black berries. Bitter condalia (Condalia globosa) is a closely related plant that has small leaves and tangled branches similar to greythorn. The barely visible flowers of this low elevation zone species fill the garden in early spring with their rich, sweet aroma.

Bloom Period and Seasonal Color
Late spring; inconspicuous white.

Mature Height × Spread
6 to 12 feet × 6 to 8 feet

Zones
1, 2, 3, 4
Hardy to 15 degrees Fahrenheit.

Guajillo
Acacia berlandieri

Guajillo is an open, rounded shrub from the Chihuahuan Desert whose delicate, airy appearance belies its extreme heat and drought tolerance. It is a quiet shrub, fading into the background most of the time. The compound light green leaves are made up of dozens of tiny leaflets, similar to mimosas, and give guajillo the appearance of floating away from the ground. But in late spring, it is transformed from a shy, green bush to a vibrant, white cloud. The creamy white, puffball-like flowers are sweetly fragrant and burst into bloom all at once in the late spring. Guajillo is evergreen in low elevation zones and briefly deciduous where winters have regular frosts. Plants are usually grown as a wide, rounded shrub but are easily trained to a small tree.

Bloom Period and Seasonal Color
April or May; creamy white puffballs.

Mature Height × Spread
10 to 15 × 10 to 15 feet

Zones
1, 2, 3, 4
Hardy to 20 degrees Fahrenheit.

When, Where, and How to Plant
Plant in fall for best results, but spring plantings may also be successful. Guajillo grows well in full or partial sun and tolerates any well-drained soil including rocky, native ones. Dig a hole three to four times wider than the container and just as deep. Add a thin layer of compost or mulch to the backfill. Set the plant in the hole slightly higher than the soil line. Fill the hole, pressing the soil gently to remove air pockets. Mulch the roots but do not allow mulch to touch the bark. Water thoroughly. Water every three to four days for two or three weeks, then water every seven to ten days for the first year.

Growing Tips
Guajillo requires no supplemental fertilizer. Water established plants every three to four weeks in summer; every month or two in winter.

Care
Prune guajillo in early spring to remove dead or damaged limbs. Guajillo may be trained into a small tree by removing the lowest two or three limbs each spring. Do not remove more than a quarter of the plant in any year. Guajillo is susceptible to infections when pruned in winter, and sunburn and stress when pruned in summer. It is not susceptible to pests or disease.

Companion Planting and Design
Mix guajillo with other drought-tolerant shrubs such as Texas ranger, hopbush, or rosewood to form an informal hedge or screen. Its delicate appearance combined with great heat tolerance makes it particularly useful against hot walls or around pools. When trained as a tree, it makes a fine focal plant for a small patio or courtyard. Guajillo can be used in any area of the garden that will receive minimal care.

Did You Know?
This plant, and many more, carries the name of the man widely regarded as the Father of Texas botany. He was Jean Louis Berlandier—a French-Swiss physician and avid student of Texas and Mexican plants in the first half of the 19th century.

When, Where, and How to Plant

Plant hibiscus after all danger of frost is past. Like many tropical species, it will tolerate being planted in summer. Hibiscus grows best in deep, well-drained, fertile soil that does not dry out quickly. Dig a hole three to four times wider than the container and just as deep. Add a thin layer of compost or mulch to the backfill. Set the plant in the hole slightly higher than the soil line. Fill the hole, pressing the soil gently to remove air pockets. Mulch the roots but do not allow mulch to touch the bark. Water thoroughly. Water every three to four days for two or three weeks, then water every four or five days.

Growing Tips

Apply slow-release or organic fertilizer two or three times during the growing season. Mulch the roots heavily during summer to prevent the soil from drying out. Water every four or five days in summer, every two to three weeks in winter.

Care

Hibiscus shrubs are semidormant in winter but rarely lose all their leaves. Prune to remove winter-damaged stems, dead wood, and to reinvigorate the plant once all danger of frost is past. Hibiscus leaves yellow during summer, both from heat damage and too infrequent or shallow watering. Maintain steady deep watering, keep roots well mulched, and provide balanced fertilizer for best results. Hibiscus is not susceptible to pests or disease.

Companion Planting and Design

Hibiscus are stunning specimen or focal plants for courtyards, patios, or small gardens. Larger varieties may be pruned to a small tree. The deep green leaves provide a good background for colorful summer perennials and shrubs such as red bird of paradise, lantana, and yellowbells. Hibiscus shrubs are extremely heat tolerant and can be used where reflected heat is intense. They grow well in containers, and this is one way to enjoy their long season of bloom in cold-winter areas.

Did You Know?

Hibiscus bloom for months, often prolifically, but each flower is open for one day only.

This tropical evergreen shrub from Asia is an icon of tropical gardens and, remarkably, prospers in many low elevation zone gardens. The wide, green leaves are so thick it makes an excellent screen. The flowers, which are large and open with paper-thin petals, occur in a bewildering range of colors and forms throughout summer. Almost all plants are hybrid forms and rarely set seed. There are countless selections and forms, but in the desert heat, the classic red shrub 'Brilliant' (also called 'San Diego Red'), 'White Wings', which has narrow white flowers with a red eye, and the 'Itsy Bitsy' selections are among the most reliable. Hibiscus schizopetalus, with its lacy petals that turn inward and look like a lantern, is uncommon but performs well.

Bloom Period and Seasonal Color

May to November; red, pink, yellow, orange, peach, and white.

Mature Height × Spread

8 to 15 feet × 5 to 8 feet

Zones

1, 2, 3
Hardy to 30 degrees Fahrenheit.

Hopbush

Dodonaea viscosa

The enormous natural distribution of hopbush—it is found worldwide—has given rise to a number of distinctive forms. There is a dark green, narrow-leafed form that is upright, evergreen, and very cold hardy. A broad leaf, dark green form from northern Mexico is somewhat cold tender. The popular purple leaf form, usually sold as 'Purpurea', has bronze to purple leaves and is the least cold hardy. The two- to four-winged seedpods can also vary from tiny and tan to showy and bright red to reddish brown. This striking evergreen shrub holds up well to the alkaline soils, high heat, and dry conditions of the low and intermediate elevation zones as well as the cold winters of the high elevation zones.

Bloom Period and Seasonal Color
Spring; inconspicuous cream or yellowish.

Mature Height × Spread
12 to 15 feet × 10 to 12 feet

Zones
1, 2, 3, 4
Hardy to 15 degrees Fahrenheit.

When, Where, and How to Plant
Plant in fall or spring in low elevation zones, in spring as soon as the soil can be worked in high elevation zones. Locate in full or partial sun. Hopbush tolerates any well-drained soil from fertile, garden soil to rocky, native ones. Dig a hole three to four times wider than the container and just as deep. Add a thin layer of compost or mulch to the backfill. Set the plant in the hole slightly higher than the soil line. Fill the hole, pressing the soil gently to remove air pockets. Mulch the roots but do not allow mulch to touch the bark. Water thoroughly. Water every three to four days for two or three weeks, then water every seven to ten days for the first year.

Growing Tips
Hopbush requires no supplemental fertilizer. In the low and intermediate elevation zones, water established plants every two weeks in summer, once a month in winter, although plants survive on less. In high elevation zones, water monthly in summer unless the weather is exceptionally hot or dry; rely on natural rainfall in winter.

Care
Hopbush has excellent natural form and seldom requires pruning to shape. Prune to reduce size or remove dead or damaged wood in spring. Hopbush becomes chlorotic when watered too shallowly, or if drainage is poor. It is not susceptible to pests or diseases.

Companion Planting and Design
Hopbush makes an excellent evergreen hedge, screen, or border plant either singly or mixed with other shrubs such as jojoba, Arizona rosewood, or sugarbush. Plant hopbush against a southern or western wall, near a pool, or other areas with high-reflected heat. With its deep evergreen foliage, hopbush is particularly useful as a backdrop for colorful perennial or annual plantings.

Did You Know?
The winged fruit are reminiscent of the true hops from which beer is made, hence the common name. Hopbush fruit has even occasionally been used to make beer.

When, Where, and How to Plant

For best results plant in fall in the low elevation zones, in spring or summer in higher elevation zones. Jojoba grows to its best form in full sun and tolerates a wide variety of soils as long as they are very well drained, including rocky, native ones. Dig a hole three to four times wider than the container and just as deep. Add a thin layer of compost or mulch to the backfill. Set the plant in the hole slightly higher than the soil line. Fill the hole, pressing the soil gently to remove air pockets. Mulch the roots but do not allow mulch to touch the bark. Water thoroughly. Water every three to four days for two or three weeks, then water every seven to ten days for the first year.

Growing Tips

Jojoba requires no supplemental fertilizer. Water established plants every two to three weeks in summer, once every other month in winter. In intermediate elevation zones and the higher parts of Zone 3, established jojoba thrives on natural rainfall alone.

Care

Jojoba naturally has a beautiful, rounded form and rarely needs pruning to shape. Prune in warm weather to remove dead or damaged branches. Jojoba responds well to formal pruning, if desired. It is not susceptible to pests and disease.

Companion Planting and Design

Jojoba is an excellent choice for an evergreen hedge or screen either alone or mixed with other shrubs such as Texas sage, Arizona rosewood, or sugarbush. The dusky leaves make a nice background for colorful perennial or annual plantings. Jojoba may be planted against a hot wall or building, near a pool, or anywhere that reflected heat is intense. It is particularly useful for areas of the garden that do not receive routine care.

Did You Know?

Early settlers in Arizona missed coffee, which was expensive and difficult to obtain. They mixed the roasted nuts of jojoba with egg yolks, sugar, and milk as a substitute.

There is an adage about desert plants that they are evaders, escapers, or endurers. Evaders are generally annuals arising only when conditions are cool and wet. Escapers are generally those that lose their leaves or go dormant when it is hot and dry. But the endurers are the real champions of desert life; they just stand out there and take all the heat and dryness. Jojoba is a classic endurer. The dusky, gray-green leaves are coated with a waxy substance and turn inward to protect the leaf's surface from the sun. Plants are evergreen and dense with a natural rounded shape. Although the flowers are inconspicuous, the fruit on the female plants is a large, dark brown nut that is edible and renowned for its oil.

Bloom Period and Seasonal Color
December to July; yellowish to white.

Mature Height × Spread
6 to 10 feet × 6 to 8 feet

Zones
1, 2, 3, 4
Hardy to 15 degrees Fahrenheit.

Little-leaf Cordia
Cordia parvifolia

White is so delightful in the summer; just looking at it makes you feel cooler. One my favorite white-flowered, summer-blooming shrubs is little-leaf cordia. The shrub is well named, as the leaves are small, crinkled, and smoky gray-green. The dark branches make fanciful turns and twists to give the plant a complicated, dense appearance. The small, paper-thin white flowers form in clusters at the ends of branches and are prolific throughout the entire warm season. The delicate beauty of the flowers entirely belies the rugged heat and drought tolerance of this shrub. Texas olive (Cordia boissieri) is a taller shrub with large, olive-green leaves and large clusters of white flowers with yellow throats. Texas olive is much less tolerant of salty soil or water than little-leaf cordia and blooms in spring and fall.

Bloom Period and Seasonal Color
February to November; pure white.

Mature Height × Spread
4 to 8 feet × 4 to 10 feet

Zones
1, 2, 3, 4
Hardy to 18 degrees Fahrenheit.

When, Where, and How to Plant
Plant in fall or spring in full sun. Little-leaf cordia tolerates any well-drained soil from fertile, garden soil to rocky, native ones, but does poorly in heavy clay. Dig a hole three to four times wider than the container and just as deep. Add a thin layer of compost or mulch to the backfill. Set the plant in the hole slightly higher than the soil line. Fill the hole, pressing the soil gently to remove air pockets. Mulch the roots but do not allow mulch to touch the bark. Water thoroughly. Water every three to four days for two or three weeks, then water every seven to ten days for the first summer.

Growing Tips
Little-leaf cordia requires no supplemental fertilizer but maintaining mulch around the roots in summer keeps soil from drying out too quickly and provides all needed nutrients. Water established plants every two to three weeks in summer, once a month or less in winter. Water much less frequently in intermediate elevation zones.

Care
Little-leaf cordia has a beautiful natural form; it is rarely necessary to prune for shape. This shrub has a complicated, twisted branching habit that makes it challenging to prune well. Prune dead or damaged wood in spring. Little-leaf cordia drops its leaves in response to severe drought stress or exceptionally cold weather, but recovers quickly. It is not susceptible to pests or disease.

Companion Planting and Design
Little-leaf cordia makes an impressive hedge or screen when planted generously. It can be used mixed with other shrubs such as jojoba, sugarbush, Texas sage, or Arizona rosewood to create an informal hedge or boundary planting. The relentless bloom through the summer makes it a splendid specimen or accent plant, particularly around small patios, courtyards, or seating areas. Use it against hot walls, near a pool, or other areas where reflected heat is intense.

Did You Know?
Little-leaf cordia was named in honor of Euricius Cordus and his son Valerius, 16th century botanists and pharmacists.

Lucky Nut
Thevetia peruviana

When, Where, and How to Plant
Plant in spring after all danger of frost is past in deep, well-drained, fertile soil. Lucky nut tolerates rocky, native soil if given adequate water. Site in full or partial sun. Dig a hole three to four times wider than the container and just as deep. Add a generous layer of compost or mulch to the backfill. Set the plant in the hole slightly higher than the soil line. Fill the hole, pressing the soil gently to remove air pockets. Mulch the roots but do not allow mulch to touch the bark. Water thoroughly. Water every three to four days for two or three weeks, then water every seven to ten days for the first summer.

Growing Tips
Lucky nut requires no supplemental fertilizer. It is very drought tolerant when established, but it blooms better and is more vigorous when watered every week to ten days in summer. Water every month or less in winter.

Care
Lucky nut has excellent natural form and does not need pruning for shape. It may be pruned to a small tree by removing the lowest three or four branches each year but be careful not to take more than a quarter of the plant in any year. Prune to remove winter-damaged limbs or dead wood in late spring. Lucky nut is not susceptible to pests or disease.

Companion Planting and Design
Mix lucky nut with other summer-flowering shrubs such as fire bush, hibiscus, or yellowbells. It also provides a colorful background for perennial plantings. When it's trained to a small tree, use it as specimen or accent plant in small patios or courtyards. Lucky nut has tremendous heat tolerance and can be planted against hot walls, near a pool, or anywhere where reflected heat is intense.

Did You Know?
The common name derives from the odd-shaped fruit, which looks like a flattened three corner hat. But I have no idea why it's lucky.

Lucky nut is in the same family as the familiar oleander and is often sold by the confusing name, yellow oleander. This subtropical shrub offers great heat tolerance, a delightfully exotic feel, and long-lasting summer bloom to low elevation zone gardens. Lucky nut is a large, openly branched shrub with long, thin, light green leaves. The flowers are bright yellow with petals that are twisted then folded inward like an origami piece. There is a white color form that looks especially cooling in the summer heat, and a charming form with pastel apricot colored flowers. The more cold tender Thevetia thevetioides is a larger plant, with long, thin, dark green leaves and clear yellow flowers, that is up to twice the size of lucky nut.

Bloom Period and Seasonal Color
From May to October; yellow, apricot, or white.

Mature Height × Spread
8 to 25 feet × 8 to 20 feet

Zones
1, 2, 3
Hardy to 30 degrees Fahrenheit.

Mexican Buckeye

Ungnadia speciosa

Mexican buckeye was common where I grew up, and a handsome one came up at the back fence of my parents' home. Every spring, the rich, dark brown branches erupted with hundreds of dark, rosy pink flowers. It didn't last long, but it was a glorious sight. The leaves are large, dark green, and shaped like a pointed hand. In fall, they turn a pale yellow. This is one of the few shrubs for low elevation zone gardens that has blooms on bare branches before the leaves emerge. The jet black seeds are held in rounded capsules that make excellent additions to dried arrangements. Mexican buckeye is a 4- to 5-foot multi-branched shrub in the desert and is generally grown as a small tree or large shrub.

Bloom Period and Seasonal Color
Spring; rosy pink, leaves yellow in fall.

Mature Height × Spread
8 to 12 feet × 8 to 12 feet

Zones
1, 2, 3, 4, 5
Hardy to 5 degrees Fahrenheit.

When, Where, and How to Plant
Plant in fall or spring in low elevation zones; in spring while it's still deciduous in intermediate elevation zones. Place in an area with only morning sun or in partial sun in the desert, but plant in full sun or partial sun in the intermediate elevation zones. Mexican buckeye grows well in almost any type of soil as long as the soil is very well drained. Dig a hole three to four times wider than the container and just as deep. Add a thin layer of compost or mulch to the backfill. Set the plant in the hole slightly higher than the soil line. Fill the hole, pressing the soil gently to remove air pockets. Mulch the roots but do not allow mulch to touch the bark. Water thoroughly. Water every three to four days for two or three weeks, then water every seven to ten days for the first year.

Growing Tips
Apply slow-release or organic fertilizer annually in spring, especially to plants growing in highly alkaline soils. Water established plants weekly in summer in low elevation zones; every two weeks in intermediate elevation zones. In winter, water occasionally in low elevation zones if the weather is exceptionally hot or dry; otherwise, rely on natural rainfall.

Care
Mexican buckeye can be trained to a small tree by removing three or four of the lowest branches each year. Do not remove over a quarter of the plant in any year. Prune in early spring while the plant is still dormant to remove damaged or dead wood. Mexican buckeye is not susceptible to pests or disease.

Companion Planting and Design
Mexican buckeye mixes well with other shrubs such as Texas sage, Baja fairyduster, or black dalea to create an informal hedge or border. When trained as a small tree, Mexican buckeye makes a lovely specimen or focal plant in a small patio or courtyard.

Did You Know?
Mexican buckeye isn't a buckeye at all, but the cupped pods that hold the large black seeds resemble the midwestern plant of the same name.

Oleander

Nerium oleander

When, Where, and How to Plant

Plant in spring after all danger of frost is past, in full sun. Oleander tolerates almost any type of soil from rocky, native soil to well-drained fertile soil. Dig a hole three to four times wider than the container and just as deep. Set the plant in the hole slightly higher than the soil line. Fill the hole, pressing the soil gently to remove air pockets. Mulch the roots but do not allow mulch to touch the bark. Water thoroughly. Water every three to four days for two or three weeks, then water every seven to ten days for the first summer.

Growing Tips

Oleander does not need supplemental fertilizer. The amount of water supplied greatly determines its size. Water every two to three weeks in summer when the plant is young; every month or less once it's mature. Rely on natural rainfall in winter.

Care

Prune in summer to shape, reduce, and remove dead or damaged wood. Prune with care; all parts of the plant are poisonous when ingested. Protect eyes and skin and do not burn or compost the leaves and stems. The brown swelling on the stem, indicative of oleander gall, is rarely more than a cosmetic problem. Oleander blight is a devastating disease that kills mature plants quickly and is transmitted by the glassy-winged sharpshooter, but it has not yet been found in Arizona. Otherwise, oleander is not susceptible to pests or disease.

Companion Planting and Design

Use as a hedge or screen or mix with other shrubs for a background for perennial or annual plantings. Single plants make excellent focal or specimen plants. Oleander is excellent near pools or against hot walls where reflected heat is intense. Smaller varieties grow well in large containers.

Did You Know?

Oleander is known to have grown in Roman gardens during the reign of Cicero. Oleander is depicted on murals from Pompeii. It was cultivated in ancient Greece and China and there are references to it in the Bible and the Talmud.

To some, oleander is a spectacular summer-flowering shrub; to others it is a monstrous pariah, indicative of all that is wrong in desert gardens. This native of the North African deserts is one of the most heat and drought tolerant shrubs for the low elevation zones. It has, however, been hideously overused—planted where too much water has caused it to grow into a towering giant that smothers small lots. When treated with care, it provides tantalizing summer flowers during the hottest time of the year with a durability to desert conditions that is unrivaled. There are numerous long, dark green leaves on each stem making the plant dense and impenetrable. There are hundreds of varieties, and plants vary greatly in size and flower color. Many varieties are sweetly fragrant.

Bloom Period and Seasonal Color

May to October; white, pink, red, mauve, and yellow.

Mature Height × Spread

3 to 30 feet × 3 to 12 feet

Zones

1, 2, 3
Hardiness depends on variety, but most are root hardy to 20 degrees Fahrenheit.

Red Bird of Paradise
Caesalpinia pulcherrima

On my first visit to Arizona, I was stunned by the brilliant flowers of red bird of paradise that I saw lining the roadways in and around Phoenix. This summer-blooming, subtropical shrub is used extensively in low elevation zones for its extravagant, showy flowers and stupendous heat tolerance. Red bird of paradise is a sparsely branched shrub with large, light green, feathery compound leaves. The inch-wide flowers have slightly ruffled petals that are a deep orange with varying amounts of yellow. The flowers are collected into loose pyramids held high above the foliage. Although these plants lose most of their leaves in winter, they recover quickly and even small plants bloom in their first year in the ground. There are forms that have pure yellow flowers.

Bloom Period and Seasonal Color
March to October, intermittently at other times; red, orange, and yellow.

Mature Height × Spread
4 to 10 feet × 4 to 6 feet

Zones
1, 2, 3
Hardy to 28 degrees Fahrenheit.

When, Where, and How to Plant
Plant in full sun in spring after all danger of frost is past. Red bird of paradise grows in any well-drained soil including rocky, native soil, and can even be found growing in lawns. Dig a hole three to four times wider than the container and just as deep. Add a generous layer of compost or mulch to the backfill. Set the plant in the hole slightly higher than the soil line. Fill the hole, pressing the soil gently to remove air pockets. Mulch the roots but do not allow mulch to touch the bark. Water thoroughly. Water every three to four days for two or three weeks, then water four or five days for the first summer.

Growing Tips
Apply slow-release or organic fertilizer annually in spring. Water established plants every four to seven days in summer, more frequently if the weather is very hot or dry. Water every month in winter or rely on natural rainfall.

Care
Once all danger of frost is past, prune to reinvigorate and remove winter-damaged or dead wood. Cut plants to within a foot or two of the ground. Remove spent flowering stalks anytime. Red bird of paradise is not susceptible to pests or disease, although plants may become chlorotic when grown in heavy or poorly drained soils.

Companion Planting and Design
Plant red bird of paradise in groups, as an informal hedge, or boundary planting for a spectacular summer show. Use it against southern or western walls, in hot barren spots, or around pools where reflected heat is intense. Red bird of paradise is excellent in large containers. Plant it with summer-flowering perennials and shrubs such as lantana, salvia, and oleander.

Did You Know?
There are three divisions of the immense bean family—the ones that bloom like peas with irregular petals that look like a bonnet, the ones that bloom like calliandra and acacia with crowded stamens that form a puffball, and the ones that bloom like this species with open, almost flat petals.

Rosemary

Rosmarinus officinalis

When, Where, and How to Plant

Plant in fall in low elevation zones; in spring as soon as the soil can be worked in high elevation zones. Locate plants in full sun even in the low elevation zones. Rosemary grows best in rocky, alkaline soil and can fail entirely in heavy, clay soil. Dig a hole three to four times wider than the container and just as deep. Add a thin layer of compost or mulch to the backfill. Set the plant in the hole slightly higher than the soil line. Fill the hole, pressing the soil gently to remove air pockets. Water thoroughly. Water every three to four days for two or three weeks, then water every seven to ten days.

Growing Tips

Rosemary does not require supplemental fertilizer. Water established plants every two to three weeks in summer in low elevation zones, much less frequently in higher elevation zones. Water every three to four weeks in winter in low elevation zones, rely on natural rainfall in high elevation zones.

Care

Prune in late fall or early spring to remove dead or damaged wood. Prune to a foot or two from the ground every two or three years to prevent a dead zone in the middle of the plant. Rosemary is not susceptible to pests or disease.

Companion Planting and Design

Plant rosemary as a low hedge or border plant. Its deep green color makes it a stunning background for bulbs, perennials, or annuals. Its heat tolerance makes it a good choice against a hot wall, around a pool or patio, or other areas where reflected heat is intense. Many of the trailing forms are reliable groundcovers for erosion control. Place near a walkway, where the foliage can be brushed often to release the fragrance.

Did You Know?

Rosemary has long been associated with friendship, loyalty, and memory. As such, it has a long history of use, beginning with the Greeks, by mourners, brides, and was routinely worn by ancient scholars while taking exams.

Many gardeners only know rosemary for its culinary qualities, but it is a valuable addition to ornamental gardens throughout Arizona in all zones. The deep green, evergreen leaves are covered with sticky, resinous oil. It is this oil that produces the sharp, clear fragrance when the leaves are touched and the rich flavor when they are cooked. The fragrant leaves are a delightful addition to fresh or dried arrangements. The blue flowers of rosemary are small and crowded on the stems. Beekeepers prize the honey made from these blossoms. There are numerous cultivars identified for upright, trailing, bushy forms, for flower color, and for taste. If you intend to cook with rosemary, taste it before you buy it; there is an astounding range of flavors.

Bloom Period and Seasonal Color
March to May; light or dark blue, purple, white, and pink.

Mature Height × Spread
3 to 6 feet × 3 to 8 feet

Zones
1, 2, 3, 4, 5
Hardy to 10 degrees Fahrenheit but m~~ ~
protection helps protect plants i~

Ruellia
Ruellia peninsularis

Ruellia is a sturdy Sonoran Desert native that grows effortlessly in low elevation zone gardens of Arizona. This small but rounded shrub easily fades into the background with small, bright green leaves that are sparse enough to reveal the grayish stems. The leaves are smooth and, in some individuals, look polished and glossy. The grayish stems twist and turn in a complicated branching pattern to give the plant a full, rounded shape. But when flowering, ruellia takes center stage. The delicate, bell-shaped flowers are a rich purple with lavender petal backs. They bloom prolifically in spring and early summer and often bloom again in fall. Ruellia californica is almost identical but the leaves are hairy. Plants of either species are sold under both names.

Bloom Period and Seasonal Color
April to June; purple.

Mature Height × Spread
4 to 5 feet × 4 to 5 feet

Zones
1, 2, 3
Hardy to 28 degrees Fahrenheit.

When, Where, and How to Plant
Plant in spring after all danger of frost is past. Grow ruellia in full sun; plants grown in shade have sparse foliage and bloom poorly. Ruellia grows in any soil with sharp drainage from well-drained fertile soil to rocky, native soil. Dig a hole three to four times wider than the container and just as deep. Add a thin layer of compost or mulch to the backfill. Set the plant in the hole slightly higher than the soil line. Fill the hole, pressing the soil gently to remove air pockets. Mulch the roots but do not allow mulch to touch the bark. Water thoroughly. Water every three to four days for two or three weeks, then water four or five days for the first summer.

Growing Tips
Ruellia does not require supplemental fertilizer. Water established plants every two to three weeks in summer. Water every month in winter or rely on natural rainfall.

Care
After all danger of frost is past in spring, prune ruellia to remove winter-damaged stems and dead wood. Every few years prune to within a couple of feet of the ground in spring to reinvigorate and keep the plant tidy. Leaves often turn black during cold snaps but recover quickly when the weather warms. Ruellia is not susceptible to pests or disease.

Companion Planting and Design
Plant ruellia in groups or as part of an informal hedge or boundary planting. Use it against southern or western walls, in hot barren spots, or around pools where reflected heat is intense. Ruellia is excellent in large containers, especially those in full sun. Plant it with summer-flowering perennials and shrubs such as lantana, salvia, and oleander.

Did You Know?
The seeds of ruellia are held in a short pod. When the seeds are ripe, the pod breaks open and they fly out. The sound is so loud that it sounds like a far away firecracker.

Shrub Althaea

Hibiscus syriacus

When, Where, and How to Plant

Plant shrub althaea in spring after all danger of frost is past, in full or partial sun. Dig a hole three to four times wider than the container and just as deep. Add a generous layer of compost or mulch to the backfill. Set the plant in the hole slightly higher than the soil line. Fill the hole, pressing the soil gently to remove air pockets. Mulch the roots but do not allow mulch to touch the bark. Water thoroughly. Water every three to four days for two or three weeks, then water weekly for the first summer.

Growing Tips

Apply slow-release or organic fertilizer in spring and once or twice in summer to maintain steady bloom. Water once a week in summer; monthly or less in winter.

Care

Prune in spring before leaves emerge to remove dead or damaged wood or to reinvigorate the plant. As plants mature, they become more open and spreading and are easily trained to a small single-trunked tree by removing the lowest three or four branches each spring. Shrub althaea is not susceptible to pests or disease.

Companion Planting and Design

Mix shrub althaea with flowering shrubs and perennials such as blue mist, summer phlox, and salvias. Whether grown as a shrub or a small tree, shrub althaea makes a striking specimen or focal plant in small courtyards or patios. Plant generously to provide long seasonal color around seating areas, patios, or pools. Shrub althaea grows quickly and helps fill in barren spots in a newly planted garden or bed.

Did You Know?

The common name althaea comes from the Greek, *althaine*, which means "to heal" and refers to medicinal properties of the related marsh mallow of Europe. While medicinal use has faded, the related *Hibiscus sabdariffa* is still renowned for a delicious tea made from its dried flowers and fruit called *jamaica* for the island where it was first made.

In both of the houses in which I grew up, shrub althaea grew outside the doorways. The lush, ruffled blooms in shades of rose and purple greeted us every day throughout the long Texas summer. This is a reliable summer-flowering, deciduous shrub for intermediate and high elevation zones. Shrub althaea is less reliable in the dry heat and soils of the low elevation zones. Related to hibiscus, shrub althaea flowers have thin, often ruffled petals, and are pastel or in paler shades than its tropical cousin. Newer selections are sterile hybrids and do not reseed as freely as the older varieties—'Aphrodite', with rosy flowers and a deep red eye, 'Helene', with white flowers and a red eye, and 'Minerva', which has ruffled lavender flowers and red to purple eyes.

Other Common Name
Rose of Sharon

Bloom Period and Seasonal Color
Summer; pink, mauve, purple, red, and white, with double and bicolor forms.

Mature Height × Spread
10 to 12 feet × 6 feet

Zones
3, 4, 5, 6
Hardy to 10 degrees Fahrenheit.

Shrubby Cinquefoil
Potentilla fruticosa

When I visit Arizona's high elevation zones in summer, one of my favorite plants is shrubby cinquefoil. This cheerful plant, with a compact vase shape and brilliant yellow flowers, is native to the high mountains of Arizona and throughout the West. Shrubby cinquefoil has dark green, deciduous leaves and the profuse, open flowers occur continuously through summer. A number of cultivars have been developed, including 'Abbotswood' that is white and the red-orange 'Tangerine'. 'Red Ace' has red flowers with a yellow center and yellow on the back of the petal; then the entire flower fades to solid yellow. Most of the red-flowered cultivars lose their color quickly in bright light and need to be grown in filtered shade for best color.

Bloom Period and Seasonal Color
Spring and summer; yellow.

Mature Height × Spread
2 to 4 feet × 2 to 4 feet

Zones
4, 5, 6
Hardy to 0 degrees Fahrenheit, or lower.

When, Where, and How to Plant
Plant in spring in full sun. Shrubby cinquefoil grows well in a wide variety of soils from well-drained fertile soil to rocky, native soil as long as the drainage is very sharp. Dig a hole three to four times wider than the container and just as deep. Add a thin layer of compost or mulch to the back-fill. Set the plant in the hole slightly higher than the soil line. Fill the hole, pressing the soil gently to remove air pockets. Mulch the roots but do not allow mulch to touch the bark. Water thoroughly. Water every three to four days for two or three weeks, then water weekly.

Growing Tips
Apply slow-release or organic fertilizer annually in spring. Water established plants every ten to fourteen days in summer, more often if the weather is especially hot or dry. Plants in very rocky soil often need more frequent irrigation. Rely on natural rainfall in winter.

Care
Shrubby cinquefoil has a fine natural form and rarely needs pruning for shape. Prune to remove dead or damaged wood in early spring just as leaves emerge. It is not susceptible to pests or disease.

Companion Planting and Design
Shrubby cinquefoil mixes well with summer-flowering shrubs or perennials such as summer phlox, hollyhocks, daylilies, and salvias. The deep green color and dense foliage make shrubby cinquefoil useful as a background for colorful plantings of small perennials or annuals. Plant generously to create a short hedge or border for a large bed. Shrubby cinquefoil is excellent for erosion control on steep slopes, areas where reflected heat is intense, or parts of the garden that receive minimal care.

Did You Know?
The word "cinquefoil" is an old Middle English word. It is derived from the Latin word *quinquefolium,* which means "five leaves." This refers to the five leaflets that make up the compound leaf.

Texas Sage
Leucophyllum species

When, Where, and How to Plant

Plant in fall or spring in low elevation zones; in spring as soon as the soil can be worked in high elevation zones. Locate in full sun. All species are extremely intolerant of heavy or poorly drained soils but grow well in both well-drained, fertile soil and rocky, native ones. Dig a hole three to four times wider than the container and just as deep. Add a thin layer of compost or mulch to the backfill. Set the plant in the hole slightly higher than the soil line. Fill the hole, pressing the soil gently to remove air pockets. Mulch the roots but do not allow mulch to touch the bark. Water thoroughly. Water every three to four days for two or three weeks, then water every seven to ten days for the first summer.

Growing Tips

Texas sage does not require supplemental fertilizer. Water sparingly in summer, even in low elevation zones. Water established plants every two to three weeks in summer; once every month or two in winter. In higher elevation zones, rely on natural rainfall unless the weather is exceptionally hot or dry.

Care

All Texas sage plants have excellent natural form and rarely need pruning for shape. Prune to remove dead or damaged wood in spring. The shrubs are susceptible to root rot and chlorosis when grown in heavy or poorly drained soils. Old plants have been known to be infected by palo verde beetles that feed on the roots and ultimately kill the plant.

Companion Planting and Design

Mix Texas sage with other shrubs such as sugarbush, jojoba, Arizona rosewood, yellowbells, or Texas mountain laurel to form an informal hedge or border planting. The tremendous heat tolerance and light-colored foliage make Texas sage particularly effective against hot walls or buildings, around pools or patios, and other areas where reflected heat is intense.

Did You Know?

Texas sages are so well timed to respond to summer rains that all plants in a given area will bloom within ten days of the last rain.

Its durability, easy care, and beautiful blooms have made Texas sage one of the most common evergreen shrubs in the lower elevation zones. They are immune to heat, extremely drought tolerant, and thrive in highly alkaline soils. Leucophyllum frutescens *is a large shrub with gray-green leaves and fragrant pink flowers. The most widely grown selections come from this species; they include* 'Green Cloud' *with dark green leaves and magenta flowers,* 'White Cloud' *with gray leaves and white flowers, and* 'Thundercloud' *with whitish leaves and deep purple flowers.* 'Silver Cloud', *a selection of* L. candidum, *has bright white foliage and dark royal-purple flowers.* L. pruinosum *has highly fragrant pink to mauve flowers. Cenizo* (L. laevigatum) *is an open shrub with small, bright green leaves and bright blue flowers.*

Other Common Names
Texas ranger, Cenizo, Purple sage, Barometer bush

Bloom Period and Seasonal Color
Late summer through fall; blue, purple, rose, mauve, or white flowers.

Mature Height × Spread
3 to 8 feet × 4 to 8 feet

Zones
1, 2, 3, 4, 5. Hardy to 18 degrees Fahrenheit, some species to 10 degrees Fahrenheit.

Turpentine Bush

Ericameria laricifolia

Turpentine bush is a small, native evergreen shrub that transforms itself from a plain, green plant into a flaming golden bush in late fall. The needlelike, dark green leaves are covered with a sticky resin. Rubbing the leaves releases its aroma that smells vaguely of turpentine, hence the common name. The plant looks like a small juniper but is actually in the sunflower family. The brilliant yellow or gold flowers are held in clusters at the ends of the stems and above the foliage. The flowers so profusely and effectively cloak the plant that it appears to change color. Turpentine bush has a tight, rounded form that blends well into a wide variety of garden styles and can be grown in all zones of the state.

Bloom Period and Seasonal Color
September to November; yellow.

Mature Height × Spread
3 to 4 feet × 3 to 4 feet

Zones
All
Hardy to 5 degrees Fahrenheit.

When, Where, and How to Plant
Plant in fall or spring in low elevation zones; in spring as soon as the soil can be worked in high elevation zones. Locate in full sun. Turpentine bush grows in any well-drained soil, even rocky, native soil, but is entirely intolerant of heavy or poorly drained soil. Dig a hole three to four times wider than the container and just as deep. Add a thin layer of compost or mulch to the backfill. Set the plant in the hole slightly higher than the soil line. Fill the hole, pressing the soil gently around the roots to remove air pockets. Water thoroughly. Water every three to four days for two or three weeks, then water weekly for the first summer.

Growing Tips
Turpentine bush needs no supplemental fertilizer. In low elevation zones, water monthly in summer, every other month in winter. In intermediate and high elevation zones, rely on natural rainfall for established plants unless it is exceptionally dry.

Care
Overwatered plants become loose and floppy, losing the characteristic regularity of the plant. To reinvigorate the plant and restore the form, prune to within a few inches of the ground in early spring. Remove dead or damaged wood or spent flowers anytime. Turpentine bush is not susceptible to pests or diseases.

Companion Planting and Design
Turpentine bush makes an excellent short hedge or border for a drive or walkway. Plant generously in a mixed planting with cacti, brittlebush, globemallow, agaves, or yuccas. Turpentine bush has tremendous heat tolerance and can be used around patios and pools for its late season color or any location where reflected heat is intense. Turpentine bush can be planted in areas that receive minimal care and will provide lovely, late season color.

Did You Know?
Plants that occur over wide ranges often exhibit interesting differences from one area to the other. Turpentine bushes growing in the Chihuahuan Desert have ray flowers with small petals. Turpentine bushes growing in the Sonoran Desert have ray flowers without petals.

Vitex
Vitex rotundifolia

When, Where, and How to Plant
Plant in early fall or throughout spring in full or partial sun. Vitex tolerates any well-drained soil from fertile, garden soil to rocky, native ones, but does poorly in heavy clay or moist soils. Dig a hole three to four times wider than the container and just as deep. Add a thin layer of compost or mulch to the backfill. Set the plant in the hole slightly higher than the soil line. Fill the hole, pressing the soil gently around the roots to remove air pockets. Mulch the roots but do not allow mulch to touch the bark. Water thoroughly. Water every three to four days for two or three weeks, then water every seven to ten days for the first year.

Growing Tips
Vitex does not need supplemental fertilizer. Mulch the roots heavily in summer to keep the soil from drying out too quickly. Water established plants weekly in summer, monthly in winter.

Care
Prune vitex in early spring to remove winter dam-aged or dead wood. This is also a good time to shape the plant by pruning it to within a foot or two of the ground. Remove spent flowering or fruiting stalks anytime. Vitex is not susceptible to pests or disease.

Companion Planting and Design
Mix vitex with spring-flowering perennials such as penstemon, red justicia, or plumbago and with summer-flowering perennials such as lantana, salvia, and verbena. Plant vitex in a group to enhance the impact of the light blue flowers or use as a short hedge or border. Vitex can be inter-planted with winter-flowering bulbs to hide its bare stems when it is dormant. Vitex grows well in large containers where the charming blue flowers can be viewed close up.

Did You Know?
Vitex is an old Latin name for the plant, *Vitex agnus-castus*. The species name *rotundifolia* refers to the round leaves. This species is used in Chinese herbal medicine for a wide variety of ailments under the name *man jing zi*.

This small deciduous shrub from Australia presents small spikes of pale blue flowers in summer. But it does not stop there. The rounded, green leaves are deciduous and turn dusky maroon to yellow in fall just in time to catch the low autumn light. New to low elevation zone gardens, this short, compact shrub has proved to be durable to the conditions there. This vitex blooms in either full or partial sun, and the cool blue color is welcome in the hottest days of summer. Vitex trifolia is a taller and wider plant with sets of three thin, light green leaves and pale blue flowers that bloom throughout summer. There is a handsome white variegated form of this species.

Bloom Period and Seasonal Color
Summer, light blue; leaves purple-red in fall.

Mature Height × Spread
3 to 4 feet × 3 to 5 feet

Zones
1, 2, 3
Hardy to 30 degrees Fahrenheit, perhaps lower.

Woolly Butterfly Bush
Buddleia marrubiifolia

Despite its delicate appearance, woolly butterfly bush is a rugged shrub for the low and intermediate elevation zones in Arizona. The small, gray-green leaves are covered with fine, white hairs giving it a soft, fuzzy look. The leaves are numerous and densely held on the stems, creating a tight, round form. Tiny, bright orange flowers are crammed into tight whorls at intervals along the blooming stalk, like lollipops piled on top of each other. Butterflies are extremely fond of the flowers, finding them a rich source of nectar. In higher elevation zones, butterfly bush, Buddleia davidii, grows easily to a 10-foot shrub with tapered leaves that are dark green above and creamy white underneath. Long spikes of purple flowers occur all summer.

Bloom Period and Seasonal Color
March to August; orange.

Mature Height × Spread
3 to 5 feet × 4 to 5 feet

Zones
1, 2, 3, 4
Hardy to 15 degrees Fahrenheit.

When, Where, and How to Plant
For best results, plant in fall although spring planting is acceptable. Locate plants in full sun for best form and overall appearance. Woolly butterfly bush grows well in any well-drained soil from fertile, garden soil to rocky, native ones but does poorly in heavy clay. Dig a hole three to four times wider than the container and just as deep. Add a thin layer of compost or mulch to the backfill. Set the plant in the hole slightly higher than the soil line. Fill the hole, pressing the soil gently to remove air pockets. Mulch the roots but do not allow mulch to touch the bark. Water thoroughly. Water every three to four days for two or three weeks, then water every seven to ten days for the first summer.

Growing Tips
Woolly butterfly bush requires no supplemental fertilizer. Water established plants every two weeks in summer, every month in winter. Plants become overgrown, floppy, and subject to rot when overwatered or grown in heavy soils.

Care
Prune in fall or very early spring to remove dead or damaged wood. Prune to within a foot or two of the ground every two or three years to maintain the shape and reinvigorate the plant. Wooly butterfly bush is not susceptible to pests or disease.

Companion Planting and Design
Woolly butterfly bush mixes well with other desert perennials such as desert marigold, black dalea, penstemon, Baja fairyduster, and salvias. Plant generously to create an informal hedge or boundary planting. The white color of the foliage is cooling in a hot spot, and its excellent heat and drought tolerance make this a good choice near a pool or other area with strong reflected heat. Place near seating areas where the continuous stream of butterflies can be enjoyed.

Did You Know?
The genus is named to honor Reverend Adam Buddle, who died in 1715. The epithet means "foliage like *Marrubium*," the genus of horehound which also has white, woolly leaves.

Wright's Bee Bush

Aloysia wrightii

When, Where, and How to Plant

Plant in fall or spring in full or partial sun. Wright's bee bush tolerates any well-drained soil from fertile, garden soil to rocky, native ones, but does poorly in heavy clay. Dig a hole three to four times wider than the container and just as deep. Add a thin layer of compost or mulch to the back-fill. Set the plant in the hole slightly higher than the soil line. Fill the hole, pressing the soil gently to remove air pockets. Mulch the roots but do not allow mulch to touch the bark. Water thoroughly. Water every three to four days for two or three weeks, then water once or twice a week for the first summer.

Growing Tips

Bee bush needs no supplemental fertilizer. Water established plants weekly in summer, more often if the weather is exceptionally hot or dry. Plants that are water stressed will drop their leaves in summer, but recover quickly when water is provided. Water monthly in winter.

Care

Prune in early spring while the plant is dormant to remove winter-damaged limbs or dead wood. When plants become too large or get leggy, prune to within a couple of feet of the ground in early spring to reinvigorate and shape it. You can also just prune out the tallest limbs to reduce the size of the plant. Bee bush is not susceptible to pests or disease.

Companion Planting and Design

The intoxicating smell of Wright's bee bush is most welcome near a patio, pool, or other seating area. Its heat tolerance makes it a good choice in areas where reflected heat is intense. Mix it with other perennials or shrubs such as flame anisacanthus, salvia, or lantana. Bee bush is a good choice for edges of gardens that receive minimal care.

Did You Know?

In some way that is hard to figure out, the genus was named to honor Maria Louisa, Princess of Parma, who died in 1819.

I used to prune our bee bush in late summer until one year, time was tight, and I didn't get around to it. That year goldfinches descended on the plant, spending a month or more devouring the virtually invisible seeds. That was a good enough reason for me to change my habits. It is also just another good reason to grow this native shrub. The tiny, gray-green leaves of this deciduous shrub smell strongly of oregano. The narrow stems are numerous on the plant and often cascade from the middle like a fountain. The diminutive white flowers bloom all summer on long spikes that have a strong vanilla fragrance. Aloysia lycioides is the Mexican oregano of commerce, and although it's very similar, it is smaller with more pungent foliage.

Other Common Names
Bee bush, Organillo

Bloom Period and Seasonal Color
Spring and summer, intermittently in fall; white.

Mature Height × Spread
5 to 8 feet × 6 to 8 feet

Zones
1, 2, 3, 4
Hardy to 15 degrees Fahrenheit.

Yellowbells

Tecoma stans

The first time I saw yellowbells in full bloom was in Key West, where it draped invitingly over a clapboard fence. It never occurred to me that it might be a native of the western deserts. Yellowbells is a tall, lanky bush with upright or arching stems covered with thin, light green leaves. The brilliant yellow flowers are trumpet-shaped and held in clusters at the ends of the stems. The variety angustata has thin, serrated leaves, and thin, yellow flowers that are rarely over 1½ inches long. It is cold hardy enough for intermediate zones. The variety stans is a small tree with deep green leaves, large, bright yellow flowers that bloom in late summer and fall, and is reliable only in the warmest areas of the state.

Bloom Period and Seasonal Color
April to November; bright yellow.

Mature Height × Spread
4 to 25 feet × 3 to 15 feet

Zones
1, 2, 3, 4
Hardy to 28 degrees Fahrenheit, root hardy to 20 degrees Fahrenheit.

When, Where, and How to Plant
Plant in spring in full or partial sun. Yellowbells tolerates any well-drained soil from fertile, garden soil to rocky, native ones, but does poorly in heavy clay. Dig a hole three to four times wider than the container and just as deep. Add a thin layer of compost or mulch to the backfill. Set the plant in the hole slightly higher than the soil line. Fill the hole, pressing the soil gently to remove air pockets. Mulch the roots but do not allow mulch to touch the bark. Water thoroughly. Water every three to four days for two or three weeks, then water every four to seven days for the first summer.

Growing Tips
Apply slow-release or organic fertilizer annually in spring. Water established plants once a week in summer, more often if the plants are growing in rocky soils or the weather is especially hot or dry. Water monthly in winter.

Care
After all danger of frost is past, prune yellowbells in spring to remove winter-damaged stems or dead wood. Yellowbells can be pruned from late spring through summer to shape or remove stems that have grown too tall or leggy. Plants will drop their leaves if water stressed, but recover quickly. Yellowbells is not susceptible to pests or disease.

Companion Planting and Design
Mix yellowbells with other shrubs such as hibiscus, red or yellow bird of paradise, and Texas sage for a colorful, informal hedge or boundary planting. When pruned to a tree form, it serves as a focal or specimen plant for small gardens or patios. Yellowbells is a fine choice to cover a hot wall or window or around a pool or patio where reflected heat is intense. It grows well in a large container.

Did You Know?
The name of the genus is the Mexican name for the plant. The epithet, *stans*, means "erect" and refers to its treelike form.

Yellow Bird of Paradise

Caesalpinia gilliesii

When, Where, and How to Plant

Plant in fall or spring in low elevation zones; in spring as soon as the soil can be worked in higher elevation zones. Locate in full or partial sun. Yellow bird of paradise tolerates any well-drained soil from fertile, garden soil to rocky, native ones, but often fails to grow well in heavy clay. Dig a hole three to four times wider than the container and just as deep. Add a generous layer of compost or mulch to the backfill. Set the plant in the hole slightly higher than the soil line. Fill the hole, pressing the soil gently to remove air pockets. Mulch the roots but do not allow mulch to touch the bark. Water thoroughly. Water every three to four days for two or three weeks, then water every four to seven days.

Growing Tips

Apply slow-release or organic fertilizer annually in spring. Adding a generous layer of mulch in summer keeps soil from drying out too quickly and also provides needed nutrients. Water yellow bird of paradise every week in summer, every month in the low elevation zones; rely on natural rainfall in intermediate elevation zones.

Care

Prune in spring to remove dead wood or winter-damaged stems. Remove suckers, unruly branches, or spent flowering heads throughout summer. Yellow bird of paradise can be trained to a small tree with careful removal of suckers and side shoots. It is not susceptible to pests or disease.

Companion Planting and Design

Plant yellow bird of paradise in groups to highlight its spectacular color. Use it against southern or western walls, in hot barren spots, or where reflected heat is intense. When trained as a small tree it makes a splendid specimen or focal plant. Mix with summer-flowering perennials and shrubs such as lantana, salvia and oleander.

Did You Know?

The genus is named for the Italian botanist and chief papal physician, Andreas Caesalpini, who died in 1603. The epithet honors John Gillies, a Scottish physician who collected plants extensively in Argentina and died in 1836.

Yellow bird of paradise is a loosely branched, multi-trunked shrub. Well suited to gardens in the low elevation zones, this species is more cold hardy than most of its relatives and grows handsomely in the intermediate elevation zone and even in very the warm spots of Zone 4. The bright green, feathery compound leaves are evergreen in low elevation zones, winter deciduous elsewhere. The flowers are remarkable with large, rich yellow petals out of which 4-inch red stamens unfurl. They are crowded into dense heads at the ends of the branches and truly look like birds ready to take flight. Mexican bird of paradise (Caesalpinia mexicana) is a large plant that grows up to 15 feet tall, with dark green, round leaflets and bright yellow flowers throughout the year.

Bloom Period and Seasonal Color
March to October; yellow.

Mature Height × Spread
5 to 10 feet × 4 to 6 feet

Zones
1, 2, 3, 4
Hardy to 20 degrees Fahrenheit.

Trees *for Arizona*

Trees are a commanding presence in the garden. Their large size dominates and defines the tone and style of the garden. Poorly placed trees look gangly, awkward, and ill at ease and they hide rather than enhance the balance of a garden. But great trees growing in just the right spot are a perfect complement to the plants that surround them and create a sense of proportion and balance that is irreplaceable.

Consider Trees Carefully

Given their importance in a garden, the location of new trees should be considered with great care. We have all seen the results of a hasty selection — a tree planted where there isn't enough room for it to mature, or placed where it quickly begins to impinge on power lines or views, or makes too much shade where it wasn't really wanted at all. It is much better to take your time, consider what the tree will be when it is mature, and how it will effect your garden when it reaches full size. It will happen sooner than you think. It isn't just the size that matters. Trees serve numerous uses and purposes in the garden and should be selected because they fulfill a particular need. For example, trees with minimal litter, large fruit that is easily skimmed from water, or varieties with few flowers are generally best to overhang or shade a pool. Trees that are dense, evergreen, and with dark green foliage might smother a good view, or close out the light and air from a room, but would be welcome as shade along the western side of the patio. Trees that have open branching and do not grow terribly tall might not be able to create the shade you imagined or anchor a large garden, but they will be beautiful accents to a small patio or make a striking focal plant. Good trees are a blessing in the garden; choosing with care before they are planted prevents them from turning into a curse.

When Less is More

When it is time to purchase a tree, think small. Buying trees is an act of faith, very much like adopting a

Citrus

184

Colorado Blue Spruce

puppy. And just like young pets, the smaller they are when they come into your home or garden, the better they fit in and mature into the sturdy, vigorous plants that we are happy to see live a long time in the garden.

Another advantage of buying and planting trees that are small is that young plants always endure the shock of transplant better than old ones. They recover quickly from the mangled root systems and erratic care that may have taken place while they were in the nursery, and they bounce back dramatically from the equally traumatic business of being wrenched from a pot and placed in the ground.

Although tempting, do not be seduced by the one specimen at the nursery that is twice the size of the rest. It has probably been in that pot too long and may be seriously rootbound. The only way to know is to remove the pot and check the roots. Roots of container grown plants should be about the size of a pencil, with a spreading network of fine, fibrous roots that cover the entire rootball and are found along the edges of the pot. There should not be any coiled or mangled roots at the bottom of the container, nor should roots be growing outside the bounds of the pot.

Plan Ahead

Figure out how you are going to water the tree before you plant it. If watering will be by hand with a hose, the most efficient way to water is to build a small basin around the plant so that water can be collected and not allowed to run off. All the water will then percolate slowly into the root zone of the tree. If you are going to water with a drip irrigation system, set at least two, and preferably four, emitters that provide a minimum of 1 gallon per hour evenly around the tree. To find the right distance from a newly planted tree, make a rough estimate of the height of the tree and set the emitters about that distance from the trunk. Later as the tree grows, both basins and emitter placement should be expanded to the drip line of the tree. In addition, place trees on a dedicated station so that the amount and timing of watering is

Fremont Cottonwood

suited to trees. Whichever way you water, provide a deep soaking (up to 3 feet deep) each time you water.

Drip systems to a great job of watering a young tree, but after about three years, the root zone of the tree has expanded and the number of emitters necessary to provide good irrigation measures in the dozens. By that time, it is better to lay a hose down for a long time, on a slow drip, to water the tree. Trees need to grow good root system to live a long and fruitful life. To keep the root system growing properly, you must expand the watering zone each year as the tree grows.

After five or six years, it becomes increasingly difficult to water a tree thoroughly with a hose—the small roots that are at the edges of the root network which take up the water and nutrients grow farther away from the main trunk. After ten years, a well-established tree has a root system that is entirely too large to water by hand, much less with drip irrigation. Unless you have a site where the entire area is flood irrigated, your tree is on its own anyway.

Remember a Few Rules

Pruning trees well is an art and if you want to be really good at it you may want to consider taking a class or two. Basic pruning, however, is not difficult if you remember a few principles.

- Always prune to a joint or junction with another branch; do not cut flush to the joining branch. Rather, leave a raised ring of tissue, called a branch collar, below the cut. This ring of growing tissue is what will heal the cut.

- Pay attention to the right time of year to prune the species that you have. While deciduous trees should be pruned in the winter when they are dormant, most desert trees are just the opposite. Legumes and other desert trees should be pruned when it is hot.

- Do not prune just because you need something to do—prune only to train a tree or remove dead wood or damaged limbs. Once training is complete, quit pruning so often.

- Use the correct size and type of tool for the job. Never prune a tree with a chain saw—that tool is strictly for removal of large or dead limbs and cutting down the entire tree.

- Sometimes an initial cut can be made with a chain saw when a large limb must be removed, but the final cut should always be done by hand.

Staking is wildly overrated as well as overused. Most trees, especially those planted when they are small, do not need staking at all. Even if the tree appears to droop and wants to fall over, leave it alone if it is small. The action of bending and moving in the wind actually strengthens the trunk and allows the tree to grow straight.

In areas that have strong winds or when trees are newly planted in a season with strong winds, temporary staking can help keep the tree in place while it is regrowing its roots. In order to stake a newly planted tree, set two poles or stakes in the ground so they form a line with the tree. Wrap tree tape or a soft collar around the tree about 2 or 3 feet from the ground and secure it to the stake. Do the same thing again about a foot or two higher up on the tree but secure this collar to the other stake. Attach the collars loosely enough to allow the tree to move in a wind. No tree should be staked for more than 4 months — if it can't stand up in that time it has greater problems than your stakes can fix.

Trees add even more vitality to a low elevation zone garden because they provide one of the best partners a garden in that zone can have—shade. All plants, even succulents, grow well under the light, high shade of most desert trees, particularly mesquites and their relatives. The sun is so intense, and the heat so great, that any small break gives your plants an extra boost. In higher zones, trees add not only shade but also shelter for the plants underneath them. Trees also provide birds and other wildlife in your garden protection during the winter.

If you choose your trees with care, they will embrace the space in which they grow. By using well-adapted or native trees, your entire garden will be filled with the look and feel of the surrounding area.

Texas Ebony

Aleppo Pine
Pinus halepensis

Aleppo pine is a massive tree with irregular, low branches that have light green needles and a billowing, cloudlike crown that seems to rise above the landscape like a tethered balloon. Native to the southern Mediterranean regions and Middle Asia, Aleppo pine is entirely at home in heat, aridity, and the soils of the low and intermediate elevation zones. However, its great size often limits its effective use. Other species for low elevation zone gardens include the Afghan pine (Pinus eldarica), which has a more upright, uniformly branched habit and dark green needles, and the Calabrian pine (P. brutia), which is a more symmetrical plant without the fantastic branching pattern of Aleppo pine. Canary Island pine (P. canariensis) also has a strong, pyramid form and long, dark green needles.

Bloom Period and Seasonal Color
Late spring and early summer; cones.

Mature Height × Spread
30 to 60 feet × 20 to 40 feet

Zones
1, 2, 3, 4
Hardy to 20 degrees Fahrenheit.

When, Where, and How to Plant
Plant in full sun when the weather is cool; pines may be planted even in midwinter. Choose one- or five-gallon containers because pines are notoriously intolerant of root disturbance and smaller plants recover from transplant more quickly. Dig a hole three to four times wider than the container and just as deep. Soil amendments are not necessary. Set the tree in the hole slightly higher than the original soil line. Fill the hole, pressing the soil gently to remove air pockets. Mulch the root zones of the plant but do not allow mulch to touch the bark. Water thoroughly. Water every three to four days for two or three weeks, then water every seven to ten days for the first year.

Growing Tips
Most pines do not need supplemental fertilizer. Water young pines every seven to ten days in summer, every three to four weeks in winter. Water established trees every month in summer, every month or two in winter. Aleppo pine also tolerates growing in lawns or where deep irrigation is provided.

Care
Prune in early spring to remove damaged or dead wood. A condition known as pine blight causes needle browning and small limbs to die back in winter. It is thought to be a physical response to heat stress and causes no permanent harm. Aleppo pine is not susceptible to pests or disease.

Companion Planting and Design
Plant Aleppo pine as a shade tree on large properties, or use as part of a mixed border planting. It makes a spectacular focal point where there is room. Plant pines some distance from buildings and driveways; the shallow roots may heave concrete. While the needles may be a nuisance around a pool, they make wonderful mulch. It gives excellent shade and frost protection for tender succulents or perennials.

Did You Know
All pines develop nuts inside the cones and birds love them. One species, Italian stone pine (*Pinus pinea*), has nuts that are enjoyed throughout the world. They are called *pignolia* in Italian.

When, Where, and How to Plant

Plant in fall in full sun in well-drained, fertile soil. Arizona ash is highly tolerant of alkaline soil. Dig a hole three to four times wider than the container and just as deep. Add a thin layer of compost or mulch to the backfill and set the tree in the hole slightly higher than the soil line. Fill the hole and press the soil gently as it is replaced to remove air pockets. Mulch the root zone, taking care that the mulch does not to touch the bark. Water thoroughly after planting and then every three to four days for two or three weeks. For the first year or two, water every seven to ten days in warm weather.

Growing Tips

Apply slow-release or organic fertilizer in fall and spring just before leaves emerge for the first four to six years. Water deeply every ten to fifteen days in summer; monthly once trees are established. Water monthly or less in winter. Expand the watering zone to the edge of the tree's canopy yearly for the first six years when watering by drip irrigation or by hand.

Care

Prune in winter when the tree is dormant to remove crossing branches or damaged wood. Arizona ash has suffered from ash blight that has killed numerous old trees in the Phoenix area. Ash blight begins as dying branches and then the entire tree will die quickly; there appears to be no cure. Trees are susceptible to limb loss from cotton root rot in some areas and can become chlorotic when watering is too shallow or too frequent.

Companion Planting and Design

Plant Arizona ash in large yards or as a street tree where its requirement for deep soils can be accommodated. This tree provides high shade for patios and buildings, and serves as a good border tree for large properties. It mixes well with other trees or pines.

Did You Know?

The genus is the classical Latin name for ash trees—*velutina*, which means "velvety," or "soft," and refers to the fine hairs on the leaves.

Native to the streams and creek-sides of southern Arizona, California, Texas, and northern Mexico, this is an attractive deciduous tree for large properties or park plantings. It has been used for decades as one of the principle deciduous shade trees in both Phoenix and Tucson. Arizona ash is an upright tree with an open, spreading crown. The bright green leaves are deciduous and turn bright yellow in fall. 'Modesto' has a rounder crown and glossy green leaves with excellent fall color. 'Rio Grande', also known as 'Fan-Tex', keeps its large, dark green leaves longer in fall and leafs out very early. 'Fan-Tex' is much more tolerant of desert heat, aridity, and alkaline soils. Gregg ash (Fraxinus greggii) is a small tree or shrub that has evergreen, dark, green leaves and smooth gray bark.

Other Common Names
Velvet ash, Modesto ash

Bloom Period and Seasonal Color
Spring; innocuous whitish flowers. Fall; bright yellow foliage.

Mature Height × Spread
30 to 45 feet × 25 to 45 feet

Zones
All
Hardy to 0 degrees Fahrenheit.

Arizona Cypress

Cupressus arizonica

Arizona cypress is found growing naturally along streams and in canyons throughout the higher elevations of Arizona. This handsome tree is used throughout the state, but in the low elevation zones it requires deep, regular irrigation. The lacy leaves resemble juniper leaves and range from light green to silver blue. Like many conifers, the bark is very ornamental. Arizona cypress bark is a rich, dark brown with rectangular plates separated by deep furrows. Arizona cypress grows in an almost perfect pyramid form, a shape that is formed when the tree is very young and continues through old age. 'Blue Pyramid' has blue-gray foliage and 'Gareei' has silvery, blue-green foliage. A related species, Cupressus glabra, is often sold as Arizona cypress but it has smooth, reddish bark and an open, flattened crown at maturity.

Bloom Period and Seasonal Color
Summer; nearly invisible flowers, bark of mature trees symmetrically plated and deep brown.

Mature Height × Spread
40 to 50 feet × 20 to 25 feet

Zones
All
Hardy to 0 degrees Fahrenheit.

When, Where, and How to Plant
Plant in fall or early spring in full sun; this species also tolerates partial shade when young, especially in the low elevation zones. Arizona cypress grows best in deep, well-drained, fertile soil, but tolerates drier soils with sufficient irrigation. Dig a hole three to four times wider than the container and just as deep, adding a thin layer of compost or mulch to the backfill. Set the tree slightly higher than the soil line, filling the hole by pressing the soil gently around the roots to remove air pockets as it is replaced. Mulch the root zone but do not allow mulch to touch the bark. Water thoroughly. Water every three to four days for two or three weeks, then water every seven to ten days for the first year.

Growing Tips
Apply slow-release or organic fertilizer annually in spring to young trees. Established trees do not require supplemental fertilizer. Water established trees every two weeks in summer in low elevation zones; monthly in higher elevation zones. In low elevation zones, water established trees monthly in winter; elsewhere rely on natural rainfall through winter.

Care
Arizona cypress has outstanding natural form and does not require regular pruning for shape. Prune in spring to remove dead or damaged wood and be sure to prune back to the junction with the main leader. Cypress bark beetles infest drought-stressed trees and cause limbs to die back. This is a particular problem for trees grown in the low elevation zones.

Companion Planting and Design
Plant at the edge of a large property to serve as a border or screen. Arizona cypress blends well with other deciduous or evergreen trees, as well as large conifers. The beautiful form and handsome foliage and bark make Arizona cypress particularly effective as a specimen or focal plant where space permits.

Did You Know?
The name of the genus is the Latin name for the Italian cypress tree, *Cupressus sempervirens*. The epithet refers to the state of Arizona where the plant was originally found.

Blue Palo Verde
Cercidium floridum

When, Where, and How to Plant

Plant in fall or spring in full sun. Blue palo verde is tolerant of a wide range of soils as long as drainage is excellent. It, and most other palo verdes, does poorly with the consistent moisture of a lawn, but thrives in rocky, native soils. Dig a hole three to four times wider than the container and just as deep. Add a thin layer of compost or mulch to the backfill and set the tree in the hole slightly higher than the soil line. Fill the hole, pressing the soil gently to remove air pockets. It is not strictly necessary to mulch the root zone but if you do, do not allow mulch to touch the bark. Water thoroughly and continue to water every three to four days for two or three weeks. Water deeply every seven to ten days for the first year.

Growing Tips

Blue palo verde needs no supplemental fertilizer. Water young trees weekly in summer; monthly in winter. Water established trees only during extended dry spells.

Care

Blue palo verde is sensitive to cold-weather pruning, which causes limb die back and may introduce infection. Prune only in warm weather to remove damaged wood. It is not susceptible to pests or disease. Although palo verde beetles are routinely found around the trees, they cause little harm to healthy trees.

Companion Planting and Design

Blue palo verde is a fast-growing shade tree for low elevation zones. Plant for shade near seating areas. The spreading crown and wide green limbs makes it a good choice for use as a specimen. The light shade of blue palo verde is ideal to protect perennials and succulents from sunburn. Unpruned trees make an excellent visual screen or border.

Did You Know?

Chlorophyll, vital for photosynthesis, is what gives leaves their green color and in most plants is only found in leaves. Palo verdes have chlorophyll in the bark as well, which makes the bark green and allows the trees to continue photosynthesis during drought when the leaves are shed.

Arizona enjoys the distinction of having two state trees—the blue palo verde and little-leaf palo verde (Cercidium microphyllum). Blue palo verde is a tall, spreading shade tree with green stems that are so numerous it looks leafy even when the small, blue-green leaves are shed. Old trees often have brown furrows and other scars up the trunk, but these are just the distinctions of old age. The brilliant yellow flowers are the first of the palo verdes to bloom in late spring. Little-leaf palo verde is a more intricately branched tree with light green bark and a shrublike form. The yellow-green leaves are minute and are shed at the first sign of dry conditions. The butter yellow flowers bloom slightly later than blue palo verde.

Bloom Period and Seasonal Color
March to April; bright yellow.

Mature Height × Spread
20 to 25 feet × 20 to 25 feet

Zones
1, 2, 3
Hardy to 15 degrees Fahrenheit.

Cascalote

Caesalpinia cacalaco

Cascalote is a relative newcomer to low elevation zone gardens but it is a stunning winter-flowering tree. This, coupled with its great heat tolerance, is winning over many low elevation gardeners. Tall spires of large, yellow flowers crowd the ends of the branches in January and they seem to glow against the deep blue winter sky. The compound leaves have large, round leaflets, which provide a dense shade through summer. Young plants are shrubby and loaded with reddish, roselike thorns. But as the tree matures, these thorns fall off revealing the rough, gray bark beneath. Mexican bird of paradise (Caesalpinia mexicana) is a smaller, more open plant that blooms throughout summer. C. platyloba has an open, upright form with thornless branches and oval, green leaves that turn burnished red in winter.

Bloom Period and Seasonal Color
December to February; bright yellow with an orange throat on a long panicle.

Mature Height × Spread
15 to 20 feet × 10 to 20 feet

Zones
1, 2, 3
Hardy to 20 degrees Fahrenheit.

When, Where, and How to Plant
Plant both in fall and spring, although fall is preferred for best establishment. Plant in full sun, although small trees will tolerate partial shade. Cascalote tolerates a wide range of soils from well-drained, fertile soil to rocky, native soil. Dig a hole three to four times wider than the container and just as deep, adding a thin layer of compost or mulch to the backfill. Set the tree slightly higher than the soil line, and then fill the hole, continuing to press the soil gently as it is replaced to remove air pockets. Mulch the root zone but do not allow mulch to touch the bark. Water thoroughly after planting, then water every three to four days for two or three weeks. For the first year, water deeply every seven to ten days.

Growing Tips
Apply slow-release or organic fertilizer in fall and spring for the first four to six years. Older or established trees do not require supplemental fertilizer. Water established trees every seven to ten days in summer; monthly in winter.

Care
Young plants are strongly multitrunked. To encourage a single trunk, prune the three or four lowest branches every spring until the tree is as tall as desired. Do not remove more than a quarter of the tree in a single year. Suckers often form at the base during summer; remove anytime. Prune dead wood, crossing branches or tangled stems in summer. Cascalote is susceptible to late spring infestations of psyllids, which resemble aphids. Treat quickly with daily, strong jets of water to prevent severe leaf loss. Trees lose leaves in a hard frost or when drought-stressed but recover.

Companion Planting and Design
Plant as a focal point or specimen. Cascalote is particularly effective when viewed over a wall or at the edge of a patio. Use as the anchor or shade for perennial or succulent plantings. Plant cascalote to protect locations where reflected heat is intense.

Did You Know?
The wood of cascalote is very hard and is used in Mexico for building material.

Chaste Tree

Vitex agnus-castus

When, Where, and How to Plant

Plant in spring after all danger of frost is past in full sun or partial shade. Chaste tree does best in well-drained, fertile soil but tolerates drier soils with sufficient irrigation. Dig a hole three to four times wider than the container and just as deep. Add a thin layer of compost or mulch to the backfill, then set the tree slightly higher than the soil line. Fill the hole and gently press the soil around the roots to remove air pockets. Mulch the root zone but be sure mulch does not touch the bark. Water thoroughly after planting and then every three to four days for two or three weeks. The first year, water every seven to ten days.

Growing Tips

Apply slow-release or organic fertilizer in fall and early spring to young plants. However, established plants do not need supplemental fertilizer. Water established trees weekly in summer; every three to four weeks in winter.

Care

To train the chaste tree to a single trunk, prune the three or four lowest branches and any suckers or side shoots each spring until the crown is as tall as you want it. Do not take off more than a quarter of the tree in any single year. Dead wood or damaged limbs may be removed in late spring. Chaste tree is a sturdy tree not susceptible to pests or disease.

Companion Planting and Design

Chaste tree complements any perennial planting with its colorful summer bloom, dark, multi-trunked habit, and dusky green leaves. It is very effective near a small patio or seating area. Chaste tree creates less litter during the summer than some trees, making it especially useful near a pool. Plant in groupings or to fill barren areas.

Did You Know?

Chaste trees were grown in monasteries throughout Europe beginning in the Middle Ages. The edible berries were thought to decrease the monks' interest in sex, hence the common name. Whether it was successful is not recorded; however, the name stuck.

Chaste tree is a splendid, moderately sized tree with a wide, spreading form, and glorious sprays of deep blue, purple, or pink flowers in early summer. Chaste trees grow to large trees in the low and intermediate elevation zones and can be grown as a shrub in the warmest parts of Zone 4. The deciduous, aromatic leaves are made up of five to seven lance-shaped leaflets that are dusky gray-green above and silver below. Trunks are dark brown, almost black, and although naturally multi-trunked, trees are often trained to a single trunk. The variety latifolia *has larger-than-average leaflets. The tall spires of flowers are usually blue to purple but white forms known as 'Alba' and 'Silver Spire' and a pink form, 'Rosea', are offered.*

Other Common Name
Monk's pepper tree

Bloom Period and Seasonal Color
May to September; blue, purple, occasionally pink and white.

Mature Height × Spread
10 to 25 feet × 10 to 25 feet

Zones
1, 2, 3, 4
Hardy to 15 degrees Fahrenheit.

Chinese Elm

Ulmus parvifolia

Chinese elm is the only elm species that can tolerate the rigors of low elevation zones of Arizona. There are lovely old trees throughout the metropolitan areas of Phoenix and Tucson because this species enjoyed great favor in the recent past. The reddish, peeling bark and the serrated, dark green leaves are distinctive. Chinese elm is a fast-growing, deciduous tree with an upright form and spreading crown making it an excellent shade tree. The American elm (Ulmus americana) is not common in Arizona, although there are some splendid individuals in Prescott. The Siberian elm (U. pumila) is widely used in the intermediate and high elevation zones, where it is particularly useful in very cold areas. Siberian elm is a weedy, fast-growing species that suffers greatly from overuse.

Bloom Period and Seasonal Color
Summer; innocuous whitish flowers, attractive red, peeling bark.

Mature Height × Spread
30 to 50 feet × 20 to 40 feet

Zones
1, 2, 3
Hardy to 20 degrees Fahrenheit, perhaps lower.

When, Where, and How to Plant
Plant in fall for best results, but trees may be set out in early spring as well. Plant in full sun. Chinese elm grows best in deep, well-drained, fertile soil but will tolerate drier soils if provided sufficient irrigation. Dig a hole three to four times wider than the container and just as deep. Add a generous layer of compost or mulch to the backfill. Set the tree in the hole slightly higher than the soil line. Fill the hole, pressing the soil gently around the roots to remove air pockets. Mulch the root zone but do not allow mulch to touch the bark. Water thoroughly. Water every three to four days for two or three weeks, then water every seven to ten days for the first year.

Growing Tips
Apply slow-release or organic fertilizer to young trees for the first four to six years. Older or mature Chinese elms do not need supplemental fertilizer. Water established plants deeply every two weeks in summer, once every month or two in winter.

Care
Prune in winter while the tree is dormant to remove dead or damaged wood and crossing branches. Although Chinese elm is tolerant of growing in lawns, it is important to water trees deeply according to the schedule above and not rely solely on lawn watering. Chinese elm is susceptible to limb die back from cotton root rot, but it is resistant to most other elm diseases.

Companion Planting and Design
Plant Chinese elm to provide high, deep shade for seating areas, patios, yards, or the roof of a building. Mix with other trees and large shrubs to form a border for large properties. Place Chinese elm trees where the beautiful reddish peeling bark can be enjoyed. Where space permits, plant as a specimen or focal plant.

Did You Know?
Ulmus is the Latin name for Chinese elm. In ancient times, the Romans used elms as supports for grape vines in their vineyards. In some parts of Italy and Portugal, elms are still used for this purpose.

Chinese Pistache

Pistacia chinensis

When, Where, and How to Plant

Plant in fall or early spring in full sun in deep, well-drained, well irrigated soil. Dig a hole three to four times wider than the container but just as deep. Soil amendments are not necessary but a generous layer of compost can be mixed with the backfill. Set the tree slightly higher than the original soil line then backfill, pressing the soil gently to remove air pockets. Mulch the root zone of the plant but prevent mulch from touching it. Water well after planting and water every three to four days for two or three weeks. Water deeply every seven to ten days the first year.

Growing Tips

Apply slow-release or organic fertilizer in fall and spring for the first four to six years. Drip irrigation is effective for the first two or three years after planting, if the emitters are evenly spaced. As trees mature, it is more effective to water with a very slow stream from a hose placed on the ground or inside a basin built around the tree to soak the entire root zone. Repeat this every ten to fifteen days in summer, monthly in winter.

Care

Prune while trees are leafless to remove dead wood or to shape. Chinese pistache is susceptible to limb die back from cotton root rot in the low desert and from severe wilting and limb die back from *Verticillium* wilt when planted in lawns. To mitigate disease problems in lawns, water as described above in addition to the water applied to lawns. Mt. Atlas pistache and mastic are not as susceptible to these diseases. Established mastic and Mt. Atlas pistache are watered once every three to four weeks in summer.

Companion Planting and Design

Use wherever a large, deciduous shade tree is needed. Mixes well with evergreens or other large trees. Exceptional in parks, roadsides, or very large properties.

Did You Know?

Pistachio nuts come from *Pistacia vera*, an Asian species. There used to be extensive groves in southern Arizona. They are now much reduced due to loss of available water.

This is the only large tree with reliable fall color for low elevation zone gardens. Chinese pistache is remarkably tolerant of heat, aridity, and alkaline soils, although it is more trouble free in the higher elevation zones where these conditions are less severe. It makes a well-formed tree with a rounded crown, and the dark green foliage provides high, dense shade in summer. Leaves turn vibrant red in late fall. The Mt. Atlas pistache (Pistacia atlantica) has similar dark green foliage and is virtually evergreen in low elevation zones. Mastic (P. lentiscus) has dark green deciduous leaves. Both of these species have greater tolerance to the heat and alkaline soils of the low elevation zones and are drought tolerant when established, but their foliage does not turn colors in fall.

Bloom Period and Seasonal Color

Spring; innocuous white flowers. Late November; red leaves in the low elevation zones.

Mature Height × Spread

30 to 60 feet × 30 to 50 feet

Zones

1, 2, 3
Hardy to 25 degrees Fahrenheit.

195

Citrus
Citrus species

In early spring, low elevation zone gardens are surrounded by the sweet, heavy fragrance of citrus trees in bloom. Citrus has been grown for centuries for its delicious fruit that ripens over a long, hot summer, but the trees are also excellent ornamentals. Trees are densely covered with firm, dark green leaves and a hedge of citrus is virtually impenetrable. The sour orange 'Seville' is planted throughout the region as a street tree and is the root stock for many grafted varieties. Other favorites for home gardeners are 'Marsh' grapefruit, 'Orlando' tangelo, and 'Lisbon' lemon, and many home gardeners grow one of the group of sweet oranges known as 'Arizona Sweet'. Mexican limes grow prolifically, blooming and setting fruit throughout the year, but may require minimal frost protection.

Bloom Period and Seasonal Color
February through April; white and highly fragrant.

Mature Height × Spread
6 to 20 feet × 6 to 20 feet

Zones
1, 2, 3
Hardiness depends on variety but most are hardy at least to 25 degrees Fahrenheit.

When, Where, and How to Plant
Plant in late winter or early spring in full sun. Citrus trees grow best in deep, well-drained, fertile soil, although they do surprisingly well in rocky, native soil. Dig a hole three to four times wider than the container and just as deep. Add a generous layer of compost to the backfill, but no other additives are necessary. Set the tree so the graft is at least 3 inches above the soil line. Fill the hole, pressing the soil gently as it is replaced to remove air pockets. If you apply mulch to the root zone, be extremely careful that it does not touch the bark. Water thoroughly after planting and every three to four days for two or three weeks. The first summer, water deeply every week.

Growing Tips
For best fruit production, fertilize citrus trees three times a year. Apply a balanced citrus fertilizer just as fruit sets (February), just before summer (May), and in late summer (August or September). Water thoroughly before and after fertilizing. Water trees deeply every ten days in summer; every three weeks in winter.

Care
Prune in spring or summer to remove dead wood, suckers, or crossing branches. Citrus bark is very thin and sunburns easily so it is best to leave low branches on trees to protect the bark. Splitting fruit in the fall is usually the result of hot, dry conditions earlier in the year or trees that have not received regular, summer watering. Healthy, vigorous plants have minimal pest and disease problems, but stressed plants can be susceptible to chlorosis, fungal infections, and borers.

Companion Planting and Design
Plant citrus as a visual screen or impenetrable hedge along a border or boundary. When grown for fruit production, plant so they are not crowding or even touching other trees. Dwarf varieties are excellent in containers, which is a fine way to grow citrus in areas with cold winters.

Did You Know?
Citrus comes originally from China where records of its cultivation date as far back as China's recorded history, well over 5,000 years.

Colorado Blue Spruce

Picea pungens

When, Where, and How to Plant

Plant in fall or early spring in full sun or partial shade in deep, well-drained, moist, fertile soil. Colorado blue spruce is intolerant of compacted or poorly-drained soils as well as hot or dry locations. Dig a hole three to four times wider than the container and just as deep. Soil amendments and treatments are unnecessary. Set the tree in the hole slightly higher than the original soil line and fill the hole by gently pressing the soil around the roots to remove air pockets. Mulching the roots helps maintain even soil moisture but be sure that it does not touch the bark. Water thoroughly after planting then every three to four days for two or three weeks. For the first year, water every seven to ten days.

Growing Tips

Established trees do not need supplemental fertilizer. Protect young trees from hot, dry winds and water every ten days to two weeks, more often if hot or dry conditions prevail. Established plants generally thrive on natural rainfall, but if the summer is unusually hot, water every two weeks until temperatures moderate. During extended dry spells water trees monthly. Apply a 4-inch layer of mulch annually to maintain soil moisture but do not let it touch the bark.

Care

Colorado blue spruce has an elegant natural form and pruning is rarely necessary. However, unlike many conifers, branches regrow after pruning. Colorado blue spruce is not susceptible to pests or disease.

Companion Planting and Design

Mix Colorado blue spruce with deciduous trees or other evergreens to form an effective border for large properties. Its gorgeous form and lovely color make it a dramatic specimen or focal point plant. Place it in a corner or barren spot in areas of the garden that receive minimal care. Use smaller varieties as a background for perennial or annual plantings.

Did You Know?

The genus name comes from the Latin, *picea*, the name for pitch pine, but that word is derived from *pix*, which means "pitch." The epithet refers to the highly fragrant needles.

This is the most common ornamental conifer for high elevation zone gardens, and rightly so. These large, dense, evergreen trees evoke mountain streams and clear blue skies. The crisp, symmetrical shape is formed from regularly spaced branches that grow almost to the ground. Branches are stiff when young and become more flexible as they age and the short, stiff needles are dense on the limbs. Cones are light brown, papery, and up to 4 inches long. Native to high elevation mountains, this beautiful evergreen grows well down to 5,000 feet in elevation. The leaves range from blue-green to silver blue. 'Glauca' has extremely blue foliage and 'Hoopsii' has foliage that is silver-blue. 'Pendula' is a weeping form. Both 'Baby Blue Eyes' and 'Fat Albert' are considered dwarf forms.

Bloom Period and Seasonal Color
Summer; light brown cones.

Mature Height × Spread
30 to 60 feet × 10 to 40 feet

Zones
4, 5, 6
Hardy to 0 degrees Fahrenheit or less.

Desert Willow

Chilopsis linearis

Few desert trees can rival the beauty of the summer-flowering desert willow. This wide-ranging species grows as either a moderately sized shrub or a large branching tree. The long, thin, willowlike leaves are light green and deciduous. The bell-shaped flowers have open, flared ends with ruffled edges in a wide range of colors from pure white to lavender and purple. There are many bicolored forms. Some color forms have been named, others have not, so it is wise to buy the plant in bloom to make a color choice. 'Burgundy' has deep, magenta flowers and 'Lois Adams' blooms are light lavender with virtually no pods. Chiltapa × tashkentensis, a hybrid between this species and Catalpa bignonioides, is a large-leafed tree with broad clusters of white or pink flowers.

Bloom Period and Seasonal Color
Summer; lavender, pink, rose, purple, white, and bicolors.

Mature Height × Spread
10 to 20 feet × 10 to 20 feet

Zones
1, 2, 3, 4, 5
Hardy to 10 degrees Fahrenheit, root hardy lower.

When, Where, and How to Plant
Plant in spring in full sun or partial shade. Plants establish best if they are leafed out before planting. Desert willow tolerates many soil conditions from deep, well-drained, fertile soil to rocky, native soil but often fails in poorly drained soils. Dig a hole three to four times wider than the container and just as deep, adding a generous layer of compost or mulch to the backfill. Set the tree slightly higher than the soil line then replace the soil, pressing it down gently to remove air pockets. Mulch the root zone heavily to retain soil moisture but take care the mulch does not touch the bark. Water thoroughly after planting and continue watering three to four days for two or three weeks. For the first year, water deeply every five to seven days.

Growing Tips
Apply slow-release or organic fertilizer annually in spring to young trees. Mature desert willow does not require supplemental fertilizer. Water established plants deeply every two weeks in summer, monthly in winter.

Care
Prune in spring just as leaves emerge to remove winter damage. To maintain a single trunk, prune the two or three lowest limbs every spring until the tree is as tall as you want it. Although this tree accepts a lot of pruning, it is best to remove only a quarter of the tree in any year. Prune lightly through summer to maintain form and keep it tidy. Seedpods are persistent and may be pruned anytime. Desert willow is not susceptible to pests or disease.

Companion Planting and Design
Mix with other large shrubs or trees such as hopbush, Texas sage, or palo verdes to form an informal border. Plant where reflected heat is intense. Desert willow mixes well with summer-flowering perennials and shrubs such as red justicia, salvias, and yellowbells. It does well in large containers.

Did You Know?
This isn't a willow at all, but a member of a family of outstanding blooming plants that includes pink trumpet vine, yellowbells, and red trumpet vine.

Douglas Fir
Pseudotsuga menziesii

When, Where, and How to Plant

Plant in winter or early spring in full sun or partial shade in deep, coarse, well-drained soil. Douglas fir fails quickly in compacted or poorly drained soils. Dig a hole three to four times wider than the container and just as deep. Although soil amendments are unnecessary, a thin layer of mulch in the backfill is helpful. Disturb the roots as little as possible. Replace the soil and gently press down to remove air. Mulch the root zones but do not allow mulch to touch the bark. Water thoroughly after planting and continue to water every three to four days for two or three weeks. The first year, water every seven to ten days.

Growing Tips

Douglas fir does not require supplemental fertilizer. Established trees grow well on natural rainfall, but if the weather is exceptionally hot or there is a prolonged dry spell, water every two weeks in summer, monthly in winter. Plants from the Northwest often perform poorly; it's wise to purchase plants that are locally grown. This species is best used in gardens above 5,000 feet.

Care

Pruning is rarely required to maintain its beautiful natural form. Prune low branches in early spring to raise the crown. Trees that are water stressed or grown where it is too hot are subject to infestations of western spruce budworm, scale, and aphids. Symptoms include leaf browning and limb die-back. Prevention through good care is the best remedy.

Companion Planting and Design

Mix Douglas fir with evergreens or other trees to form an effective border for large properties. Use it as a focal or specimen plant in gardens that have the space. Plant in areas that receive minimal care. Use smaller varieties in mixed plantings or as a background for perennial or annual plantings.

Did You Know?

The common name honors David Douglas, a Scottish plant explorer sent to North America in 1823 to bring back plants for the Royal Horticultural Society in London. The epithet honors another famous 19th century botanist and plant explorer, Archibald Menzies.

When I studied conifers in college, I fell in love with the botanical name of this plant; it is a delight on the tongue. But I rarely saw the plant in Texas. However, in the high elevation forests of Arizona these magnificent trees are common. Rising over 70 feet tall at maturity, Douglas fir has a regular, pyramid shape. The deep green leaves are flat and provide a striking contrast to the orange-flecked, brown bark. The leaves have a strong spicy, woodsy smell that for many people is the essential smell of the Christmas season. The distinctive cones are small and tan with flat scales that end in a three-pronged tip. The variety 'Little Jon' is shorter and 'Pendula' is a weeping form.

Bloom Period and Seasonal Color

April to May; cones are tan.

Mature Height × Spread

70 to 100 feet × 30 feet

Zones

4, 5, 6
Hardy to 0 degrees Fahrenheit, probably lower.

Feather Tree
Lysiloma watsoni

The open, delicate foliage of the feather tree provides a graceful, tropical effect to low elevation zone gardens. Despite its appearance, this low desert native is fantastically heat and drought tolerant. Feather tree used to be uncommon, but in the last few years, it is beginning to be used in streetside and median plantings all over the region. A small tree, it is often multitrunked and can be exquisite when a few of the trunks are left to develop to maturity. Tiny pale green leaflets crowd the compound leaf giving feather tree its distinctive, mimosa-like appearance. It is briefly deciduous in winter, but recovers quickly in the warmth of spring. In late spring, feather tree is covered with creamy white, puffball-like flowers.

Other Common Names
Desert fern, Feather bush

Bloom Period and Seasonal Color
April to June; white or cream colored puffball blooms.

Mature Height × Spread
15 to 45 feet × 15 to 25 feet

Zones
1, 2, 3
Hardy to 25 degrees Fahrenheit.

When, Where, and How to Plant
Plant in fall or spring in full sun or partial shade. Feather tree grows well in almost any type of soil from deep, well-drained, fertile soil to rocky, native soil, but often fails in heavy or poorly drained soils. Dig a hole three to four times wider than the container and just as deep, adding a generous layer of compost or mulch to the backfill. Place the tree slightly higher than the soil line and backfill the hole, pressing the soil gently as it is replaced to remove air pockets. Mulch the root zone generously but prevent the mulch from touching the bark. Water thoroughly after planting and continue to water every three to four days for two or three weeks. For the first year, water every seven to ten days.

Growing Tips
In spring, apply slow-release or organic fertilizer to young trees, although mature feather trees do not require supplemental fertilizer. Water deeply every ten to fourteen days in summer; monthly in winter.

Care
Feather tree has a strong multitrunk habit, particularly when it's young. Each year in late spring or early summer, prune out the lowest two or three branches until the crown is as high as you want it to encourage a single trunk or selected multiple trunks. Plants are extremely responsive to watering—generous watering will result in large trees and less frequent watering will keep trees smaller. Feather tree is not susceptible to pests or disease.

Companion Planting and Design
Feather tree is an excellent choice to anchor or complement a perennial bed and provide light summer shade. Use as a shade or specimen tree for small patios, courtyards, or seating areas. Plant alone or in groups against hot walls, around pools, or other areas where reflected heat is intense.

Did You Know?
Like the mesquite tree, the pods of feather tree were pounded into flour that was stored and used through the winter by the Native American people who lived in the Sonoran Desert before the arrival of the Spanish.

Fig Tree
Ficus species

When, Where, and How to Plant

Plant in full sun or partial shade in spring after all danger of frost is past. Fig trees may also be planted in the summer. Figs are one of the few trees that thrive with hot weather planting. Fig trees grow best in deep, well-drained, fertile soil but tolerate rocky, native soil if provided sufficient irrigation. Dig a hole three to four times wider than the container and just as deep, adding a generous layer of compost or mulch to the backfill. Set the tree slightly higher than the soil line. Fill the hole, pressing the soil gently to remove air pockets. Mulching the root zone generously helps retain soil moisture, but mulch should not touch the bark. Water thoroughly, then water every three to four days for two or three weeks. Continue watering every five to seven days for the first year.

Growing Tips

Apply slow-release or organic fertilizer in spring for the first four to six years; however, established trees do not require supplemental fertilizer. Water deeply every seven to ten days in summer, and every month or two in winter. Figs rot easily in wet, cold soils so avoid watering when the temperature is below 60 degrees Fahrenheit.

Care

Prune in late spring or summer to remove winter damage or to shape. If plants become too tall, prune the central leader to reduce their size. Although figs are occasionally susceptible to a mite infestation that is hard to control and will ultimately kill the tree, they are generally not susceptible to pests and disease.

Companion Planting and Design

Use taller figs as dense, evergreen shade trees. Smaller species are useful both as shade or background plants around patios, in small courtyards, or in shady gardens. Figs are easily maintained as a shrub with regular, careful pruning and when planted generously, make a good visual screen. Fig trees are not recommended around pools because their shallow roots can lift concrete.

Did You Know?

Buddha is thought to have reached enlightenment under the boughs of the bo tree, *Ficus religiosa*.

As the urban areas of Phoenix have become warmer, tropical fig trees have become more prominent in the ornamental landscape. Figs are tall, smooth-trunked trees with hard, evergreen, deep green leaves. Their great heat tolerance and dense shade make them particularly useful in areas with lots of pavement or reflected heat. The ornamental species rarely bloom, and their fruit is not edible, although birds often find it tasty. The rubber tree (Ficus elastica) typically grows to 15 feet as a multistemmed shrub. Indian laurel fig (F. microcarpa), formerly F. retusa and F. nitida, is a 40-foot-tall tree with a smooth, gray trunk that is widely planted as a street tree. The tall, stately F. benjamina grows to a mature height of 50 feet in low elevation zone gardens.

Bloom Period and Seasonal Color
Late spring and early summer; innocuous pale white.

Mature Height × Spread
20 to 50 feet × 20 to 35 feet

Zones
1, 2, 3
Hardy to 28 degrees Fahrenheit but will die at prolonged temperatures below 22 degrees Fahrenheit.

Flowering Plum

Prunus cerasifera

Flowering plum is widely planted throughout Arizona not for the fruit, but for its early spring flowering and colorful foliage. Flowering plum is often a short-lived plant in low elevation zone gardens but is a durable, small deciduous tree both in intermediate and high elevation zones. The leaves are wide and dark green. The small but prolific flowers bloom in early spring just before the leaves emerge and are generally white or pink. The variety 'Newport' has excellent cold hardiness for the high elevation zones. Although most flowering plum varieties set no fruit, 'Thundercloud' sets small red fruit after its bright pink flowers fade. One of the most commonly used varieties is 'Atropurpurea', which is also called purple-leaf plum. The foliage is a rich, wine color that remains throughout the growing season.

Bloom Period and Seasonal Color
Late winter to early spring; white, white edged in pink, pink, red to reddish purple foliage year-round in selected varieties.

Mature Height × Spread
20 to 30 feet × 15 to 25 feet

Zones
All
Hardy to 0 degrees Fahrenheit.

When, Where, and How to Plant
In high elevation zones, plant in spring after all danger of frost is past; in low elevation zones, plant in fall or early spring. Flowering plum grows best in full sun in deep, well-drained, fertile soil, although protection from afternoon sun is advisable in the hottest zones. Dig a hole three to four times wider than the container and just as deep and add a generous layer of compost or mulch to the backfill. Replace the soil and press gently to remove air pockets. Mulch the root zone generously taking care not to let mulch touch the bark. Water thoroughly, and every three to four days for two or three weeks. Water every five to seven days the first year.

Growing Tips
Apply slow-release or organic fertilizer in fall and again in spring just before leaves emerge. Water established plants weekly in low elevation zones, every two weeks in all others. In low elevation zones, water established plants once a month in winter; rely on natural rainfall in higher elevation zones.

Care
Prune flowering plum in winter while it is dormant to remove damaged or dead wood and crossing branches. Where sawflies are common, flowering plum is susceptible to the leaf damage caused by their larvae. Healthy trees generally tolerate mild infestations; remove larvae with strong jets of water. Plants grown in low elevation zones are easily stressed by high heat and dry soils and may become chlorotic and short-lived. Maintain deep watering regularly in summer to keep plants healthy.

Companion Planting and Design
Plant flowering plum as a shade tree for small patios or seating areas. Group around pools, patios, or in mixed shrub plantings to maximize the effect of the early spring bloom. The purple-leaf plum makes a dramatic specimen or focal plant.

Did You Know?
The genus is the Latin name for the plant and also includes apricots, peaches, cherries, and almonds in it. The epithet means "looking like a cherry" and refers to the fruit.

Fremont Cottonwood

Populus fremontii

When, Where, and How to Plant

Plant in spring in full sun, although young plants will tolerate partial shade. Cottonwoods grow best in moist, deep, well-drained, fertile soil. Cottonwood does not tolerate soils that dry out quickly. To plant, dig a hole three to four times wider than the container and just as deep, adding generous amounts of compost or mulch to the backfill. Place the tree in the hole slightly higher than the soil line and as you replace the soil, press it gently to remove air pockets. Mulch the root zone heavily but do not allow mulch to touch the bark. Water thoroughly after planting and water every three to four days for two or three weeks. Water weekly for the first year.

Growing Tips

A heavy mulch applied annually not only maintains even soil moisture, but also provides all the nutrients cottonwood needs. Established trees do not require supplemental fertilizer. Cottonwood requires steady, deep moisture that is difficult to provide with irrigation. In summer, water deeply at least once a week in low elevation zones, every other week in higher elevation zones. In winter, water once or twice a month in low elevation zones, rely on natural rainfall in higher elevation zones.

Care

Prune cottonwood in winter while it is dormant to remove dead wood, suckers, or damaged limbs. Prune excessive twiggy growth and suckers at the base of the plant anytime in spring or summer. Cottonwood is not susceptible to pests or disease.

Companion Planting and Design

Use cottonwood as a fast-growing shade tree in large yards or the edge of the property. Mix cottonwood with other water-loving trees such as ash to create shady groves on large properties. Plant cottonwood as a focal plant in gardens that have adequate space.

Did You Know?

The Hopi tribe of northern Arizona has long valued cottonwood roots and small stems as carving material. Most of the kachina representations made by artists today are carved from a single piece of cottonwood.

Cottonwoods are denizens of areas where springs arise near the surface as well as the remaining free-flowing waterways throughout Arizona. Most cottonwoods find their way into gardens as large, deciduous shade trees, but few reach the massive proportions of their wild relatives. Cottonwoods have a broad crown crowded with light green leaves that appear to shimmer in the faintest breeze. In fall the leaves turn yellow contrasting well with the gray, furrowed bark. The related Quaking aspen (Populus tremuloides) is a striking plant for high elevation zones where its requirement for moist, deep soils can be met. The white, mottled bark and bright green, ever-moving, heart-shaped leaves that turn a dazzling yellow in fall make quaking aspen a consistent favorite.

Bloom Period and Seasonal Color
February; yellow-green catkins. Fall; bright yellow foliage.

Mature Height × Spread
40 to 70 feet × 20 to 40 feet

Zones
All
Hardy at least to 5 degrees Fahrenheit or more.

Gum Tree
Eucalyptus species

Reviled by some, appreciated by others, gum trees have had a mixed history in the low elevation zones of Arizona. Some of most widely planted species are towering giants, suitable only for golf courses and public rights-of-way. But with over 500 species there are eucalyptus trees to suit any garden scale. Coolibah, Eucalyptus microtheca, a tall tree with thin, silver leaves and whitish bark, is regularly planted. The round, shrubby Forman's eucalyptus (E. formanii) has light green leaves and attractive, twisted branches and Bookleaf mallee (E. kruseana) is a dainty shrub that has blue-gray leaves. Narrow-leafed gimlet (E. spathulata) is a handsome tree with red bark and delicate, deep green leaves and the ghost gum (E. papuana) has a weeping form and striking white bark.

Bloom Period and Seasonal Color
Spring to summer; red, yellow, or white.

Mature Height × Spread
6 to 30 feet × 10 to 30 feet

Zones
1, 2, 3, 4
Hardiness varies by species but most are hardy to 20 degrees Fahrenheit.

When, Where, and How to Plant
Plant in spring or fall in full sun. Gum trees have a wide soil tolerance and grow well in deep, well-drained, fertile soil or rocky, native soil. Many are very salt tolerant and a few grow in moist soils. Dig a hole three to four times wider than the container and just as deep. Add a thin layer of compost or mulch to the backfill. Set the tree in the hole slightly higher than the soil line. Fill the hole, pressing the soil gently to remove air pockets. Mulch the root zone but do not allow mulch to touch the bark. Water thoroughly. Water every three to four days for two or three weeks, then water every seven to ten days for the first year.

Growing Tips
Established gum trees need no supplemental fertilizer. Water established trees carefully; overwatering is the cause of most of the problems with these trees. Water deeply, every three to four weeks in summer, rely on natural rainfall in winter unless the weather is exceptionally hot or dry.

Care
Prune in early spring to remove dead wood or damaged limbs. Many species are brittle and lose limbs in high winds; prune to make a clean cut as soon as possible. Gum trees are not susceptible to pests or disease in Arizona but California is experiencing an increasing problem with borers.

Companion Planting and Design
Plant tree form species as shade trees or mix with other trees for large, border plantings. Some of the shrubby species and those with showy bark make excellent specimen or focal plants. Use the smaller species of gum trees mixed with shrubs to form an informal hedge. Gum trees grow well against hot walls or other areas with high-reflected heat and are particularly useful around pools.

Did You Know?
The name is from the Greek words *eu* meaning "well," and *kalypto,* meaning "to cover," and refers to the cap formed on the flower bud.

Honey Locust
Gleditsia triacanthos

When, Where, and How to Plant

Plant in spring as soon as the soil is warm enough to work. Honey locust grows in full sun or partial shade in deep, well-drained, fertile soils but does not tolerate heavy or poorly drained soil. Plant by digging a hole three to four times wider than the container and just as deep and add a generous layer of compost or mulch to the backfill. Set the tree in the hole slightly higher than the soil line then fill the hole, all the time pressing the soil gently to remove air pockets. Mulch the root zone but do not allow mulch to touch the bark. Water thoroughly after planting and every three to four days for two or three weeks. For the first year or two, water every seven to ten days.

Growing Tips

Apply slow-release or organic fertilizer in fall and late spring to young trees. Water established trees every two to three weeks in summer; rely on natural rainfall in winter. In low elevation zones, water weekly in summer and monthly in winter.

Care

Prune during winter when trees are dormant to remove dead wood, crossing branches, and damaged or diseased limbs. Honey locust leafs out early and sometimes suffers foliage loss from late spring frosts, but it recovers quickly. The thin bark is particularly susceptible to injury from mowers or string cutters and young trees in particular should be protected from such injury. Honey locust is not susceptible to pests and disease.

Companion Planting and Design

Plant honey locust as a solitary shade tree near patios, walkways, and seating areas. Mix with other tall deciduous or evergreen trees to create a large informal boundary planting. Honey locust grows well in lawns but water deeply according to the schedule above in addition to lawn watering.

Did You Know?

The genus honors Johann Gottlieb Gleditsch, who was director of the Botanical Garden of Berlin and died in 1786. The epithet *tri* means "three," and *akantha* means "spined."

Honey locust is a tall, deciduous shade tree that is widely planted in the intermediate and high elevation zones, although it grows nearly as well in low elevation zones. Honey locust has an upright, vase shape and can develop multiple trunks. Flowers are small and unremarkable but result in 6- to 10-inch-long, flat brown pods. The dark brown to black bark highlights the dark glossy green, compound leaves. The leaves turn golden yellow in early fall. 'Shademaster' is a thornless variety with few pods that holds its foliage longer in fall. 'Imperial' has dense foliage making it a particularly good shade tree. 'Sunburst' is a thornless variety with no pods and new leaves that are bright, yellow-green that revert to dark, glossy green as they age.

Bloom Period and Seasonal Color

Summer; inconspicuous green to yellow. Fall; gold to yellow foliage.

Mature Height × Spread

25 to 75 feet × 20 to 50 feet

Zones

All
Hardy to 0 degrees Fahrenheit.

Ironwood

Olneya tesota

The first time I was in Arizona, I took a drive into the hills surrounding Phoenix. The roadsides were resplendent with a large, rounded tree with an odd, smoky purple color. As I got out to investigate, I found the small, pealike blooms of the rugged native ironwood gave it its hue. Found only in the low Sonoran Desert, ironwood is exceptionally drought and heat tolerant, although it does not like the cold. This is a slow-growing tree with intricate branching. The wood is hard and dark brown, almost black, and so heavy that it will not float. The tiny compound leaves are dusky gray and thickly cover the dark, gray limbs. Branches are covered with small, sharp spines until they are old and woody.

Bloom Period and Seasonal Color
April and May; lavender, purple, occasionally white.

Mature Height × Spread
15 to 30 feet × 15 to 25 feet

Zones
1, 2, 3
Hardy to 25 degrees Fahrenheit.

When, Where, and How to Plant

Plant in spring after all danger of frost is past in full sun. Ironwood grows best and more quickly in deep, well-drained soil, but fails to grow or survive long in heavy, wet, or poorly drained soils. To plant, dig a hole three to four times wider than the container but just as deep, adding generous amounts of compost or mulch to the backfill. Set the tree in the hole slightly higher than the soil line and fill the hole, pressing the soil gently as it is replaced to remove air pockets. Water thoroughly after planting and continue to water every three to four days for two or three weeks. Thereafter, water the tree every seven to ten days for the first summer.

Growing Tips

Ironwood requires no supplemental fertilizer. To maintain steady growth and overall vigor, water established plants deeply every month in summer, but mature trees rely entirely on natural rainfall. Water ironwood trees in winter only during prolonged hot or dry spells.

Care

Prune in spring or summer to remove dead or damaged wood. Ironwood is a complicated, multi-branched tree that can be difficult to prune well. To establish a single trunk, prune the lowest three or four branches from young trees in early spring. Repeat every year until the desired crown height is achieved. Ironwood is not susceptible to pests or disease.

Companion Planting and Design

When grown naturally, without pruning, ironwood makes an excellent large visual screen or hedge either singly or mixed with large shrubs. When pruned to a high-crowned shade tree, ironwood can be used as a tall, low-water-use shade tree for patios or seating areas.

Did You Know?

The wood of ironwood is so hard that it resists rot. For many years, the Seri Indians of Baja California carved dead wood into delightful sculptures. In recent times, this practice has been severely controlled because of overuse of live trees by other carvers.

Jacaranda

Jacaranda mimosifolia

When, Where, and How to Plant

Plant in spring after all danger of frost is past in full sun. Jacaranda grows either in deep, well-drained, fertile soil or rocky, native soil, although it grows taller in deep soils. Dig a hole three to four times wider than the container and just as deep. Add a generous layer of compost or mulch to the backfill. Set the tree slightly higher than the soil line and press the soil gently as it is replaced to remove air pockets. Mulching the root zone helps retain soil moisture, but keep mulch away from the bark. Water thoroughly and continue to water every three to four days for two or three weeks, then water every five to seven days for the first year.

Growing Tips

Apply slow-release or organic fertilizer to young trees in fall and again in spring just as leaves emerge. Mature trees do not generally require supplemental fertilizer. Water established trees deeply every seven to ten days in summer, every three to four weeks in winter.

Care

Jacaranda is naturally multitrunked as a young tree but can be trained to a single trunk by removing the lowest three or four branches every spring until the canopy is as tall as you want it. Suckers and small side shoots form in late spring and early summer and should be removed promptly. Jacaranda will grow in a lawn, but be sure it is deep watered in addition to the lawn watering. Jacaranda is not susceptible to pests or disease, but becomes chlorotic when not watered deeply.

Companion Planting and Design

Jacaranda is an outstanding shade tree. Mix with other large trees to form a border. Jacaranda is wonderful as a specimen or focal plant in large gardens. It can be grown as a multibranched shrub for smaller gardens if carefully pruned. The roots are not invasive so it can be used close to walkways, driveways, or patios.

Did You Know?

The genus is the Brazilian name for the plant. The epithet means "foliage like mimosa."

Jacaranda is used in all the warm regions of the world for its tall, stately form and outstanding spring color display. This Brazilian native brings its late spring color and high, graceful shade into Arizona's low elevation zone gardens as well. Jacaranda is an upright, open-crowned tree that is generally much taller than it is wide. This fast-growing, semievergreen tree has soft, dark green, mimosa-like foliage. The large, blue to purple flowers are clustered into showy heads at the end of the branches in late spring. They are followed by round, flat pods that are useful in dried arrangements. Plants are naturally multi-trunked but are easily trained to one or a few main trunks. Although jacaranda sheds most of its leaves in winter, trees recover quickly in the warmth of spring.

Bloom Period and Seasonal Color
May; lavender, blue, and purple, occasionally pink or white.

Mature Height × Spread
25 to 50 feet × 15 to 30 feet

Zones
1, 2, 3
Hardy to 25 degrees Fahrenheit.

Kidneywood

Eysenhardtia orthocarpa

As yards get smaller, and patios take the place of an entire garden, small, attractive trees become especially useful. Heading up my list of underused, small trees is kidneywood, a 10- to 12-foot-tall, semievergreen tree that is the perfect size for small gardens or crowded patios. Kidneywood is an openly branched tree with dark, gray stems that are lightly covered with small, light green compound leaves. Tiny flowers occur in loose spikes at the ends of the branches intermittently through summer and smell of vanilla. The flat, tan pods are crammed into clusters that look like miniature pagodas. The closely related Texas kidneywood (Eysenhardtia texana) has much darker green leaves, a spicier aroma, and grows more as a shrub than a tree.

Bloom Period and Seasonal Color
April to September; white.

Mature Height × Spread
3 to 10 feet × 3 to 10 feet

Zones
1, 2, 3, 4
Hardy to 17 degrees Fahrenheit.

When, Where, and How to Plant
Plant in fall for best results, although trees may be successfully planted in early spring. Place in full sun or partial shade, and protect from western sun in the hottest zones. Kidneywood grows equally well in all but heavy or poorly drained soils. Dig a hole three to four times wider than the container and just as deep, adding a generous layer of compost or mulch to the backfill. Set the tree slightly higher than the soil line and press the soil gently as it is replaced to remove air pockets. Mulching the root zone is helpful to maintain soil moisture, but do not allow mulch to touch the bark. Water thoroughly and water every three to four days for two or three weeks, then every five to seven days for the first year.

Growing Tips
Kidneywood does not require supplemental fertilizer. Established plants should be deeply watered twice a month in summer; once a month or less in winter. The bloom is not as prolific if plants are overwatered.

Care
Plants are often multitrunked when young but can be trained to a single trunk by annually removing the suckers and the lowest two or three branches in late spring until the tree is the desired height. Do not remove more than a quarter of the tree in any year. Prune dead wood or damaged limbs in late winter and early spring. Kidneywood is not susceptible to pests or disease.

Companion Planting and Design
Kidneywood is a superb small tree for a patio or courtyard. Use it as light shade for tender succulents or perennials or place it near walkways, seating areas, or near a pool where the lovely summer fragrance can be enjoyed. Mix unpruned kidneywood with Texas sage, desert senna, or black dalea to form an informal hedge.

Did You Know?
This plant gets its odd common name from its medicinal use in Mexico. The wood was steeped as a tea and used to treat kidney and bladder problems and as a diuretic.

Maple
Acer species

When, Where, and How to Plant

Plant in early spring in a full sun location leaving plenty of room for the spreading crown. Maples grow best in deep, moist, well-drained soil that does not dry out regularly and is close to a neutral pH. Dig a hole three to four times wider than the container and just as deep and add a generous layer of compost or mulch to the backfill. Set the tree slightly higher than the soil line, and then refill the hole, pressing the soil gently as it is replaced to remove air pockets. Mulch the root zone generously to maintain steady soil moisture, but do not allow mulch to touch the bark. Water thoroughly, then water every three to four days for two or three weeks; every seven to ten days for the first year.

Growing Tips

Fertilize young trees annually with slow-release or organic fertilizer; established trees do not require supplemental fertilizer. Water established trees every three to four weeks in summer; every other month in winter. Young trees may need more frequent watering when the weather is warm and dry. Protect young trees with shade cloth or screens from hot, drying winds.

Care

Prune in winter while trees are dormant to remove dead wood, crossing branches, and damaged limbs or to shape and thin the tree. Maples are not susceptible to pests and disease in Arizona, but may die prematurely if they are not provided enough steady moisture.

Companion Planting and Design

Maples can be used wherever deep shade is required. The smaller size and general durability of Amur maple make it particularly useful in smaller gardens, near patios, or seating areas. Plant maples as specimens to show off their stunning fall color. Mix maples with other deciduous trees or conifers for an informal boundary or border planting.

Did You Know?

The name *Acer* is the Latin word for maple trees but it also means "sharp." That meaning refers to the hardness of the wood, which was used in Roman times as the handle of a spear.

Maples are prized by gardeners around the world for their spectacular fall display and dense crown of hand-shaped leaves. In Arizona, maples grow best in moist soils in the cooler parts of the intermediate elevation zone and throughout the high elevation zones. One of the most durable is the Amur maple (Acer tartaricum var. ginnala) with its dome-shaped crown formed from large, nearly round, dark green leaves. This deciduous tree grows to only 20 feet tall and turns red or yellow in fall. The much larger bigtooth maple (A. grandidentatum) grows well in areas of the high elevation zone where its need for cool, moist soils can be met. Bigtooth maple grows to 40 feet tall and the leaves turn yellow, gold, red, and deep rose in fall.

Bloom Period and Seasonal Color

Summer; innocuous. Fall; shades of red, gold, and yellow foliage.

Mature Height × Spread

15 to 20 × 10 to 15

Zones

4, 5, 6
Hardy to -5 degrees Fahrenheit and lower.

Netleaf Hackberry

Celtis reticulata

Netleaf hackberry is a dependable, native shade tree for intermediate and high elevation zones. This hackberry does remarkably well in low elevation zones when given ample water and deep soils. The smooth, gray bark is marked by bumps and knobby warts, but they are the marks of maturity, not of disease. The gray-green leaves are finely serrated and rough, and although they are deciduous, they are not especially colorful in fall. Winter exaggerates the complicated, fanciful branching of the tree making it a particularly handsome specimen during that season. The related desert hackberry (Celtis pallida) is more shrub than tree with the same complex branching, and rough, green leaves. Desert hackberry is evergreen. Both species produce prodigious amounts of small, red fruit that is devoured by birds.

Bloom Period and Seasonal Color
March to June; white.

Mature Height × Spread
20 to 30 feet × 30 feet

Zones
All
Hardy to 0 degrees Fahrenheit or more.

When, Where, and How to Plant
Plant in fall or spring in low elevation zones, in spring in higher elevation zones. Plant trees in full sun. Netleaf hackberry grows best in deep, well-drained, fertile soil. Dig a hole three to four times wider than the container and just as deep. Add a generous layer of compost or mulch to the backfill. Set the tree in the hole slightly higher than the soil line. Fill the hole, pressing the soil gently around the roots to remove air pockets. Mulch the root zone but do not allow mulch to touch the bark. Water thoroughly. Water every three to four days for two or three weeks, then water every seven to ten days for the first year.

Growing Tips
Fertilize young trees annually in spring with slow-release or organic fertilizer. Mature trees do not require supplemental fertilizer. Water established trees every two to three weeks in summer; every other month in winter. Water young trees more frequently during extended hot, dry weather.

Care
Prune while the tree is dormant to remove dead or damaged wood and crossing branches. To maintain an upright, single-trunk form, prune the lowest three or four branches each year during dormancy and repeat annually until the desired crown height is achieved. Do not remove more than a quarter of the tree in any single year. Tent caterpillars show up in early summer; remove them promptly from small trees by cutting out the infected area. Psyllids and nipple galls appear from time to time on the leaves but cause only cosmetic damage.

Companion Planting and Design
Plant netleaf hackberry as a tall shade tree near patios, houses, or seating areas. Mix netleaf hackberry with other deciduous trees and conifers to form a boundary planting. Netleaf hackberry tolerates growing in a lawn but water deeply in addition to lawn watering. Birds will visit in stupendous numbers when the fruit is ripe.

Did You Know?
The genus is the Greek name of a similar tree. The epithet means "covered with a net."

New Mexican Locust

Robinia neomexicana

When, Where, and How to Plant

Plant in spring in full sun or partial shade. New Mexican locust grows best in deep, well-drained soil. Dig a hole three to four times wider than the container and just as deep, adding a generous layer of compost or mulch to the backfill. Set the tree slightly higher than the soil line, and back fill, pressing the soil gently as it is replaced to remove air pockets. Mulch the root zone generously but keep mulch away from the bark. Water thoroughly after planting then water every three to four days for two or three weeks; every seven to ten days for the first year.

Growing Tips

New Mexican locust trees need no supplemental fertilizer, even as young plants. Deeply water established plants every month or two during the growing season; rely on natural rainfall in winter.

Care

Prune unwanted stems and root suckers, dead or damaged wood, and crossing branches in spring. To maintain a single trunk or selected trunks, cut out the three or four lowest branches each spring and regularly remove any root suckers that appear. Do this yearly until the tree is the height you want. Continue to remove the root suckers every spring to keep the plant tidy and in good shape. New Mexican locust is not susceptible to pests or disease.

Companion Planting and Design

New Mexican locust is lovely mixed with other summer-flowering shrubs or small trees in a mixed hedge or border. This species is very drought tolerant when mature, and its suckering habit makes it a good choice for erosion control on steep slopes or for areas of the garden that receive minimal care. When pruned to a single or few-trunked tree, use as a specimen or focal plant for small patios, courtyards, or near a pool.

Did You Know?

It was first proposed to name the genus after the great American botanical explorer, Thomas Coulter, but that name was taken. It was named instead for his close friend, the astronomer Thomas Romney Robinson, who died in 1882.

New Mexican locust is a fast-growing, multitrunked, deciduous tree that is native to the high elevations of the Arizona mountains and other areas of the West. This locust is easily trained to a small tree with regular pruning. The compound leaves are made up of large, dark green leaflets that are in handsome contrast to the dark brown to black bark. But the full glory of New Mexican locust is its spring bloom. Dozens of pale pink, pealike flowers are clustered in drooping heads at the ends of the stems each spring. Black locust (Robinia pseudoacacia) is a much larger multitrunked tree, up to 75 feet tall, with inky black trunks and large, deep green, compound leaves.

Bloom Period and Seasonal Color

May to July; light and dark pink, occasionally white.

Mature Height × Spread

6 to 30 feet × 6 to 20 feet

Zones

4, 5, 6

Hardy to 0 degrees Fahrenheit or lower.

Oak

Quercus species

Oaks in Arizona are rarely the towering, deciduous shade trees so familiar to Eastern gardeners. One of the largest, Emory's oak (Quercus emoryi) is an evergreen with dark green leaves that grows up to 50 feet tall. The shrubby, evergreen scrub oak (Q. turbinella) has gray-green, holly-shaped leaves, and like Emory's oak, grows best in the intermediate elevation zones. Gambel oak (Q. gambelii) with its wide, irregular crown, and deciduous leaves that turn yellow or orange in fall grows easily in high elevation zone gardens. 'Heritage', a selection of Q. fusiformis, has dark green, evergreen leaves and dark bark and grows extremely well in the low elevation zones of the state. The deciduous Texas red oak (Q. texana), also called Q. buckleyi, has deeply cut leaves that turn brilliant red; it also grows well in low elevation zones.

Bloom Period and Seasonal Color
Spring; inconspicuous creamy catkins. Fall; shades of red or yellow foliage.

Mature Height × Spread
30 to 60 feet × 10 × 40 feet

Zones
All
Hardiness varies by species but most are hardy at least to 15 degrees Fahrenheit.

When, Where, and How to Plant
Plant in fall in low zones; in fall or early spring in other zones. Oaks grow best in full sun. Oaks grow in a wide variety of soils but most species do best in deep, well-drained soil, although scrub oak grows well in dry, rocky soil. Dig a hole three to four times wider than the container and just as deep and add a generous layer of compost or mulch to the backfill. Set the tree slightly higher than the soil line filling the hole by pressing the soil gently around the roots as it is replaced to remove air pockets. Oaks respond well to heavy mulch around the root zone, but take care it does not touch the bark. Water thoroughly, then water every three to four days for two or three weeks. Water deeply every week for the first year, and through the second year in the hottest zones.

Growing Tips
Established oaks do not require supplemental fertilizer. In low elevation zones, water established plants weekly in summer; monthly in winter. In intermediate and high elevation zones, established native oaks need irrigation only during extended hot, dry weather.

Care
Prune in late winter to remove damaged wood or to shape young trees. Most oaks have wonderful natural form and do not need aggressive pruning. Oaks are resistant to most pests and diseases of the area, but decline in the low elevation zones when provided insufficient water.

Companion Planting and Design
Scrub oak in particular makes an excellent hedge or visual screen whether planted singly or mixed with other shrubs and small trees. Plant taller species near patios, houses, or around play or seating areas for shade. The dark green color of evergreen oaks provides a good background for colorful perennial or annual plantings.

Did You Know?
The genus is the Latin word for "oak." Renowned since ancient times for their strength and longevity, oaks have been used in religious practice, for construction, as a tanning agent, and the acorns as food both for animals and humans.

Orchid Tree
Bauhinia species

When, Where, and How to Plant

Plant in spring or fall in full sun or partial shade, however it is best to plant deciduous species after they leaf out. Tropical orchid trees require deep, well-drained, fertile soil that does not dry out. The others grow equally well in well-drained, fertile soil or rocky, native soil. Dig a hole three to four times wider than the container and just as deep, adding a generous layer of compost or mulch to the backfill. Fill the hole, pressing the soil gently around the roots as it is replaced to remove air pockets. All orchid trees thrive with a thick layer of mulch around the roots, but be careful that it does not touch the bark. Water thoroughly at planting and every three to four days for two or three weeks. Continue deep watering every five to seven days for the first year.

Growing Tips

Fertilize tropical orchid trees annually in spring with slow-release or organic fertilizer and apply iron and sulphur amendments in summer. The other species do not require any supplemental fertilizer beyond a steady application of mulch. Deeply water established tropical orchid trees weekly in summer, every two to three weeks in winter. Water established trees of the other species every seven to ten days in summer, monthly in winter.

Care

Prune to shape or remove frost damaged limbs and dead wood in early spring. Tropical orchid trees are highly susceptible to salt burn, heat stress, and chlorosis in summer. None are susceptible to any pests or disease.

Companion Planting and Design

Mix orchid trees with large shrubs to form an informal hedge. The spectacular blooms make them effective as specimen or focal plants, particularly in small gardens. The two desert species listed are useful to fill barren corners or serve as accent plants for small patios.

Did You Know?

This genus, *Bauhinia*, is easily recognized by its oddly shaped pair of leaves. The pair looks like a hoof, joined at the very end, separate in the middle, with a point at the tip.

Gardeners really are a perverse lot who cling to familiar plants, regardless of the difficulties. The common orchid tree, Bauhinia variegata, *with its brief pink or white spring bloom, suffers from salt burn, heat stress, and needs generous irrigation. The Hong Kong orchid tree (B. × blakeana) with its corsage-sized amethyst flowers has the same struggles, in addition to which, both are very cold tender. Anacacho orchid tree (B. lunarioides) prefers rocky, alkaline soils and high heat and although individual white flowers are small, they are prolific over a long season in spring and early summer. The Chihuahua orchid tree (B. macranthera) brings out its large, pink flowers flat along the stems in May and thrives in the hottest parts of the state. Both of these species are undamaged to 15 degrees Fahrenheit.*

Bloom Period and Seasonal Color
Spring to summer; pink, purple, mauve, and white.

Mature Height × Spread
6 to 30 feet × 5 to 25 feet

Zones
1, 2, 3, 4
Tropical orchid trees are hardy to 28 degrees Fahrenheit; others, to 15 degrees Fahrenheit.

Palo Blanco
Acacia willardiana

The delicate beauty of palo blanco belies its desert origins. Native to Sonora, Mexico, palo blanco is a loose, open tree that is a striking choice for a small narrow place or a crowded courtyard. Plants have a solitary trunk with few branches giving it an overall vase shape. Branches are covered with thin, white bark that gracefully peels away to reveal the cream-colored trunk. The odd, draping foliage is made up of elongated petioles, called phyllodes, that are up to 12 inches long. These leaf mimics cascade and fall from tall, thin stems floating gracefully in the slightest breeze. The real leaves are tiny, at the ends of the phyllodes, and occur briefly in spring along with the creamy white flowers.

Bloom Period and Seasonal Color
February to June; white or yellowish cream.

Mature Height × Spread
10 to 20 feet × 5 to 10 feet

Zones
1, 2
Hardy to 25 degrees Fahrenheit.

When, Where, and How to Plant
Plant in fall or early spring in a full sun location. Palo blanco grows well both in deep, well-drained, fertile soil or rocky, native soil but cannot tolerate heavy or poorly drained soils. Plant by digging a hole three to four times wider than the container and just as deep. Add a generous layer of compost or mulch to the backfill. Fill the hole, pressing the soil gently around the roots as it is replaced to remove air pockets. Water thoroughly after planting and continue deep watering every three to four days for two or three weeks. Water newly planted trees every seven to ten days for the first year.

Growing Tips
Palo blanco does not require supplemental fertilizer, even as a young tree. Established trees should be watered every two to three weeks in summer; every month in winter.

Care
Prune lightly to remove dead or damaged branches in early spring or summer. It is tempting to stake young trees because the trunk is so thin, but trees straighten quickly and are much stronger if they are grown without staking. Palo blanco is not susceptible to pests or disease.

Companion Planting and Design
Use palo blanco in small patios to provide light shade. The delicate appearance and upright form make palo blanco useful in narrow, or crowded patios, courtyards, or between structures. The peeling bark and graceful form make palo blanco a good specimen or focal point. Plant in groups to create groves for barren areas or to fill corners in hot, dry locations. Plant against hot walls, around a pool or other areas where reflected heat is intense.

Did You Know?
Phyllodes are elongated leaf petioles that function as leaves. This is a common adaptation in the Australian species of *Acacia* that grow in arid or desert regions, but palo blanco is the only species in the Americas with this leaf form. It is also the only New World species with peeling bark.

Palo Brea
Cercidium praecox

When, Where, and How to Plant

Plant in fall, spring, or summer in full sun; young trees also grow well in partial shade. Palo brea grows well both in deep, well-drained, fertile soil or rocky, native soil but does not tolerate heavy or poorly drained soils. To plant, dig a hole three to four times wider than the container and just as deep, adding a thin layer of compost or mulch to the backfill. Set the tree in the hole slightly higher than the soil line and fill the hole, pressing the soil gently around the roots as it is replaced to remove air pockets. Water thoroughly after planting then every three to four days for two or three weeks. Continue watering every seven to ten days for the first year or two.

Growing Tips

Fertilize young trees annually in spring with slow-release or organic fertilizer; established trees do not require supplemental fertilizer. Water established trees every ten to fourteen days in summer; once a month in winter.

Care

Prune to remove dead or damaged wood or crossing branches only in warm weather; cold weather pruning encourages bacterial infections. The bark of palo brea is extremely thin and easily damaged by tools or equipment, rough handling, and even by the action of an impact sprinkler. Palo brea is not susceptible to pests and diseases. It does not grow well in a lawn without supplemental watering because it does not like frequent, shallow watering.

Companion Planting and Design

Plant palo brea as the principal shade tree in the yard or around a patio or seating area. The phenomenal limbs and brilliant bloom make palo brea an excellent choice for a specimen or focal plant where room permits. Plant against hot walls or windows where reflected heat is intense.

Did You Know?

The genus *Cercidium* means "referring to *Cercis*," the genus of redbuds. The epithet means "very early" and probably refers to the bloom period in April.

There are not very many old, mature palo brea trees in the low elevation zones of Arizona; they are a fairly recent addition to the ornamental offerings. But one look at these majestic desert trees and you are hooked into finding a place for their elegant beauty in your own yard. Palo brea has a wide, open, and spreading crown, making it a favored shade tree for low elevation zone gardens. The few, widely spaced branches twist and turn gracefully as they mature and look as if they were painted with the smooth, light green bark. The small, blue-green compound leaves are numerous and remain on the plant most of the year. Palo brea blooms in late spring and the plant is completely covered by the vivid yellow flowers.

Bloom Period and Seasonal Color
April and May; vivid yellow.

Mature Height × Spread
15 to 30 feet × 20 to 25 feet

Zones
1, 2, 3
Hardy to 25 degrees Fahrenheit; recovers quickly from sun damage.

Pinyon Pine
Pinus edulis

Pinyon pine is a small, multibranched native pine that grows throughout the intermediate and high elevation zones of Arizona. Pinyon pine has numerous, erratically shaped limbs that form a symmetrical pyramid of a tree when young. As trees mature, the crown spreads to form a low dome-shaped or flat crown. The stiff dark green needles are prolific and create a beautiful contrast with the shaggy, reddish bark. In summer, multitudes of small cones ripen on female trees. Inside are the delectable nuts that have served as an important food for native peoples of the region for centuries and are still roasted and enjoyed today. The very similar single-leaf pinyon, Pinus monophylla, is a more heat tolerant species and a better choice for lower elevation zone gardens.

Other Common Name
Colorado pinyon pine

Bloom Period and Seasonal Color
Summer; inconspicuous.

Mature Height × Spread
10 to 20 feet × 8 to 16 feet

Zones
3, 4, 5, 6
Hardy to 0 degrees Fahrenheit or lower.

When, Where, and How to Plant
Plant pinyon pine in fall in full sun in any fast draining soil from deep, well-drained, fertile soil to rocky, native soil. However, pinyon pine does not tolerate heavy, poorly drained soils or those that are very alkaline or salty. Plant by digging a hole three to four times wider than the container and just as deep and providing a generous layer of compost or mulch to the backfill. Set the tree in the hole slightly higher than the soil line and fill the hole, pressing the soil gently around the roots as it is replaced to remove air pockets. Water thoroughly after planting and water every three to four days for two or three weeks. After that, water every seven to ten days for the first year.

Growing Tips
Established trees do not require supplemental fertilizer and when growing within their natural range need supplemental irrigation only during extended hot, dry spells in summer or during extremely dry periods in winter. Water young plants once a month in summer; every other month in winter.

Care
Pinyon pine has a remarkable natural form and should be left to develop naturally. Prune only to remove dead or damaged wood in spring. Pinyon pine is not susceptible to pests or disease.

Companion Planting and Design
Mix pinyon pine with other conifers or tall shrubs to create an informal border planting. Plant as a specimen or focal plant where there is ample room for the symmetrical form to develop. Pinyon pine trees make an effective background for colorful perennials or annual plantings.

Did You Know?
People are not the only creatures that enjoy the rich nuts; birds are also wild for them. Most birds that eat pine nuts have specialized bills to open the cone and get the seed. In order for blue jays to get at the seed, they take a cone to a large limb, hold it with their feet, and use their bill as a chisel to pry out the nuts.

Pomegranate
Punica granatum

When, Where, and How to Plant
Plant in winter or early spring while plants are dormant. Place in full sun or partial shade. Pomegranate grows well in deep, well-drained, fertile soil or rocky, native soil but does not grow well in moist, heavy, or poorly drained soils. Dig a hole three to four times wider than the container and just as deep and set the tree slightly higher than the soil line. Add a generous layer of compost or mulch to the backfill then fill the hole, pressing the soil gently around the roots to remove air pockets. Mulch the root zone generously, but do not allow mulch to touch the bark. Water thoroughly and continue to water deeply every three to four days for two or three weeks. Water newly planted trees every week for the first year.

Growing Tips
Apply slow-release or organic fertilizer in fall and spring. Mulching roots heavily helps maintain even soil moisture in summer. Established plants should be watered every ten days in summer; monthly in winter. Although pomegranate is quite drought tolerant it has better quality and quantity of fruit when it's regularly watered.

Care
Prune in winter while the plant is dormant to remove suckers, crossing branches, and dead or damaged wood. Plants are easily trained to a single trunk or even an espalier by removing suckers and unwanted branches annually in early spring. Pomegranate is not susceptible to pests or disease but leaf-foot plant bugs may eat holes in the fruit. These insects rarely occur in large numbers and there is no known preventive.

Companion Planting and Design
Pomegranate makes a spectacular espaliered plant. When grown as a shrub it makes a good visual screen hedge either alone or mixed with other shrubs. Plants trained as a small tree make good specimen or accent plants for small patios or courtyards. Pomegranate also grows well in a large container.

Did You Know?
The distinctive shape of the fruit was recreated in the jewelry of the ancient cultures of Egypt and the Middle East.

Pomegranate is the tree of many colors. In spring, the dark green, glossy leaves coat the stems and the plants look cool and refreshing. Then the tree is covered in flaming red-orange flowers that give way to large, round fruit with its characteristic flared end, like the mouth of a marine creature. Fruits stay on the plant for months and deepen in color to a rich, wine red. Finally, in fall, leaves turn a blazing yellow before they fall leaving the bare stems holding the red globes of fruit. The fruit and seeds are delicious. 'Wonderful' has rich, red fruit and red-orange flowers. 'Chico' and 'Nana' are dwarf varieties with colorful, decorative fruit that is not edible.

Bloom Period and Seasonal Color
Spring through summer; red, red-orange, yellow, apricot, and white. Fall; bright yellow foliage.

Mature Height × Spread
12 to 20 feet × 10 to 15 feet

Zones
1, 2, 3, 4
Hardy to 20 degrees Fahrenheit.

Ponderosa Pine
Pinus ponderosa

Ponderosa pine is the hallmark of the high, mountain areas of Arizona. Huge forests of this species extend from the northeastern corner of the state in a wide diagonal to the New Mexico border. It is not only a prized landscape pine but also an important timber plant for the region. Ponderosa pines are very tall trees that grow almost perfectly straight with widely spaced branches that form a symmetrical, pyramidal crown. The long, deep green needles are held toward the ends of the branches in bundles of three. In young trees, the bark is black, but as trees mature the bark develops distinctive reddish yellow plates. The small cones are prolific in good years providing food for countless birds and animals in the northern forests.

Other Common Name
Western yellow pine

Bloom Period and Seasonal Color
June; evergreen needles.

Mature Height x Spread
50 to 100 feet × 25 to 30 feet

Zones
4, 5, 6
Hardy to 0 degrees Fahrenheit and lower.

When, Where, and How to Plant
Plant in early spring while weather and soils are still cool. Ponderosa pine grows best on dry slopes or in well-drained soil in full sun but fails in compacted heavy soil or those with poor drainage. Plant by digging a hole three to four times wider than the container and just as deep. Soil amendments and treatments are not necessary; however, pines are sensitive to root disturbance so plant as small a tree as possible. Set the tree in the hole slightly higher than the original soil line. Fill the hole, pressing the soil gently around the roots as it is replaced to remove air pockets. Mulch the root zones of the plant generously but be careful the mulch does not touch the bark. Water thoroughly when completed and continue to water every three to four days for two or three weeks. For the first year or two, continue to water every seven to ten days.

Growing Tips
Apply slow-release or organic fertilizer annually in spring to young trees. Water maturing plants deeply once a month in summer, every other month in winter. When grown within its native range, established ponderosa pines grow well with supplemental water needed only during unusually dry spells.

Care
Prune in spring just as the new needles emerge to remove unwanted branches or lift the crown. Ponderosa pine self prunes old branches naturally. Remove dead wood anytime. Ponderosa pine is not susceptible to pests or disease although stressed plants may show significant needle and limb loss from pine bark beetles.

Companion Planting and Design
Ponderosa pine is an outstanding specimen tree where space permits. Mix it with other large conifers and deciduous trees to form border planting for large properties. Ponderosa pine provides excellent high shade and the fallen needles provide ample mulch for perennial and vegetable gardens.

Did You Know?
Flagstaff gets its name from a flagpole made from a ponderosa pine which was erected on the Fourth of July, 1876, to mark the trail from Santa Fe to San Francisco.

Redbud
Cercis species

When, Where, and How to Plant

In low elevations, plant in fall or early spring while plants are dormant. Plant in partial shade. In higher elevations zones, plant in spring in full sun or partial shade. Redbuds grow in a wide range of soils but grow best in well-drained, fertile soil. Dig a hole three to four times wider than the container and just as deep. Set the tree slightly higher than the soil line. Add a generous layer of compost or mulch to the backfill then as it is replaced, press the soil gently around the roots to remove air pockets. Mulch the root zone generously, but be careful the mulch does not touch the bark. Water thoroughly when done and then water every three to four days for two or three weeks. For the first year, continue to water weekly.

Growing Tips

Apply slow-release or organic fertilizer in fall and spring for the first four to six years. Keep roots heavily mulched in summer to keep soil from drying out. Water every seven to ten days in summer; every month or less in winter when the tree is dormant.

Care

Prune in winter while the tree is dormant to remove dead or damaged wood, remove suckers or unwanted stems, and shape. Redbud is naturally multitrunked but can be trained to a single trunk by removing suckers and unwanted branches annually in winter. Plants bloom on new wood, so prune only those branches that must be pruned to preserve the bloom. Redbud is not susceptible to pests and disease.

Companion Planting and Design

Mix redbud with large perennials or shrubs to provide early spring color. Redbud grows well in shady locations, particularly in the low elevation zones, and can be used to provide needed color and texture to shady beds. Use the deep green leaves as a background for colorful summer perennial or annual beds.

Did You Know?

There are redbuds in Europe and the genus was named for the Greek word, *kerkis*, which was one of the species.

There was a huge redbud in the yard of our house when I was young. Every spring, the barren, dark branches were smothered in deep pink flowers—our first sign of spring. Here in Arizona, we, too, can enjoy the glorious burst of early spring pink flowers that these small trees or large shrubs provide. Eastern redbud (Cercis candensis) grows best in intermediate and high elevation zones. Mexican redbud (C. candensis var. mexicana) also known as C. mexicana with its round, leathery leaves and light pink flowers is well-suited to the heat and aridity of the low elevation zones. Western redbud (C. occidentalis) is a reliable, drought tolerant, small tree with bright pink flowers and foliage that turns yellow or red in fall.

Bloom Period and Seasonal Color
February to March; light pink to dark pink flowers before the leaves emerge. Fall; shades of red and yellow foliage.

Mature Height × Spread
6 to 20 feet × 6 to 15 feet

Zones
All
Hardiness varies by species.

Shoestring Acacia
Acacia stenophylla

It is often difficult to find a tree for a narrow spot that needs high shade, but shoestring acacia is a first-rate choice. Trees grow straight up with minimal branching but spread somewhat as they age. The long, dusky green foliage hangs gracefully off the spare branches and, like all Australian acacias, is made up of flattened leaf petioles called phyllodes. The true leaves are briefly seen in spring. The bark is maroon in youth but ages to dark gray. There appear to be at least two recognizable growth forms—one that remains narrow and columnar even in maturity, and the other grows a wide, full, spreading crown as it ages. The creamy yellow flowers are sparsely arranged on the tree.

Bloom Period and Seasonal Color
Fall to spring; cream to yellowish white.

Mature Height × Spread
15 to 25 feet × 15 to 20 feet

Zones
1, 2, 3
Hardy to 18 degrees Fahrenheit.

When, Where, and How to Plant
Plant in fall or spring in full or partial sun. Shoestring acacia grows in a wide variety of soil conditions from deep, well-drained, fertile soil to rocky, native soil but does not tolerate heavy or poorly drained soils. Plant by digging a hole three to four times wider than the container and just as deep. Set the tree in the hole slightly higher than the soil line. Add a generous layer of compost or mulch to the backfill then replace it, pressing the soil gently around the roots as you fill to remove air pockets. Water thoroughly when planting is complete and every three to four days for two or three weeks. Water every seven to ten days for the first year.

Growing Tips
Shoestring acacia does not need supplemental fertilizer. Water maturing plants every ten to fourteen days in summer; every three to four weeks in winter. Established plants survive on monthly watering in summer; every other month in winter.

Care
Prune in late spring or early summer to remove dead wood, damaged limbs, or crossing branches. Shoestring acacia has excellent natural form and rarely needs pruning for shape. It is not susceptible to pests or disease.

Companion Planting and Design
Shoestring acacia is an excellent shade tree for a tight spot, such as between buildings, or for a small patio or courtyard. Shoestring acacia has very little litter compared to most trees making it particularly useful around pools or other areas where litter is a problem. Mix shoestring acacia with other large trees to form a boundary planting. Use shoestring acacia to protect hot walls or other areas where reflected heat is intense. Plant in groups to create a shady grove where space permits.

Did You Know?
The genus, *Acacia*, is derived from the Greek word, *akakie*, which means "a sharp point." The epithet is from the Greek, *steno*, meaning "narrow" and the Greek, *phyllon*, which means "leaf."

Sweet Acacia
Acacia farnesiana

When, Where, and How to Plant

Plant in fall or spring in full or partial sun. Sweet acacia tolerates rocky, native soil, but grows best in deep, well-drained, fertile soil. Dig a hole three to four times wider than the container and just as deep and set the tree slightly higher than the soil line. After adding a generous layer of compost or mulch to the backfill, refill the hole, pressing soil gently around the roots to remove air pockets. Mulch the root zone but do not allow mulch to touch the bark and water thoroughly. Water every three to four days for two or three weeks, then water every seven to ten days for the first year.

Growing Tips

Apply slow-release or organic fertilizer annually in spring to young plants; established trees do not generally need fertilizer. Water established plants twice a month in summer, and every three to four weeks in winter. Plants growing in dry or rocky soils may require more frequent irrigation.

Care

Prune in late spring or early summer to remove damaged limbs and to shape. Trees are strongly multitrunked when young but can be trained to a single trunk by removing lower branches and suckers annually in spring. Sweet acacia grows a thick crown that makes it susceptible to falling over in high winds. Thin the crown every two or three years to allow ample air flow. Sweet acacia is occasionally infested with borers, which cause lesions on the trunk or limb die back. Healthy trees usually recover quickly.

Companion Planting and Design

Plant sweet acacia for shade in small yards, courtyards, or near patios. Unpruned sweet acacia makes an impenetrable hedge. Sweet acacia will grow in a lawn, but water deeply in addition to lawn watering.

Did You Know?

Although native to the Americas, this species has been cultivated in Europe since 1611 and is still an important component of the French perfume industry. It has naturalized in parts of southern Europe on the Mediterranean coast as well as Africa, tropical Asia, and Australia.

Sweet acacia is a charming small tree for gardens of the low and intermediate elevation zones of Arizona. This is an intricately branched, thorny tree with a heavy, spreading crown. The tiny, dark green leaves are congested along the many dark, brown branches. The small, golden, puffball-like flowers are so prolific in winter and spring that the tree appears to change from a deep green to gold overnight. The sweet fragrance fills the garden over the entire cool season and gives the tree its common name. Sweet acacia is often sold as Acacia smallii, but this is a smaller tree, more of a shrub that is much cold hardier and blooms only in spring. There are countless hybrids between these two that are sold under either name.

Bloom Period and Seasonal Color
October to March; deep gold.

Mature Height × Spread
15 to 25 feet × 15 to 25 feet

Zones
1, 2, 3, 4
Hardy to 15 degrees Fahrenheit.

Texas Ebony
Pithecellobium flexicaule

Texas ebony naturally occurs in what is left of the tangled thorn forests lining the southern Rio Grande river valley of southern Texas and adjacent Mexico. This medium-sized, evergreen tree has deep green leaves that are densely clustered on the twisted gray branches. The thorny branches twist and change direction repeatedly, which makes this tree a favored tree for nesting cactus wrens. The dense crown and complex branching give Texas ebony more substance in the garden than most desert trees. The white, puffball-like flowers are sweetly fragrant and are followed by large, curved, dark brown pods. Pithecellobium mexicanum is a taller tree with an open, spreading crown and light green leaves. The smaller tenaza (P. pallens) has medium green leaflets and intensely fragrant flowers in summer.

Bloom Period and Seasonal Color
May to October; white to cream and fragrant.

Mature Height × Spread
15 to 30 feet × 15 to 20 feet

Zones
1, 2, 3
Hardy to 25 degrees Fahrenheit.

When, Where, and How to Plant
Plant in fall or spring in full or partial sun. Texas ebony tolerates almost any soil conditions from deep, well-drained, fertile soil to rocky, native soil, or heavy clay. Plant by digging a hole three to four times wider than the container and just as deep. Set the tree in the hole slightly higher than the soil line. After adding a generous layer of compost or mulch to the backfill, fill the hole, pressing the soil gently around the roots to remove air pockets. Mulch the root zone but do not allow mulch to touch the bark. Water thoroughly. Water every three to four days for two or three weeks, then water every seven to ten days for the first year.

Growing Tips
Apply slow-release or organic fertilizer to young plants, but established plants do not require supplemental fertilizer. Water established plants twice a month in summer, monthly in winter.

Care
Texas ebony has a complicated, twisted branching pattern that makes pruning for shape difficult. Prune a few side branches every summer until the crown is the desired height, then prune in summer only to remove dead wood or damaged branches. Texas ebony is not susceptible to pests or disease.

Companion Planting and Design
When pruned to a tree, plant Texas ebony as a shade tree or focal plant for small patios, courtyards, or yards. Plant against hot walls or around pools and other areas where reflected heat is intense. If left unpruned, use Texas ebony to make an impenetrable hedge or mix it with other small trees or large shrubs to form an informal hedge or boundary planting. The deep green of this evergreen tree makes a good background for colorful perennial or annual plantings.

Did You Know?
The wood of Texas ebony is not black as the name suggests, but is a deep mahogany red, almost purple. It is extremely hard and the heartwood is occasionally used to build furniture.

Velvet Mesquite

Prosopis velutina

When, Where, and How to Plant

Mesquites may be planted almost anytime, but they establish best when planted in fall. Grow mesquites in full sun. Velvet mesquite tolerates almost any soil conditions from deep, well-drained, fertile soil to rocky, native soil but does not tolerate heavy or poorly drained soils. Dig a hole three to four times wider than the container and just as deep and add a generous layer of compost or mulch to the backfill. Fill the hole, pressing the soil gently around the roots to remove air pockets. Mulching the root zone helps retain soil moisture but do not allow mulch to touch the bark. Water thoroughly and continue to water every three to four days for two or three weeks. For the first year or two, water every seven to ten days.

Growing Tips

Velvet mesquite does not require supplemental fertilizer, even when the trees are young. Established trees should be watered deeply every three to four weeks in summer, once a month or less in winter. Mesquites are often overwatered or watered too shallowly resulting in a huge crown and insufficient roots that cause them to fall in high winds. For best results, water deeply at long intervals.

Care

Prune to thin, shape, or raise the crown in late summer. Pruning in winter invites bacterial infections and pruning in spring and early summer encourages rampant growth. Prune dead wood anytime. Velvet mesquite is not susceptible to pests or disease.

Companion Planting and Design

Velvet mesquite is unrivaled as a large, fast-growing, spreading shade tree. The light shade provides protection for tender succulents such as small cacti and agaves as well as most perennials without impeding growth or bloom. It tolerates growing in a lawn, but water deeply in addition to lawn watering.

Did You Know?

The purple streaked pods of velvet mesquite are sweet and nutritious. They were routinely gathered in the summer by native peoples of the Southwest and pounded into a flour that was mixed with flour and stored as winter food.

Mesquites have historically marked the most precious commodity in the desert—water. Long used by both Native American and later Anglo settlers of the Southwest for construction, food, and medicine, these graceful trees are now a mainstay of gardens in the low desert. Velvet mesquite has dusky, gray-green soft leaves that are deciduous in only the coldest weather. The new leaves emerge in early spring and are bright, yellow-green. Velvet mesquite is a low-branched, open tree with dark, almost black, shaggy bark. Chilean mesquite (Prosopis chilensis) and Argentine mesquite (P. alba) both have wide, spreading crowns and narrow, green leaflets. There are countless hybrids between the two offered under both of these names. Honey mesquite (P. glandulosa) has wide, pale green leaflets and is winter deciduous.

Bloom Period and Seasonal Color

March to June; cream to yellow-white.

Mature Height × Spread

20 to 30 feet × 25 to 30 feet

Zones

1, 2, 3, 4, 5
Hardy to 0 degrees Fahrenheit.

Willow Acacia
Acacia salicina

There are hundreds of acacias around the world. They are generally thorny shrubs or trees except in Australia; there they are thornless with flattened petioles called phyllodes which stand in for the ephemeral leaves. Willow acacia is a handsome Australian tree that provides a thornless shade tree for low elevation zone gardens. The flat, gray-green foliage falls gracefully from the branches; the tiny leaves emerge briefly in spring. However, this delicate appearance is deceptive; willow acacia is immune to heat, alkaline soils, and drought. Willow acacia blooms in fall, and the small clusters of creamy-white, puffball-like flowers are lightly fragrant. Blue-leaf wattle (Acacia saligna) is a more multitrunked, rounded tree with blue-gray leaves. The flowers are bright yellow or gold in spring.

Other Common Names
Weeping wattle, Cooba

Bloom Period and Seasonal Color
Late summer to winter, intermittently year-round; cream to white.

Mature Height × Spread
20 to 40 feet × 10 to 20 feet

Zones
1, 2, 3, 4
Hardy to 18 degrees Fahrenheit.

When, Where, and How to Plant
Plant in fall or spring in full sun or partial shade. Willow acacia tolerates almost any soil condition from deep, well-drained, fertile soil to rocky, native soil. It does not tolerate heavy or poorly drained soils, however. Dig a hole three to four times wider than the container and just as deep. Add a generous layer of compost or mulch to the backfill. Set the tree in the hole slightly higher than the soil line. Fill the hole, pressing the soil gently around the roots to remove air pockets. Mulch the root zone but do not allow mulch to touch the bark. Water thoroughly. Water every three to four days for two or three weeks, then water every seven to ten days for the first year.

Growing Tips
Willow acacia does not require supplemental fertilizer. Water established trees sparingly—every three to four weeks in summer even in the lowest elevation zones; every other month in winter.

Care
Willow acacia has a graceful natural form and does not need pruning for shape. Prune dead wood or damaged limbs in fall or early spring. Willow acacia becomes chlorotic when grown in poorly drained soils or with frequent, shallow watering. Watering deeply at long intervals helps prevent this problem. Otherwise, willow acacia is not susceptible to pests or disease.

Companion Planting and Design
The thornless branches make willow acacia a fine choice to use as a shade tree near walkways, patios, or areas of heavy traffic. The minimal litter makes it useful near pools; in fact, it can even overhang a pool successfully. Plant against hot walls, around pools, or other areas where reflected heat is intense. Willow acacia mixes well with other shrubs or trees to form an informal border or visual screen. Its drought and heat tolerance make it a good choice for areas of the garden that receive minimal care.

Did You Know?
The wood is very hard, dark brown, and shines beautifully when polished.

Vines *for Arizona*

Vines are the explorers in the garden, seeking out any congenial place to catch a ride to the sun, wandering high up a tree, or out over the roof of a shed. This audacious growth is what makes them useful and attractive in gardens; they cover quickly, bloom fast, and provide a vivid show in very little space.

The Many Faces of Vines

Many vines have tendrils that twirl around a stem, a leaf, or a branch to give the plant a stepping stone approach to growing. Vines such as Arizona grape ivy and Queen's wreath grow like this. To control the growth of vines like these, gently pinch out the tendrils and side shoots throughout the growing season. Others simply fling out long, slim branches that hang over the branches of trees or shrubs letting the host's branches hold it up. Bougainvillea and pink trumpet vine grow this way. To control the growth of these kinds of vines, prune severely at the beginning of the growing season to remove wayward stems when they are actively growing.

Vines can be delicate and wispy such as purple butterfly vine. Fine textured vines make a gentle complement to a larger planting when raised to prominence on a trellis or a pole. They are often best where they can be viewed closely or where there is less visual competition during their flowering.

Arizona Grape Ivy

Others are robust plants such as bougainvillea or trumpet creeper, full of leaves and with gaudy, showy flowers. These kinds of vines cover anything that gets in their way, practically shouting their way

225

Queen's Wreath

through the other plants in the garden. They usually look best where they can be seen from a distance or against a plain background where their vivid flowers and abundant bloom can be highlighted. These vines look inviting when spilling over a wall or cascading down an embankment.

Some vines such as pink trumpet vine are really shrubs that have long stems that can be trained up a trellis or a wall. We treat them as if they were vines, but if left to their own devices they would just crawl and wander from a woody center. These are excellent types of vines to cover the roofs of patios or hide an unattractive view.

There are vines that are entirely unexpected such as the succulent vining aloe or the rain forest species of cacti that snake through the stems of a bush. If you have a shady spot, try one or several of these succulent vines for a real treat in a desert garden.

Vines are endlessly useful in a garden. Trained up a trellis or wire, vines create living walls or roofs for patios to protect them from the hot sun or drying winds. Using a plant, instead of block, wood, or metal to cover a patio has many advantages. Not only does the mass of the plant reflect the full blast of the sun's rays from the surface of the patio and its inhabitants, but the leaves absorb some of the sun's heat as well. In addition, each leaf is transpiring all day long, releasing minute amounts of water vapor that help lower the air temperature. But these uses are just part of the bonus package, because the real reason we love to plant vines is their propensity to have vivid flowers over a long season.

Because of this trait, vines can be used to create a sense of density in an otherwise spare space. Trellises do not have to be against a wall, but can be free standing, which makes the vine that files them up appear to be an exuberant, free standing plant.

Vines also are good at adding surprise to a garden. When planted at the base of a tree, rather than against a trellis, it becomes a pleasant shock to see a mesquite suddenly spring out in the large, yellow flowers of yuca vine, or watch a palo verde appear to bloom pink in late summer from its Queen's wreath companion.

Up to the Challenge

In very small gardens, where vines could get out of control fast, they can be planted to great effect on a solitary pole or dead tree trunk. With only minimal pruning and training, a vine can be encouraged to be vertical and the effect can be dramatic, adding both height and interest to a limited space. It can also help clear up the decision about what to do with an ugly stump that is too difficult to remove.

Vines can be just as useful on the ground as they are in the air. Many are well suited to use as ground covers. I am particularly fond of Arizona grape ivy, which looks a lot like small-leaved English ivy but is much more drought tolerant, when used this way in a dry, shady courtyard.

Whatever we ask of them, vines are ready to perform. They hide ugly views, perk up mundane fences, provide quick

Lilac Vine

color, and offer soothing shade. Arbors covered with a vine become a focal point in the garden, and walls taken over by a traveling rose or lush bougainvillea become an intriguing destination rather than a solid barricade.

Arizona Grape Ivy
Cissus trifoliata

Vines as a group are sun-loving plants; after all, their rapidly growing stems are an adaptation for reaching the sun. But Arizona grape ivy is the reverse—a vine that grows best in the shade. This native Arizona vine is frost tender and best suited for use in low and intermediate elevation zone gardens. Throughout summer, it is densely covered with glossy, dark green, three-lobed leaves. Vines grow rapidly and the tiny tendrils attach easily to limbs, trellises, or walls. The small, white flowers are practically invisible, and the minute grapes are not edible, except to birds. Arizona grape ivy can be left to trail along the ground like other garden ivy but is much better adapted to the soils and heat of the desert.

Bloom Period and Seasonal Color
Late spring and summer; white.

Mature Height × Spread
20 to 30 feet × 10 to 20 feet

Zones
1, 2, 3
Hardy to 30 degrees Fahrenheit, root hardy to 20 degrees Fahrenheit.

When, Where, and How to Plant
Plant in spring or early summer in partial to full shade. Arizona grape ivy grows in a wide variety of soils from well-drained, fertile soil to rocky, native soil. Dig a hole that is two to three times the width of the container and as deep. Add compost or mulch to the backfill. Place the plant gently in the soil, making certain the roots are two to three inches below the surface. Fill the hole and press the soil gently to remove air pockets. Water thoroughly. Water every two to three days for the first three or four weeks, then every five to seven days until established.

Growing Tips
Apply slow-release or organic fertilizer to young plants in spring. Mulch the roots to keep soil from drying out too quickly and to protect the roots in winter. Water established plants every three or four weeks in summer; rely on natural rainfall in winter.

Care
Arizona grape ivy is semideciduous in most winters but loses all its leaves in a hard freeze. Prune back frost-damaged or dead stems only after all danger of frost is past. Plants can be pruned to within a few inches of the ground in early spring to reduce their size or reinvigorate them. Arizona grape ivy is not susceptible to pests or disease.

Companion Planting and Design
Use Arizona grape ivy to cover bare walls or bare tree limbs in shady locations. Provide the plant with a trellis or arbor. Arizona grape ivy is effective as ground cover in dry shade and will quickly cover bare ground. It grows well in containers either as a hanging plant or as a vine in a small or confined space.

Did You Know?
Even though Arizona grape ivy rarely looks large or vigorous when it is sold in a container, it doesn't matter. For this plant, it is the swollen root that counts and the merest slip of a plant will grow into a vigorous vine in one year.

Bougainvillea
Bougainvillea species

When, Where, and How to Plant
Plant in spring in full sun. Although bougainvillea tolerates some shade, it does not bloom well in such locations. Bougainvillea is tolerant of a wide range of soils including rocky, native soil and deep, garden soil. Dig a hole two to three times the width of the container and as deep adding a thin layer of compost or mulch to the backfill. Set the plant in the hole and fill the hole, pressing the soil gently to remove air pockets. Water thoroughly after planting and every two to three days for two weeks, then water weekly through the first summer.

Growing Tips
Apply slow-release or organic fertilizer to plants in spring and fall for the first two to three years. Fertilize established plants only once every year or two. Overfertilized plants grow leaves at the expense of blooms. Water established plants every ten days in summer; once a month in winter.

Care
Prune to remove dead or frost damaged limbs in spring after all danger of frost is past. Bougainvillea may be pruned lightly in summer to control the plant's size or to train it up a trellis or wall. Bougainvillea is not susceptible to pests or disease although leaf cutters and flea beetles may cause cosmetic damage to the leaves in spring.

Companion Planting and Design
Bougainvillea is a dramatic specimen or accent plant when grown as a freestanding shrub. When grown as a vine, provide a sturdy wall, trellis, or arbor to support the plant. Use bougainvillea near patios or pools for long seasonal color. It is excellent against hot walls or anywhere that reflected heat is intense. Plant bougainvillea as a colorful background to winter-flowering annuals and perennials. Bougainvillea grows well in containers.

Did You Know?
The colorful part of the bloom is not the flowers; they are tiny and usually white. But they are embraced by large, papery, vividly colored bracts, which are modified leaves. This is also why they are colorful for such a long time.

Bougainvillea is a tough shrubby vine that can withstand the extremes of heat and alkalinity that mark the low elevation zones of Arizona. More drought tolerant than one would guess based on the places where it is typically grown, bougainvillea needs a sturdy trellis or a wall to serve as its support. Although it blooms almost year-round in the low elevation zones, the bloom is most prolific and the colors most intense in late winter and early spring. In cooler areas, it blooms in summer. There are numerous varieties in almost every imaginable color but two of the most common are 'Barbara Karst', a deep, magenta color and 'San Diego Red' (also sold as 'Scarlet O' Hara' or 'San Diego'), a vivid red with purple undertones.

Bloom Period and Seasonal Color
October to May, intermittently at other times; magenta, pink, red, white, orange, salmon.

Mature Height × Spread
15 to 30 feet × 10 to 20 feet

Zones
1, 2, 3
Hardy to 30 degrees Fahrenheit, but root hardy to 20 degrees Fahrenheit.

Lilac Vine
Hardenbergia violaceae

This evergreen Australian native is virtually immune to the heat and dry conditions of the low elevation zones of Arizona. Lilac vine has long, thin leaves with a dash of purple on the edges. The leaves are so profuse you cannot see through the plant. This dense foliage provides ample cover for patios and porches in the heat of summer. There is both a vine and a shrub form of this species, although the shrub form is unknown in Arizona. Lilac vine has small deep purple flowers that hang off the plant in gentle cascades. This charming vine blooms a long season, from fall through the following spring. In milder summer areas, it blooms in summer. There are white-flowered and pink-flowered forms.

Bloom Period and Seasonal Color
Summer; deep blue to purple, also white, and occasionally pink.

Mature Height × Spread
10 to 15 feet × 6 to 15 feet

Zones
1, 2, 3
Hardy to 25 degrees Fahrenheit.

When, Where, and How to Plant
Plant in either fall or spring in full sun. Lilac vine tolerates a wide range of soils from well-drained, fertile soil to rocky, native soil but it does not perform well in heavy or poorly drained soils. Dig a hole that is two to three times the width of the container and as deep, adding one or two inches of compost or mulch to the backfill. As you fill the hole, press the soil gently around the roots to remove air pockets making sure the base of the stem is even with the soil surface. Water thoroughly after planting. Water every two to three days for two weeks, then every five to seven days until established.

Growing Tips
Apply slow-release or organic fertilizer in fall and spring until plants are a mature size. Fertilize established plants every year or two in spring or fall because plants with too much fertilizer grow abundant leaves at the expense of bloom. Water established plants every two weeks in summer even in the lowest elevation zones. Water monthly in winter.

Care
Lilac vine has twining stems but not clasping tendrils so provide sturdy support for the vines. Prune in spring after bloom is complete to remove dead or damaged wood or clear out tangled stems. Do not prune in summer; exposed stems are easily sunburned and do not recover quickly. Lilac vine is not susceptible to pests or disease.

Companion Planting and Design
Lilac vine is an outstanding choice to cover a sunny fence or provide a privacy screen for courtyards or small seating areas. The dense, evergreen foliage makes a splendid living ceiling for a patio or ramada. Plant lilac vine on an arbor or trellis for a burst of cool-season color. A dwarf selection makes a good specimen or focal plant as well as a colorful container plant.

Did You Know?
The genus was named for Franziska, Countess von Hardenberg, a member of the immense 19th century Austrian aristocracy and a botanical patron. The word *violaceae* refers to the color of the flowers.

Pink Trumpet Vine

Podranea ricasoliana

When, Where, and How to Plant

Plant in fall or spring in full sun or partial shade. Pink trumpet vine tolerates a wide range of soils including well-drained, fertile soil as well as rocky, native soil. However, it does not grow well in heavy clay or poorly drained soils. Dig a hole that is two to three times the width of the container and as deep, adding a generous layer of compost or mulch to the backfill. Set the plant in the hole with the base of the stem level with the soil surface and fill the hole, pressing the soil gently to remove air pockets. Water thoroughly after planting and continue watering every two to three days for the first two weeks, then every five to seven days through the first summer.

Growing Tips

Apply slow-release or organic fertilizer annually in spring. Keep three or four inches of mulch around the roots in summer to prevent the soil from becoming too dry. Water established plants weekly in summer, every ten to fourteen days in fall and spring, and monthly in winter.

Care

Prune in spring just as the leaves emerge to remove dead or winter damaged wood and to cut back unruly stems. Prune lightly in summer to maintain shape and remove unwanted stems. Every other year in spring just as the leaves emerge, prune back to the main trunk, or to within a few feet of the ground, to reinvigorate the plant. Pink trumpet vine stems will root along the ground; remove these stems regularly when growing it as a vine. Pink trumpet vine is not susceptible to pests or disease, but leaves may yellow from chlorosis in infertile soils or when watered too shallowly. Water deeply.

Companion Planting and Design

Provide a pole, wall, or trellis to support pink trumpet vine. This vine makes an excellent screen or ceiling for seating areas, patios, or porches. When allowed to grow as a shrub, pink trumpet vine is useful for erosion control on steep slopes.

Did You Know?

Podranea is an anagram of *Pandorea,* the former genus. The epithet *ricasoliana* commemorates the Ricasoli garden in Italy where the plant was grown and came to the attention of botanists.

This large, rambunctious, flowering vine is a South African native but came to the attention of most Arizona gardeners from plants grown in Mexico. It thrives in the gardens of the low elevation zone with its exuberant fall bloom. It can often take a year or two for this vine to become well established, but once it is, plants grow quickly and need a trellis or arbor for support. Pink trumpet vine has compound pale-green leaves that are semideciduous and loses most of them in the coldest part of winter. The flared, trumpet-shaped flowers are in full heads at the ends of the branches. Flowers vary from pale pink or mauve to purple and have light striping on the back of the petal.

Other Common Name

St. John's trumpet vine

Bloom Period and Seasonal Color

September to January; pink, mauve, purple.

Mature Height × Spread

10 to 20 feet × 6 to 10 feet

Zones

1, 2, 3
Hardy to 25 degrees Fahrenheit.

Queen's Wreath
Antigonon leptopus

It seems that anywhere you garden there is a vine that somehow defines the look and feel of the area. For desert gardens, Queen's wreath produces bountiful clusters of small, pink flowers throughout the brutal summer season. I remember this vine from Louisiana gardens where it was half wild, crawling up huge trees, sneaking blooms out of their dark green crowns. The wide, raspy, heart-shaped leaves are dense enough to provide welcome shade in summer but are deciduous in winter. The flowers are small, in loose clusters, and are usually a light, refreshing shade of pink. There is a dark pink, almost red, form that is sold as 'Baja Red' and is very showy. Occasionally white-flowered forms are available.

Other Common Names
Coral vine, Rosa de Montana

Bloom Period and Seasonal Color
Spring until frost; clusters of small pink flowers, occasionally darker pink, red, or white.

Mature Height × Spread
20 to 40 feet × 10 to 40 feet

Zones
1, 2, 3
Hardy to 28 degrees Fahrenheit, root hardy to 20 degrees Fahrenheit.

When, Where, and How to Plant
Plant in spring in full sun or partial shade. Queen's wreath is tolerant of almost any fast-draining soil from well-drained, fertile soil to rocky, native soil. Dig a hole that is two to three times the width of the container and as deep. Add a generous layer of compost or mulch to the backfill. Set the plant in the hole, pressing the soil gently to remove air pockets as you backfill. Water thoroughly and spread three to four inches of mulch around the roots to maintain soil moisture. Water every two to three days for two weeks, then every five to seven days through the first summer.

Growing Tips
Apply slow-release or organic fertilizer annually in spring, especially when plants are young. Mulch plants heavily with three to four inches of mulch to prevent the soil from drying out too quickly and to protect the roots in winter. Water weekly in summer; rely on natural rainfall in winter.

Care
Prune in spring just as the leaves begin to emerge to remove winter-damaged stems and shape the plant. Prune lightly through summer to maintain shape and train the plant. Provide a trellis or arbor to support the vine. Queen's wreath is not susceptible to pests or disease.

Companion Planting and Design
Queen's wreath makes a stunning summer display when planted on a trellis or arbor or is left to grow through the branches of a palo verde or mesquite. Use this vine to cover the roof of a ramada or patio for summer shade or as a specimen or focal plant in a small courtyard or patio. Plant along a fence as a background for summer flowering perennials and shrubs such as lantana, hibiscus, red bird of paradise, or yellowbells.

Did You Know?
Antigonon is derived from the Greek words *anti*, meaning "against," and *gonia*, meaning "an angle," and refers to the flexible stems. The epithet *leptopus* is also Greek and means "slender stalk;" it's a reference to the blooming stalk.

Trumpet Creeper
Campsis radicans

When, Where, and How to Plant
Plant in early spring in low or intermediate elevation zones; in spring in warm soils in high elevation zones. Plant in full sun in all zones although it will perform well in partial shade in the lowest elevation zones. Trumpet creeper will grow in almost any type of soil but grows best in deep, well-drained, fertile soil. Dig a hole that is two to three times the width of the container and as deep. Add a generous layer of compost or mulch to the backfill. As you fill the hole, press the soil gently to remove air pockets. Water thoroughly. Water every three or four days for two weeks, then weekly through the first summer.

Growing Tips
Apply slow-release or organic fertilizer in spring. In low elevation zones, water established plants that have been in the ground at least two years deeply every week in summer, monthly in winter. In higher elevation zones, water established plants every two weeks in summer, every month or less in winter.

Care
Prune in spring just as leaves emerge to remove winter-damaged limbs, dead wood, or to shape the plant. Prune in spring to within a few feet of the ground to reduce plants that have become too large or to reinvigorate plants. Suckers that form at the base can be removed anytime. Trumpet creeper is not susceptible to pests or disease.

Companion Planting and Design
This is a brilliant splash of summer color for northern gardens providing much of the same drama that bougainvillea provides in southern Arizona gardens. Plant trumpet creeper against a wall, up a trellis or arbor, or over a ramada or patio roof. Plant along a fence to serve as a background for summer-flowering perennials, bulbs, and shrubs such as penstemon, summer phlox, blue mist, or shrubby cinquefoil. If left to grow without supports, trumpet creeper makes an excellent plant for erosion control on steep slopes.

Did You Know?
Campsis is from the Greek *kampe*, meaning "something bent," and refers to the curved stamens. The epithet *radicans* is also Greek and means "with rooting stems."

Trumpet creeper is a large, fast-growing, deciduous vine with aerial roots that enable it to climb and cling to almost any surface. Trumpet creeper has long, glossy, dark green, compound leaves that deepen to a maroon or red color in fall before they drop. Native to the eastern United States, trumpet creeper does well in all zones of Arizona but in low elevation zones requires deep soils and steady summer irrigation. The large, flared, trumpet-shaped flowers are red-orange and bloom continuously through summer. Hummingbirds and orioles are particularly fond of the nectar. The variety 'Flava' has yellow flowers and light green leaves. The much less common Chinese trumpet creeper (Campsis grandiflora) has deep red flowers and is not as hardy in the high elevation zones.

Other Common Name
Trumpet vine

Bloom Period and Seasonal Color
Summer; red to red-orange, occasionally yellow.

Mature Height × Spread
30 to 40 feet × 30 to 40 feet

Zones
All
Hardy to 0 degrees Fahrenheit.

Yellow Butterfly Vine

Mascagnia macroptera

Yellow butterfly vine is an elegant plant that provides marvelous spring color for low elevation zone gardens. The numerous, small flowers have irregular, paddle-shaped petals that are both unusual and striking. However, the resulting fruit pods are nearly as attractive and remain on the plant for months. Seeds are held within large chartreuse pods with four wide, ruffled wings. As the seed matures, the pods fade to a pale tan and are the source of the common name. They are highly valued for use in dried arrangements. Yellow butterfly vine is vigorous, although it does not grow with the blinding speed of many other vines. In cold winters, it is briefly deciduous. The closely related lilac butterfly vine (Mascagnia lilacina) has small, widely spaced purple flowers.

Bloom Period and Seasonal Color
March and April; bright yellow.

Mature Height × Spread
10 to 15 feet × 6 to 10 feet

Zones
1, 2, 3, 4
Hardy to 15 degrees Fahrenheit.

When, Where, and How to Plant
Plant in spring after all danger of frost is past in full sun or partial shade. Yellow butterfly vine is tolerant of a wide range of soils from well-drained, fertile soil to rocky, native soil. Dig a hole that is two to three times the width of the container and as deep, adding a generous layer of compost or mulch to the backfill. Set the plant in the hole, making sure the base of the stem is level with the soil surface. Fill the hole, pressing the soil gently to remove air pockets. Spread three or four inches of mulch around the roots and water thoroughly. Water every two to three days for two weeks, then every five to seven days through the first summer.

Growing Tips
Apply slow-release or organic fertilize to young plants in spring once the plant is beginning to set out new leaves. Established plants do not require supplemental fertilizer. Water established plants weekly in summer, more often if the weather is exceptionally hot or dry. Water established plants monthly in winter.

Care
Prune to remove winter damage, dead wood, or to shape the plant in spring after all danger of frost is past. Prune in spring to within a foot or two of the ground to reduce the size of a plant that has become too large or to reinvigorate it. Yellow butterfly vine is not susceptible to pests or disease.

Companion Planting and Design
Provide a trellis, arbor, fence, or other support for yellow butterfly vine. Plant as a specimen or focal point where both the brief spring bloom and the charming pods can be enjoyed. Plant along a fence to use as a background for colorful spring-flowering perennials and annuals such as penstemon, salvias, poppies, or globemallow. Interplant with the other vines such as Queen's wreath to provide year-round color. Yellow butterfly vine also grows well in a large container.

Did You Know?
The genus was named in honor of Paolo Mascagni, an Italian anatomist and chemist who died in 1815. The epithet is a combined form meaning "large" (*macro*) "wing" (*ptera*).

Common Pests and Diseases

Diseases

In comparison to most parts of the country, Arizona has a low incidence of diseases on ornamental plants. In most instances, a healthy, well-grown plant that is not stressed by heat, cold, or inappropriate watering is the best defense against disease. Prevention is always best, but when trouble strikes use the following steps. (1) Identify the problem correctly—take a sample to a nursery or your County Extension Office if you aren't sure. (2) Use the mildest form of control possible first, and if that is insufficient, move up to more heavy-duty poisons. (3) Even when using so-called organic controls, read the labels thoroughly. Apply any product according to the directions for amount, time of year, and any temperature constraints.

Bacteria Galls
Symptoms: Swollen masses on the stems or leaves; erratic but rarely extensive twig die back.
Agent: *Pseudomonas* species.
Control: Prune out infected areas in dry weather; most pesticides do not work on this condition in oleander, but fortunately it is rarely more than a cosmetic problem.
Favorable Conditions: Because the bacteria can only enter through wounds, damaged plants or unsterilized tools usually spread it around.
Usually Seen On: Oleander and oaks.

Bacterial Necrosis
Symptoms: Black, foul-smelling ooze from a hole or wound in saguaro.
Agent: Bacteria *Erwinia* species.
Control: Prevention is best. Protect plants from wounds or holes in the skin, cold damage at the tip, or severe sunburn when transplanting. Birds do not cause or encourage this disease.
Favorable Conditions: Old plants often die of this infection as do plants that are severely stressed or wounded.
Usually Seen On: Saguaro.

Canker
Symptoms: Lesions on stems or trunks that ooze when wet; flower or tip die back.
Agent: A variety of fungal, bacterial, or environmental agents.
Control: Remove dead leaves and old fruit around trees; prune out any infected limbs in dry weather; avoid overhead watering to prevent spread; fertilize correctly for the species. Bordeaux mix in the spring often reduces the level of infestation.
Favorable Conditions: Overly fertilized trees; plant is stressed or in poor condition.
Usually Seen On: Citrus, and many other species of woody plants.

Cotton Root Rot

Symptoms: Sudden death of all or a portion of the plant or a limb of a tree.

Agent: Fungus *Phyotochrichum omnivorum*.

Control: Difficult and usually unsuccessful; use resistant species where soil is widely infected.

Favorable Conditions: Fungus is indigenous, but more active when weather is hot and there is ample soil moisture.

Usually Seen On: Almost any woody plant that is not a low desert native.

Crown Rot

Symptoms: Sudden collapse of the crown or growing point of the plant; decay of the bud or leaf bases.

Agent: Bacteria of many types causes these symptoms in succulents; in palms, a number of fungi are thought to be the agents of this condition but this has not been proven.

Control: Prevention is the best remedy in succulents; avoid overhead watering and especially do not allow water or leaf litter to accumulate in the leaf bases or crown. Research is ongoing to find a control for palms.

Favorable Conditions: Warm, humid conditions appear to encourage both the agents in succulents and those in palms.

Usually Seen On: Aloes, agaves, nolina, dasylirions, many rosette-forming succulents, and palms.

Fire Blight

Symptoms: Sudden browning of leaves; shoots and dead leaves persist; then a rapid spread of this scorched look all over the plant.

Agent: Bacteria *Erwinia amylovora*.

Control: Remove infected branches at least six inches below infection; using a weak Bordeaux mix in the spring when the plant is blooming helps control the spread.

Favorable Conditions: Proximity of infected plants; this bacteria is spread by insects, entering the plant through the flowers.

Usually Seen On: All members of the rose family are susceptible, but in Arizona it is most prevalent on pyracantha.

Mildew

Symptoms: White, powdery growth on the surface of the leaf or stems.

Agent: Many species of fungi depending on the plant and location.

Control: Good air circulation, pick off and destroy infected leaves immediately, spray susceptible plants often to prevent spore germination; use sulphur when temperatures are mild enough to use it.

Favorable Conditions: Shade, poor air circulation around the bush, moderate temperatures.

Usually Seen On: Sunflowers, roses, plumbago, and many other perennials.

Oleander Blight

Symptoms: Sudden death of a mature plant.

Agent: Bacteria *Xylella* that is carried to the plant by glassy-winged sharpshooters.

Control: None at this time. Although the disease is currently not evident in Arizona, it has been spreading in California.

Favorable Conditions: Unknown if any special or specific ones apply but is the subject of intensive research in California and Florida.

Usually Seen On: Oleander and grapes.

Root Rot

Symptoms: Dark, soft to mushy stems, slow decline with shoot die back, soft, blackened, decaying roots, and death.

Agent: Many species of *Rhizoctonia* and *Pythium* fungus.

Control: Prevent through good care, using well-drained soils for plants that are susceptible; reduced watering when the weather is hot and humid, especially in low zones; infrequent watering in cactus rather than continuous watering.

Favorable Conditions: Poor drainage, watering too much or too frequently during hot, humid weather.

Usually Seen On: Almost any type of plant can succumb to one or several of these types of fungi if conditions are right. Succulents are particularly susceptible.

Rust

Symptoms: Orange or yellow spore masses on leaves, leaf drop.

Agent: Numerous species of parasitic fungi.

Control: Avoid overhead watering; clean up thoroughly under infected plants; prune out infected stems except on roses when annual pruning should take care of the problem.

Favorable Conditions: Build up of leaf or stem litter from infected plants. The spores overwinter on leaves, thriving on mild, moist conditions.

Usually Seen On: The many kinds of rusts usually have specific hosts so it can occur on almost any plants.

Texas Root Rot See Cotton Root Rot.

Verticillium Wilt

Symptoms: Foliage fades to pale green or yellow, with scattered wilting, especially on woody plants. Shoot die back occurs and in small plants, sudden death results.

Agent: Fungus *Verticillium dahliae*.

Control: Grow resistant varieties; keep woody plants healthy and prune out any infected branches.

Favorable Conditions: Stressed or damaged trees or heavily infected soil.

Usually Seen On: Ash, Chinese pistache, roses, and herbaceous plants, including vegetables.

Pest Problems

Insects

I like to approach insects cautiously; not because I am afraid of them but because there are so many and most of them wandering through our gardens cause little or no harm. Some are a huge help in the garden, feeding on other various problem insects, helping maintain a healthy balance of predatory and prey species throughout the garden. The best strategy with insects on your plants is (1) be sure they are causing a real problem; (2) find out what they are—you can't treat the problem if you do not know what it is; and (3) apply a solution that won't cause more harm than the insect is causing. There are countless ways to manage and control many insect populations. Become familiar with as many as you can and do not just reach for a jar of chemical pesticide when you see a bug idly walking by on the limb of the palo verde tree.

Agave Snout Weevil

Symptoms: Sudden collapse of all the leaves but those on the central bud of an agave.
Agent: Larvae of the weevil.
Control: Pesticides like Diazinon™ are often applied to kill the adult but success is uncertain because timing is critical. Certain species are highly susceptible and infestations usually prevent blooming in these species so it is best not to grow clones of such individual plants but look for individuals that successfully bloomed.
Favorable Conditions: Susceptible plants that are nearing bloom.
Usually Seen On: Large, softer leaved agaves, occasionally on yucca.

Aphids

Symptoms: Crowded clumps of yellow, green, or black insects on the bud or tip of a plant, mottled or decrepit leaves, leaf drop in severe cases. The clear to yellow honeydew often results in growth of a black sooty mold.
Agent: Tiny, sucking insects.
Control: Light infestations can be removed by hand, or with strong jets of water. Use insecticidal soap for large infestations.
Favorable Conditions: The appearance of aphids corresponds to certain times in their life cycle and is generally short-lived. Most plants suffer no more than cosmetic damage, although their feeding action can mar flowers, especially roses.
Usually Seen On: Almost any plant that is in bloom when they are active, but particularly on roses, desert milkweed, and brittlebush.

Borers

Symptoms: Lesions or holes in trunks or limbs that ooze a thick, dark substance; sudden decline or death of a limb or branch; hollowed out stems of cacti; round entry holes; or hollow tunnels in dead branches after pruning.

Agent: There are hundreds of different insects including beetles and moths whose larvae feed inside woody plants and are generically known as borers.

Control: Often difficult, sometimes unnecessary, because the initial entry hole to lay the eggs is tiny. Pruning out the infected limb will help limit damage but most pesticides are ineffective or require specific application techniques and timing. Healthy, vigorous plants usually withstand small infestations with only cosmetic damage.

Favorable Conditions: Old, diseased, or highly stressed plants are most susceptible to large infestations of borers.

Usually Seen On: Bulbs, hedgehog cactus, pincushion cactus, prickly pear cactus, yuccas, roses, and many species of trees and shrubs.

Flea Beetle

Symptoms: Chewed or cut out portions of the leaf.

Agent: A number of species of small, rounded beetles.

Control: There is little that can be done; by the time damage is seen, the beetle has moved on. Most damage is merely cosmetic. Formulations of *Bacillus thuringiensis* var. *san diego* can reduce extremely large infestations.

Favorable Conditions: Infestations occur in the greatest numbers in spring.

Usually Seen On: Primrose and other soft-leaved ground covers as well as a number of other soft-leaved ornamentals.

Leaf Beetle   See Flea Beetle.

Leaf Foot Plant Bug

Symptoms: Holes in the fruit of pomegranate.

Agent: The adult insect.

Control: There is little that works well. Monitor fruit carefully, covering it if these insects are a special problem. They rarely result in large infestations.

Favorable Conditions: Ripening fruit.

Usually Seen On: The many species of this insect can find their way to many different kinds of plants, but in the low zones the desert pomegranate is especially vulnerable.

Mites including **Red Spider Mite**

Symptoms: Depending on the plant, growth can be contorted or distorted (aloes), large areas of dead tissue that becomes corky (agave), or stippled, distorted, or pale leaves, and stunted growth.

Agent: Tiny, almost microscopic creatures that are related to spiders.

Control: Controls vary by the type of mite and the species affected, but in general, mites are not a serious problem or cause huge infestations. Ironically, many chemical controls have the reverse effect, causing explosions of mite populations after application.

Favorable Conditions: Many species appear to be more vulnerable if they are grown with too much nitrogen-heavy fertilizer. Where dust and ants appear to assist in mite population growth, regular overhead sprays are helpful; this is especially true for spider mites.

Usually Seen On: Almost any plant; succulents, perennials, and woody plants can have infestations of mites from time to time.

Palo Verde Beetle

Symptoms: Death of limbs or portions of the tree; usually seen on old or stressed trees.

Agent: Larvae of the large, flying palo verde beetle.

Control: Prevention is best. These are long-lived, subterranean larvae that are difficult to control with chemicals. Healthy, vigorous plants are usually unaffected by the feeding of this beetle.

Favorable Conditions: Old, diseased, or deeply stressed plants.

Usually Seen On: Palo verde trees, Mexican palo verde, or Texas rangers; however, any woody plant could be infected.

Pearl Scale

Symptoms: Circular patch of weakened or dead grass; roots often have minute "pearls" in the dying area.

Agent: Small, sucking insects.

Control: Early detection is the key; remove and dispose of affected plants and adjacent soil to a depth and circumference of one foot. Chemical controls are inadequate as a general rule.

Favorable Conditions: Common in alkaline soils.

Usually Seen On: Bermuda and St. Augustine lawn grasses.

Pine Bark Beetle See borers.

Psyllids

Symptoms: Large numbers of tiny yellow or clear dots on the surface of the leaves, stippled or yellowed leaves, and leaf drop.

Agent: A small, sucking insect that strongly resembles an aphid.

Control: Spray with strong jets of water to remove psyllids from the leaf; use insecticidal soap on larger or longer-lasting infestations. Reduce watering and delay fertilization on plants that are susceptible or have had infestations in the past until new growth is well established.

Favorable Conditions: Succulent new growth on woody species.

Usually Seen On: Any plant, but cascalote and other members of the genus *Caesalpinia* are particularly vulnerable.

Sawfly

Symptoms: Chewed leaves or needles, skeletonized leaves.

Agent: Small insects related to ants, wasps, and bees.

Control: General insecticides like insecticidal soap work well, but most infestations are small and intermittent.

Favorable Conditions: They are common insects that will take advantage of available plants to feed.

Usually Seen On: Most species of this insect are attracted to a particular type of plant; pear sawflies are the greatest problem in Arizona.

Tent Caterpillars

Symptoms: White filmy covering on the tip of the branch full of small caterpillars.

Agent: Larvae of a moth in the genus *Malacosoma*.

Control: Prune off the affected branch or in large infestations and use a *Bacillus thuringiensis* formula with a power jet application to penetrate the "tent." Because the larvae are especially attracted to young, succulent growth, delay fertilizing and reduce watering if insects are a particular problem.

Favorable Conditions: New growth.

Usually Seen On: Texas mountain laurel and pecans, but they will feed on a wide variety of woody species.

Thrips

Symptoms: A curled, or stunted leaf. In citrus, the leaf is often rolled and folded; in some plants, thrips cause stippling of the leaf.

Agent: Small, sucking insect.

Control: None is necessary; the damage is of a short duration and is only cosmetic.

Favorable Conditions: Common year-round but more numerous in the spring.

Usually Seen On: Roses and citrus, but can be found on almost any ornamental plant.

Western Pine Beetle See borers.

Whiteflies

Symptoms: Yellowing of the leaves, especially in a splotched pattern, masses of clear or white exudate on the underside of the leaves. These tiny, white insects fly and will rise in a cloud when the plant is touched.

Agent: Small, sucking insects that are not flies but are related to psyllids and aphids.

Control: Monitor populations with yellow sticky tape and spray with insecticidal soap when infestations begin to rise. Strong jets of water often help reduce populations, but nothing eliminates them entirely.

Favorable Conditions: It is unclear what makes populations change so much—some years insect levels are merely annoying; other years levels can be lethal. Most damage in low desert areas occurs in late summer and early fall, but insects occur year-round.

Usually Seen On: Soft-leaved perennials like lantana and hibiscus. Peppers and tomatoes are particularly vulnerable.

Animals

Animal pests are often some of the most difficult of all pests to control. Scaring them away is rarely good enough, and in some areas fencing them out is impractical or impossible. But a good fence is usually the best defense against most of the animals that want to ravage the garden with the exception of the underground marauders.

Gophers

Symptoms: Sudden disappearance of plants, or quick death of newly planted ornamentals, occasionally dead patches in lawns are caused by these animals. Ground squirrels and moles can cause similar damage where they are present.

Agent: Gophers are ground-dwelling rodents that eat roots.

Control: Trap and remove; or in particularly valuable plants, use wire casing to enclose the plant.

Favorable Conditions: Gophers like any place that they can dig, especially soft or sandy soils.

Usually Seen On: Any plant can be attacked but newly planted ornamentals and bulbs (especially narcissus) are the most common victims.

Rabbits

Symptoms: Plants that seem to disappear overnight, girdling low on cacti or other succulents, loss of leaves or stems on shrubs or perennials, especially within a foot or two of the ground.

Agent: Both cottontail and jack rabbits.

Control: Fencing the yard against entry, wire cages around newly planted shrubs until they are large enough to withstand the attack.

Favorable Conditions: Dry seasons bring rabbits into gardens in increasingly large numbers and, at these times, they will eat anything. In good years, they are particularly attracted to new plantings, young growth, and lawns.

Usually Seen On: Rabbits will eat almost anything including barbed plants, agaves, cacti, and any kind of shrub, perennial, or ground cover.

Slugs and Snails

Symptoms: Chewed leaves or stems; sudden disappearance of small shoots or stems.

Agent: Numerous species of snails and soft-bodied slugs.

Control: Trap into shallow containers using a bait of orange juice or beer, then kill them.

Favorable Conditions: Cool, wet conditions, thick layers of mulch or areas that remain continually moist in the shade.

Usually Seen On: Bulbs, young seedlings, soft herbaceous perennials, or in the vegetable garden.

Environmental Conditions

Some things that go wrong with plants are related to the weather or with the type of soil in which they grow. These conditions often look like disease or even insect damage, but are caused by changes in the environment in which the plants grow, or when plants are grown in unfavorable or difficult conditions. When trying to determine if it is an environmental condition or a disease or pest that is affecting the health and vigor of your plant, consider whether this is a new phenomenon or an old one, if you always see the same symptoms at the same time of the year, or if anything has changed drastically for the plant. The loss of a large shade tree or a limb of a tree alters the amount of sun for the plants underneath it. A sudden cold snap, late in the season, damages new growth and possibly fruit set. An unusually long, hot, or dry summer or conversely, an unusually wet or cold winter can dramatically affect plants in ways that might look like disease. If in doubt, check around the area and see if your gardening friends are having the same problems.

Chlorosis

Symptoms: Yellowing of the leaf between the veins.

Agent: This is a mineral deficiency, and it can be any mineral that the plant needs but iron chlorosis is the most common problem in low desert zones.

Control: Apply regular applications of iron chelate to the soil around the plants; use resistant plants; water deeply.

Favorable Conditions: Many plants are inherently susceptible; alkaline dry soils increase susceptible plants probability of having this condition.

Usually Seen On: Queen palms, plants from areas of acid soils, a wide range of shrubs and trees that are not from desert areas, many Australian species used in the low desert.

Cold Damage

Symptoms: Pale or translucent or flaccid stems (in succulents), browned or blackened tips, sudden leaf drop, blackened or decayed leaves, shoot or branch die back.

Agent: Cold temperatures beyond the plant's tolerance.

Control: Know the limits of your plants and protect tender plants with cloth, frost blankets, or cardboard for occasional cold nights. Never use plastic directly on the plant for cold protection. Protect roots in any climate from severe cold by mulching heavily.

Favorable Conditions: Cold beyond the plant's tolerance; sudden unexpected cold spells, even if the temperature was not particularly severe.

Usually Seen On: Any plant, but it is especially common in species grown on the edge of their cold tolerance.

Heat Stress

Symptoms: Yellowed or pale leaves that develop suddenly; loss of vigor or cessation of growth; dried tips or ends of leaves or branches.

Agent: Prolonged hot weather and exposure to more sun than the plant can handle, especially afternoon sun.

Control: Shade the plant if possible using shade cloth, or other coverings but never anything plastic. If the plant is young, it may grow out of it. If not, consider relocating it in the fall. Keep affected plants well watered even if symptoms persist; symptoms often disappear when the weather cools.

Favorable Conditions: Newly planted species that are not acclimated to full sun; sudden change in sun exposure; unusually long or hot spells.

Usually Seen On: Succulents such as agave or cacti and tender perennials that are planted against hot walls; but heat stress is possible for almost any plant.

Pine Blight

Symptoms: Sudden death of small limbs, or browning and dropping of needles on pines.

Agent: It is thought to be an environmental condition following hot, dry weather.

Control: Keep plants healthy and well irrigated during long hot, dry spells.

Favorable Conditions: Hot, dry summers.

Usually Seen On: Aleppo pines.

Landscape Watering Guidelines

How Much and How Often Water to the outer edge of the plant's canopy and to the depth indicated. Watering frequency will vary depending on season, plant type, weather, and soil.		Seasonal Frequency—Days Between Waterings				Water This Deeply (Typical Root Depth)
		Spring Mar.–May	Summer May–Oct.	Fall Oct.–Dec.	Winter Dec.–Mar.	
Trees	Desert adapted	14–30 days	7–21 days	14–30 days	30–60 days	24–36 inches
	High water use	7–12 days	7–10 days	7–12 days	14–30 days	24–36 inches
Shrubs	Desert adapted	14–30 days	7–21 days	14–30 days	30–45 days	18–24 inches
	High water use	7–10 days	5–7 days	7–10 days	10–14 days	18–24 inches
Groundcovers and Vines	Desert adapted	14–30 days	7–21 days	14–30 days	21–45 days	8–12 inches
	High water use	7–10 days	2–5 days	7–10 days	10–14 days	8–12 inches
Cacti and Succulents		21–45 days	14–30 days	21–45 days	if needed	8–12 inches
Annuals		3–7 days	2–5 days	3–7 days	5–10 days	8–12 inches
Warm Season Grass		4–14 days	3–6 days	6–21 days	15–30 days	6–10 inches
Cool Season Grass		3–7 days	none	3–10 days	7–14 days	6–10 inches

These guidelines are for established plants (1 year, 3 years for trees). Additional water is needed for new plants or unusually hot or dry weather. Less water is needed during cool or rainy weather. Drip run times are typically 2 hours or more for each watering.

These guidelines were developed by the Arizona Municipal Water Users Association and their member cities.

Public Gardens

The Arboretum at Flagstaff

200 acres of gardens and natural areas, including several specialty gardens, representing over 2,500 plant species.

    4001 Woody Mountain Road

    Flagstaff, AZ 86001

    928-774-1442

    http://www.thearb.org

    Fee, open April 1 to December 15, daily.

Arizona Sonora Desert Museum

A zoo, natural history museum, and botanical gardens including 2 miles of paths.

    2021 Kinney Road

    Tucson, AZ 85743

    520-883-1380

    http://www.desertmuseum.org

    Fee, open every day.

Boyce Thompson Southwestern Arboretum

Large collection of desert plants, especially trees and legumes.

    37615 U.S. 60

    Superior, AZ 85273

    520-689-2723

    http://ag.arizona.edu/BTA

    Fee, open every day but Christmas.

Desert Botanical Garden

Large collection of agaves, yucca, cacti, and other desert plants.

    1201 N. Galvin Parkway (Papago Park)

    Phoenix, AZ 85008

    480-941-1225

    http://www.dbg.org

    Fee, open every day but Christmas and July 4th.

Glendale Public Library Demonstration Garden

Extensive plantings using desert plants; many unusual varieties, including a large succulent garden.

5959 W. Brown Street (corner of 59th Ave. and Brown)

Glendale, AZ 85302

623-930-3530

http://www.glendaleaz.com/library

No fee, open every day.

Maricopa County Extension Service Demonstration Garden

A variety of gardens including vegetable, herb, desert ornamental, heirloom rose, tropical, and pond gardens.

4341 East Broadway Road

Phoenix, AZ 85040

602-470-8086

http://www.ag.arizona.edu/Maricopa/garden/

No fee, open every day (self-guided tour).

Mesa Community College, AARS Rose Garden

Extensive rose garden at the entrance on Southern.

1833 W. Southern (Campus located at Southern and Dobson)

Mesa, AZ 85202

480-461-7000

http://www.mc.maricopa.edu

No fee, open every day.

Sharlot Hall Museum Grounds

Museum, historical buildings, and four specialty gardens including an 1870s kitchen garden and a pioneer herb garden.

415 W. Gurley Street

Prescott, AZ 86301

928-445-3122

http://www.sharlot.org

Fee (donations), open every day, hours vary by season. (Museum closes for major holidays.)

Tohono Chul Park

A variety of specialty gardens including a hummingbird garden, a children's garden, and a demonstration garden.

> 7366 N. Paseo del Norte
>
> Tucson, AZ 85704
>
> 520-742-6455
>
> http://www.tohonochulpark.org
>
> Fee (donation), open every day but New Year's, July 4th, Thanksgiving, Christmas.

Tucson Botanical Garden

A five-acre collection of 15 specialty gardens including a historical garden, an herb garden, a butterfly garden, and a cactus and succulent garden.

2150 N. Alvernon Way

Tucson, AZ 85712

520-326-9686

http://www.tucsonbotanical.org

Fee, open every day but New Year's, July 4th, Thanksgiving, Christmas.

Glossary

Alkaline soil: soil with a pH greater than 7.0. It lacks acidity, often because it has limestone in it.

All-purpose fertilizer: powdered, liquid, or granular fertilizer with a balanced proportion of the three key nutrients—nitrogen (N), phosphorus (P), and potassium (K). It is suitable for maintenance nutrition for most plants.

Annual: a plant that lives its entire life in one season. It is genetically determined to germinate, grow, flower, set seed, and die the same year.

Bare root: describes plants that have been packaged without any soil around their roots. Bulbs are often sold this way. (Often young shrubs and trees purchased through the mail arrive with their exposed roots covered with moist peat or sphagnum moss, sawdust, or similar material, and wrapped in plastic.)

Barrier plant: a plant that has intimidating thorns or spines and is sited purposely to block foot traffic or other access to the home or yard.

Basal leaves: leaves that are congested near the ground to form a rosette or as a small mound. Typically, a large blooming stalk or other leafy stems arise out of these leaves.

Beneficial insects: insects or their larvae that prey on pest organisms and their eggs. They may be flying insects, such as ladybugs, parasitic wasps, praying mantis, and soldier bugs, or soil dwellers such as predatory nematodes, spiders, and ants.

Berm: a narrow raised ring of soil around a tree used to hold water so it will be directed to the root zone.

Bract: a modified leaf structure on a plant stem near its flower that resembles a petal. Often it is more colorful and visible than the actual flower, as in bougainvillea.

Bud union: the place where the top of a plant was grafted to the rootstock; usually refers to roses and citrus.

Canopy: the overhead branching area of a tree, usually referring to its extent including foliage.

Chlorosis: a mineral deficiency. The typical symptom is a yellowing of the leaf between the veins; in extreme cases the entire leaf turns yellow.

Cold hardiness: the ability of a perennial plant to survive the winter cold in a particular area.

Composite: a flower that is actually composed of many tiny flowers. Typically, they are flat clusters of tiny, tight florets, sometimes surrounded by wider-petaled florets. Composite flowers are highly attractive to bees and beneficial insects.

Compost: organic matter that has undergone progressive decomposition by microbial and macrobial activity until it is reduced to a spongy, fluffy texture. Added to soil of any type, it improves the soil's ability to hold air and water and to drain well.

Corm: the swollen, energy-storing structure analogous to a bulb under the soil at the base of the stem of plants such as crocus and gladiolus.

Crown: the base of a plant at, or just beneath, the surface of the soil where the roots meet the stems.

Cultivar: a CULTIvated VARiety. It is a naturally occurring form of a plant that has been identified as special or superior and is purposely selected for propagation and production. A cultivar can also be created through breeding.

Deadhead: a pruning technique that removes faded flower heads from plants to improve their appearance, abort seed production, and stimulate further flowering.

Deciduous plants: unlike evergreens, these trees and shrubs lose their leaves all at once, usually in the fall.

Desiccation: drying out of foliage tissues usually due to drought or wind.

Division: the practice of splitting apart perennial plants to create several smaller-rooted segments. The practice is useful for controlling the plant's size and for acquiring more plants; it is also essential to the health and continued flowering of certain ones.

Dormancy: the period, usually winter, when perennial plants temporarily cease active growth and rest. Dormant is the adverb form, as used in this sentence: "Some plants, like spring-blooming bulbs, go dormant in the summer."

Espalier: A pruning practice where a plant, usually a fruit tree, is pruned to force it to grow flat against a wall or fence.

Established: the point at which a newly planted tree, shrub, or flower begins to produce new growth, either foliage or stems. This is an indication that the roots have recovered from transplant shock and have begun to grow and spread. In this book, I have used "established" (particularly with woody shrubs and trees) to mean plants that have been in the ground long enough to have their watering regimen extended.

Evergreen: perennial plants that do not lose their foliage annually with the onset of winter. Needled or broadleaf foliage will persist and continues to function on a plant through one or more winters, aging and dropping unobtrusively in cycles of three or four years or more.

Foliar: of or about foliage—usually refers to the practice of spraying foliage, as in fertilizing or treating with insecticide; leaf tissues absorb liquid directly for fast results, and the soil is not affected.

Floret: a tiny flower, usually one of many forming a cluster, that comprises a single blossom.

Germinate: to sprout. Germination is a fertile seed's first stage of development.

Glochid: A fine spine, often invisible, at the base of the larger spines on prickly pear and cholla cactus.

Graft (union): the point on the stem of a woody plant with sturdier roots where a stem from a highly ornamental plant is inserted so that it will join with it. Roses are commonly grafted.

Hardscape: the permanent, structural, nonplant part of a landscape, such as walls, sheds, pools, patios, arbors, and walkways.

Herbaceous: plants having fleshy or soft stems, the opposite of "woody."

Hybrid: a plant that is the result of intentional or natural cross-pollination between two or more plants of the same species or genus.

Low-water demand: describes plants that tolerate dry soil for varying periods of time. Typically, they have succulent, hairy, or silvery-gray foliage and tuberous roots or taproots.

Mulch: a layer of material over bare soil to protect it from erosion and compaction by rain, and to discourage weeds. It may be inorganic (gravel, fabric) or organic (wood chips, bark, pine needles, chopped leaves).

Naturalize: a. to plant seeds, bulbs, or plants in a random, informal pattern as they would appear in their natural habitat; b. to adapt to and spread throughout adopted habitats (a tendency of some nonactive plants).

Nectar: the sweet fluid produced by glands on flowers that attract pollinators such as hummingbirds and honeybees for whom it is a source of energy.

Organic material, organic matter: any material or debris that is derived from plants. It is carbon-based material capable of undergoing decomposition and decay.

Peat moss: organic matter from peat sedges (United States) or sphagnum mosses (Canada), often used to improve soil texture. The acidity of sphagnum peat moss makes it ideal for boosting or maintaining soil acidity while also improving its drainage.

Perennial: a flowering plant that lives over two or more seasons. Many die back with frost, but their roots survive the winter and generate new shoots in the spring.

pH: a measurement of the relative acidity (low pH) or alkalinity (high pH) of soil or water based on a scale of 1 to 14, 7 being neutral. Individual plants require soil to be within a certain range so that nutrients can dissolve in moisture and be available to them.

Pinch: to remove tender stems and/or leaves by pressing them between thumb and forefinger. This pruning technique encourages branching, compactness, and flowering in plants. It is also a technique to remove aphids clustered at growing tips.

Pollen: the yellow, powdery grains in the center of a flower—the plant's male sex cells. They are transferred to the female plant parts by means of wind or animal pollinators to fertilize them and create seeds.

Psillids: Tiny sucking insects that resemble aphids.

Raceme: an arrangement of single stalked flowers along an elongated, unbranched axis.

Rhizome: a swollen energy-storing stem that lies horizontally in the soil, with roots emerging from its lower surface and growth shoots from a growing point at or near its tip, as in bearded iris.

Rootbound (or potbound): the condition of a plant that has been confined in a container too long, its roots having been forced to wrap around themselves and even swell out of the container. Successful transplanting or repotting requires untangling and trimming away of some of the matted roots.

Root flare: the transition at the base of a tree trunk where the bark tissue begins to differentiate and roots begin to form just before entering the soil. This area should not be covered with soil when planting a tree.

Root hardy: term describing plants that may lose all foliage and stems to freezing temperatures but the root remains undamaged and will resprout stems and leaves in spring.

Self-seeding: the tendency of some plants to sow their seeds freely around the yard. It creates many seedlings the following season that may or may not be welcome.

Semievergreen: tending to be evergreen in a mild climate but deciduous in a rigorous one.

Shearing: the pruning technique whereby plant stems and branches are cut uniformly with long-bladed pruning shears (hedge shears) or powered hedge trimmers. It is used when creating and maintaining hedges and topiary.

Slow-acting fertilizer: fertilizer that releases its nutrients gradually as a function of soil temperature, moisture, and related microbial activity. Typically granular, it may be organic or synthetic.

Succulent growth: the sometimes undesirable production of fleshy, water-storing leaves or stems that results from overfertilization.

Sucker: a new growing shoot. Underground plant roots produce suckers to form new stems and spread by means of these suckering roots to form large plantings or colonies. Some plants produce root suckers or branch suckers as a result of pruning or wounding.

Tuber: swollen roots in which nutrients are stored (example: dahlia).

Variegated: having various colors or color patterns. The term usually refers to plant foliage that is streaked, edged, blotched, or mottled with a contrasting color, often green with yellow, cream, or white.

White grubs: fat, off-white, wormlike larvae of Japanese beetles. They reside in the soil and feed on plant roots (especially grass) until summer when they emerge as beetles to feed on plant foliage.

Wings: a. the corky tissue that forms edges along the twigs of some woody plants such as winged euonymus; b. the flat, dried extension of tissue on some seeds, such as maple, that catch the wind and help them disseminate.

Bibliography

Arizona Native Plant Society, Urban Landscape Committee (Eds.). *Desert Wildflowers, Desert Bird Gardening, Desert Butterfly Gardening, Desert Trees, Desert Shrubs, Desert Accent Plants, Desert Groundcovers and Vines.* Tucson, Arizona: Arizona Native Plant Society, 1990-1997.

Beck, Hallie. *Roses in a Desert Garden.* Phoenix, Arizona: P H G, Inc., 1996.

Blombery, Alec, and Tony Rudd. *Palms.* Australia: Angus and Robertson Publishers, 1982.

Bown, Deni. *The Herb Society of America Encyclopedia of Herbs and Their Uses.* London: Dorling Kindersley, 1995.

Brickell, Christopher and Judith D. Zuk (Eds.). *The American Horticultural Society A-Z Encyclopedia of Garden Plants.* New York: DK Publishing, 1996.

Brenzel, Kathleen N. (Ed.). *Sunset Western Garden Book.* Menlo Park, California: Sunset Publishing Corp., 2001.

Bryan, John (Ed.). *Manual of Bulbs.* Portland, Oregon: Timber Press, 1995.

Correll, Donovan Stewart, and Marshall Conring Johnston. *Manual of the Vascular Plants of Texas.* Richardson, Texas: University of Texas at Dallas, 1979.

Cromell, Cathy, Linda Guy, and Lucy Bradley. *Desert Gardening for Beginners: How to Grow Vegetables, Flowers and Herbs in an Arid Climate.* Phoenix, Arizona: Arizona Master Gardener Press, 1999.

Cromell, Cathy (Ed.). *Desert Landscaping for Beginners: Tips and Techniques for Success in an Arid Climate.* Phoenix, Arizona: Arizona Master Gardener Press, 2001.

Darke, Rick. *The Colour Encyclopedia of Ornamental Grasses.* London: Weidenfeld and Nicolson, 1999.

Dinchak, Ronald K. *An Illustrated Guide to Landscape Shrubs of Southern Arizona.* Mesa, Arizona: 3D Press, 1981.

Dinchak, Ronald K. *An Illustrated Guide to Landscape Trees of Southern Arizona.* Mesa, Arizona: 3D Press, 1981.

Dreistadt, Steve H., Jack Kelly Clar, and Mary Louise Fline. 1994. *Pests of Landscape Trees and Shrubs: An Integrated Pest Management Guide.* Oakland, California: University of California Publication 3359, University of California, 1994.

Duffield, Mary Rose and Warren Jones. *Plants for Dry Climates.* Cambridge, Massachusetts: Perseus Publishing, 2001.

Felger, Richard Stephen, Matthew Brian Johnson, and Michael Francis Wilson. *The Trees of Sonora, Mexico*. Oxford University Press, 2001.

Gomez, Tom and John Duff Bailey. *Beyond the Ponderosa: Successful Landscape Trees for Higher Elevations in the Southwest*. Flagstaff, Arizona: Flagstaff Community Tree Board, 1998.

Howard, Thad M. *Bulbs for Warm Climates*. Austin, Texas: University of Austin Press, 2001.

Johnson, Eric and Scott Millard. *How to Grow the Wildflowers*. Tucson, Arizona: Ironwood Press, 1993.

Jones, Warren and Charles Sacamano. *Landscape Plants for Dry Regions*. Tucson, Arizona: Fisher Books, 2000.

Kearney, Thomas H. and Robert H. Peebles. *Arizona Flora*. Berkeley, California: University of California Press, 1960.

Mielke, Judy. *Native Plants for Southwestern Landscapes*. Austin, Texas: University of Texas Press, 1993.

Morrow, Baker H. *Best Plants for New Mexico Gardens and Landscapes*. Albuquerque, New Mexico: University of New Mexico Press, 1995.

Nabhan, Gary Paul and Jane Cole (Eds.). *Arizona Highways Presents Desert Wildflowers*. Arizona Department of Transportation, State of Arizona: Phoenix, Arizona, 1988.

Phillips, Judith. *New Mexico Gardener's Guide*. Franklin, Tennessee: Cool Springs Press, 1998.

Roberts, Annie Lisse. *Cornucopia: The Lore of Fruits and Vegetables*. New York, New York: Knickerbocker Press, 1998.

Wasowski, Sally, with Andy Wasowski. *Native Texas Plants: Landscaping Region by Region*. Austin, Texas: Texas Monthly Press, 1988.

Wrigley, John W., and Murray Fagg. *Australian Native Plants*. Reeds Books, 1996.

Photography Credits

Thomas Eltzroth: pages 12, 15, 17 (upper), 22, 23, 26, 31, 32, 34, 36, 37, 39, 40, 42, 43, 44, 46, 47, 54, 63, 64, 67, 68, 71, 72, 73, 75, 78, 79, 85, 86, 87, 88, 89, 91, 93, 95, 97 (lower), 102, 103, 106, 111, 112, 119, 123, 126, 128, 132, 133, 134, 135, 136, 137, 138, 139, 140, 141, 142, 143, 151, 154, 161, 163, 167, 169, 172, 175, 184, 185, 195, 196, 197, 198, 202, 204, 205, 207, 227, 229, 230, 233, and the back cover

Charles Mann: Front cover and pages 10, 49 (both), 52, 57, 61, 76, 82, 83, 84, 97 (upper), 99, 100, 105, 107, 113, 117, 120, 129, 146, 148, 152, 158, 159, 160, 168, 186, 203, 211, 218, 221, 223, 225, 228

Jerry Pavia: pages 14, 16, 17 (lower), 21 (lower), 24, 27, 28, 29, 35, 41, 48, 50, 51, 55, 58, 60, 74, 80, 101, 110, 114, 115, 116, 121, 125, 155, 174, 193, 199, 217, 219

Judy Mielke: pages 69, 70, 77, 81, 90, 94, 108, 109, 145 (lower), 147, 149, 150, 153, 165, 166, 170, 178, 189, 190, 191, 200, 201, 214, 216, 220, 234

Mary and Gary Irish: pages 13, 25, 45, 53, 59, 98, 104, 144, 162, 164, 176, 182, 183, 188, 213, 271

Liz Ball and Rick Ray: pages 20, 21 (upper), 30, 33, 38, 96, 122, 145 (upper), 156, 171, 226, 232

Scott Millard: pages 118, 124, 131, 157, 180, 187, 192, 206, 215, 222, 224

Christine Douglas: pages 62, 173, 208, 210

Pam Harper: pages 130, 194, 209

William Adams: pages 181, 231

Michael Dirr: pages 177, 179

Lorenzo Gunn: page 92

George Hull: page 212

Dency Kane: page 127

Plant Index

Primary plant entries are denoted by boldface type.

Meet Mary Irish

Mary Irish has an extensive background in horticulture, having served as an author, lecturer, educator, and garden writer. She is an accomplished gardener who has lived in Arizona for more than 16 years. Irish assisted thousands of gardeners through the years as the Director of Public Horticulture at the Desert Botanical Garden in Phoenix, during which time she managed the botanical garden's Plant Introduction and Sales Program.

Irish's educational background includes a Bachelor of Arts from the University of Texas, Austin, and a Master of Science from Texas A&M University, College Station. Irish has written extensively for periodical publishing, as well as serving as the host of a call-in radio program, *The Arizona Gardener*. Irish currently appears twice weekly on the *Jan D'Atri Heart and Home Show*, on KAZ-TV.

Irish is the author of another book for Cool Springs Press, *Month-by-Month Gardening in the Desert Southwest*. Other books authored or co-authored by Mary include *Agaves, Yuccas, and Related Plants*, and *Gardening in the Desert*.

In addition to her frequent contributions to regional and national publications, Irish regularly teaches classes on desert gardening, the use and cultivation of agaves, and the care and cultivation of succulents. Although Irish is interested in all plants, agaves and their relatives, bulbs, and desert perennials are her primary interest.

Irish and her husband, Gary, live in Scottsdale, where she enjoys birding and quilting.